The Campus History Series

Southern Arkansas University

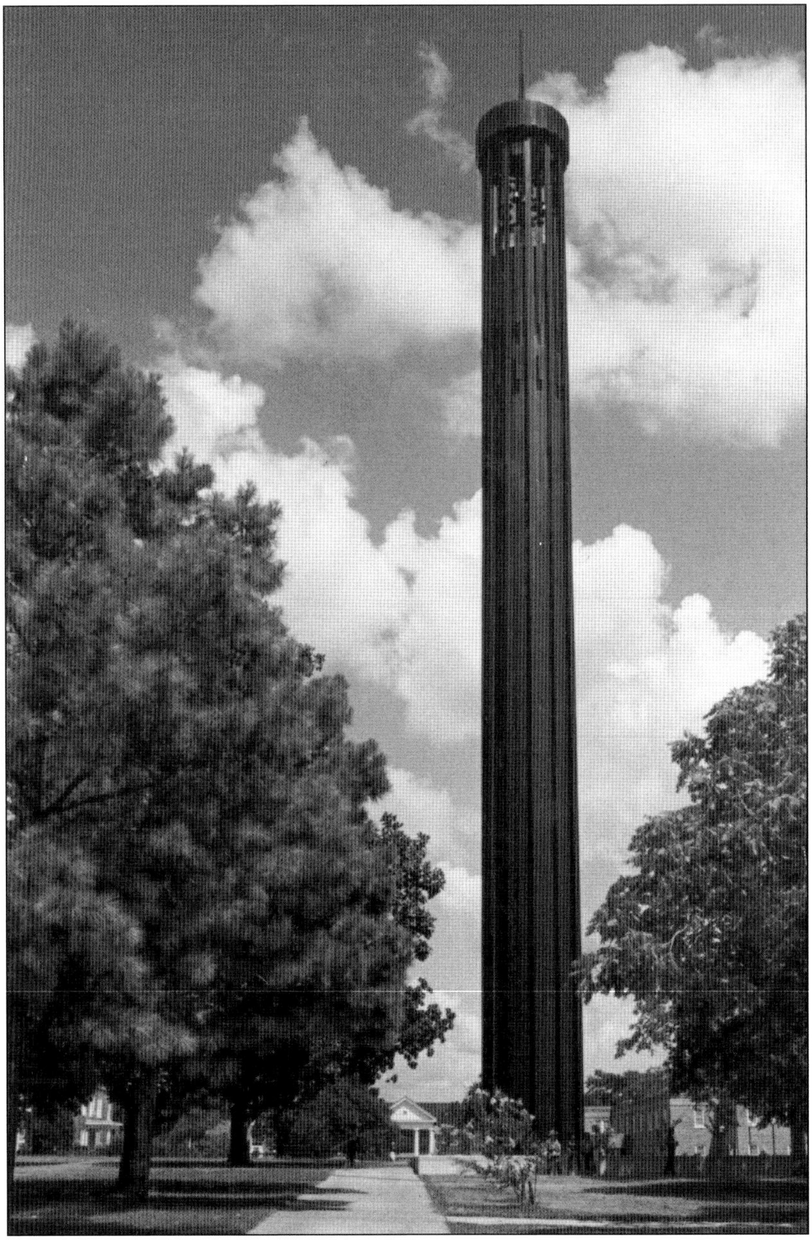

Today, the Bell Tower, originally an ornamental water tower, is among the images most used as a symbol of Southern Arkansas University (SAU). Built in 1976–1977, it stands at the center of campus and is visible from a distance. In 1980–1981, a 14-bell carillon from France was placed in the top of the tower to ring out chimes, telling the university community the hours of the day. (Courtesy of Southern Arkansas University Archives.)

On the Cover: Bussey Hall is seen here as it appeared in the late 1950s. It is the oldest SAU women's residence hall. When first completed in 1950, it housed all female students on the campus. It remains one of the principal student residences at SAU. (Courtesy of Southern Arkansas University Archives.)

The Campus History Series

SOUTHERN ARKANSAS UNIVERSITY

JAMES F. WILLIS AND DEL DUKE

ARCADIA
PUBLISHING

ISBN 978-1-4671-2665-6

Published by Arcadia Publishing
Charleston, South Carolina

Printed in the United States of America

Library of Congress Control Number: 2017935580

For all general information, please contact Arcadia Publishing:
Telephone 843-853-2070
Fax 843-853-0044
E-mail sales@arcadiapublishing.com
For customer service and orders:
Toll-Free 1-888-313-2665

Visit us on the Internet at www.arcadiapublishing.com

Contents

ACKNOWLEDGMENTS

The Southern Arkansas University Archives were established in 2007. At that time, the director of Magale Library, Peggy Walters, with the approval of SAU president Dr. David F. Rankin, directed library staff to consolidate materials related to the history of the university, long stored in various places. A large, secure room was designated for the organization and permanent storage of these materials. Librarian Gayle Coston was primarily responsible for these initial steps. Librarian Donna McCloy was given continuing responsibility for the SAU Archives. A strategic plan was devised, one part of which stated that the archives would accept only photographs and documents dealing with the history of the school. Without the earlier work of these librarians, this book would have been impossible to prepare.

More immediately, the authors wish to thank Jeanie Bismark, the SAU Foundation's executive director, for supporting the writing of this book. All authors' proceeds from the sale of this book have been transferred through copyright assignment to the foundation.

The authors wish to thank the Communications Center and Magale Library staff, including Donna McCloy, Anne Lee, and Holli Howard, for their assistance in the preparation of this book.

All images appear courtesy of Southern Arkansas University Archives.

INTRODUCTION

Over the course of a century, four schools occupied the same campus, one and a half miles from the town square of Magnolia, Arkansas. The three earlier schools began traditions that continue to influence today's Southern Arkansas University. All of the schools offered educational opportunities primarily for people living in the southwest region of the state, especially working and middle class youngsters, often the first members of their families to seek degrees. The strongest tradition shared by the four schools has been a nurturing faculty and staff, giving personal attention and assistance to each individual student.

In 1907, Pres. Theodore Roosevelt called for agricultural schools as a progressive reform to raise educational and living standards in rural America. Agricultural high schools were to teach the latest scientific agricultural practices and modern home economics as well as math, English, and other subjects sufficient for a high school diploma. The Farmer's Educational and Cooperative Union, the largest farm organization in the United States at the time, lobbied in many states, especially in the South, for such schools and played a role in their creation in Georgia, Mississippi, Oklahoma, Virginia, North Carolina, and Arkansas.

In 1908, the Farmers' Union actively supported George W. Donaghey's successful campaign to become Arkansas's governor. He had pledged to seek legislative approval for four agricultural schools, which was accomplished with Act 100 in 1909. Boards of trustees sought financial support from local communities and awarded schools to those providing the most money. In addition to the Third District Agricultural School (TDAS) in Magnolia, schools were located near Jonesboro, Russellville, and Monticello. Arkansas's investment in buildings and infrastructure was so large during the schools' first decade—ranking second among 29 states with agricultural schools—that the schools were able to evolve into residential colleges rather than disappear, as happened to many agricultural schools in other states.

In the mid-1920s, with Act 229 of 1923 and Act 45 of 1925, Arkansas elevated the agricultural schools to junior colleges in order to improve public education through better preparation of rural schoolteachers. The school's official name was Arkansas State Agricultural and Mechanical College, Third District, but it was known everywhere as Magnolia A&M College or often, in Magnolia, just A&M.

In addition to public school teacher preparation, Magnolia A&M offered two-year associate degrees that included freshman and sophomore coursework needed to transfer to a four-year bachelor's degree–granting college. New faculty with master's degrees taught Spanish and French, humanities courses, and math and advanced science classes. The college established a flourishing drama program, an orchestra, numerous extracurricular activities, and winning athletic teams.

During World War II, Magnolia A&M lost so many male students to the war effort that it nearly closed. Afterward, so many veterans enrolled that the school became overcrowded. Demands from local citizens combined with changes in higher education funding led the school's board of trustees to vote in 1949 to add junior and senior level coursework. In 1951, the Arkansas legislature recognized the board's decision to become a four-year college with Act 11, naming the school Southern State College.

From 1951 to 1976, Southern State College (SSC) grew into an excellent regional state college. Increasing the number of faculty with doctoral-level degrees, acquiring larger library holdings, and constructing needed buildings were required to gain accreditation.

Academically, SSC was organized into six divisions: business and commerce, education, fine arts, humanities, natural sciences, and social sciences. Each created bachelor degree programs. Greater academic performance was demanded of students. In 1958, a chapter of the national scholarship fraternity Alpha Chi was established to recognize high academic achievement.

Large baby boomer student increases in the 1960s brought many changes, including a crash program of construction. New buildings of every kind, from athletic to academic to residential, transformed the campus. The most dramatic change was the enrollment of African American students.

With Act 171 in 1975, the Arkansas legislature added two community college branches, one at El Dorado and another at Camden, to create a three-campus SSC system. However, after 15 years in an uneasy relationship, El Dorado gained its independence, leaving only the branch at Camden as partner to the main branch at Magnolia.

The same legislative session that created the three-campus system also changed SSC's status to that of a university with Act 343. The school was the last of the original four agricultural schools to become a regional university.

Southern Arkansas University organized academically into four colleges, including business, education, liberal arts and humanities, and science and technology. The university at first offered only master's degrees in education but later offered master's degrees in a variety of fields, including business, computer science, library science, agricultural science, athletic training, criminal justice, public administration, kinesiology, nursing, social work, and counseling, with more degrees always in development. By 2011, the Carnegie Foundation for the Advancement of Teaching ranked SAU as a Master's M level institution.

The university gained accreditation from numerous professional agencies. The College of Business was one of only 570 colleges and universities worldwide to gain accreditation by the Association to Advance College Collegiate Schools of Business. New innovative undergraduate programs also appeared, including marine biology, computer game and animation design, engineering-physics, entrepreneurship, cyber security, and a bachelor of fine arts degree with several emphases, including musical theater.

An especially important development that began during SAU's early years—the creation of the SAU Foundation—led to an endowment exceeding $30 million and the awarding each year of hundreds of scholarships to students. In 2017, SAU launched a Love and Loyalty campaign aimed at raising an additional $22.5 million.

An extensive building program occurred at SAU after 2001. The Blue and Gold Vision led to $100 million worth of construction.

Enrollment increased exponentially at SAU after 2010, and the school became the fastest growing university in Arkansas. By 2016, total enrollment reached 4,771. Additional construction of residence halls and other facilities was begun to meet the needs of the multiplying numbers of students.

One

Third District Agricultural School

On January 3, 1911, five teachers welcomed 75 students to register for classes and to live on the campus of the Third District Agricultural School at Magnolia, Arkansas. All entering students were required to be at least 15 years old; many were older. Almost all were from rural areas. Arkansas at that time had high schools only in the major cities. Elsewhere, there were one-room schools where education stopped at the eighth grade.

During the first semester in spring 1911, students lived in buildings not fully completed. In those months, students in the original two residence halls studied by candlelight and kept warm with wood-burning heaters, as neither the electrical lines nor the steam heat pipes were finished. However, the rural students from farmhouses without electricity or steam heat were used to these conditions.

TDAS's curriculum included sufficient math, English, history, and science courses to offer a degree like those of regular high schools. But its four-year course of study, as explained in early catalogues, was "primarily technical." In 1915, when the catalogue was fully developed, there were 74 courses. Of these, 48 were in agricultural subjects, home sciences, mechanics, and bookkeeping.

Conflict between the board of trustees and faculty and students led to the dismissal of Principal Elbert E. Austin and most of the faculty in 1921, just as a new Arkansas governor, Thomas McRae, sought major improvements in public schools. McRae encouraged the transformation of agricultural schools into junior colleges with a new mission of supporting public education. At TDAS, a new school head, Charles A. Overstreet, and a new faculty made the change. The older agriculture mission continued, but with diminished emphasis.

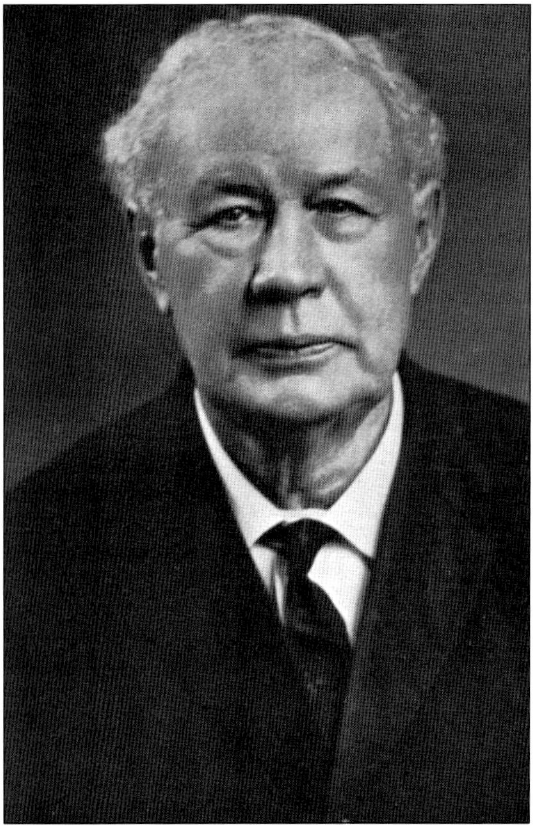

William R. Cross, insurance agent and civic booster, led an effort to raise $40,000 from Columbia County citizens to match the state appropriation for the Third District Agricultural School. The money was used to outbid other communities and to persuade the board of trustees in 1909 to place the school near Magnolia.

On August 24, 1910, hundreds of citizens who had given money for the school watched in celebration as a group of Masons and members of the TDAS board of trustees laid the cornerstone of Old Main, the school's first building. Afterwards, the crowd engaged in festivities, including a meal, speeches, and the awarding of prizes in a competition for the best stock and crop entries.

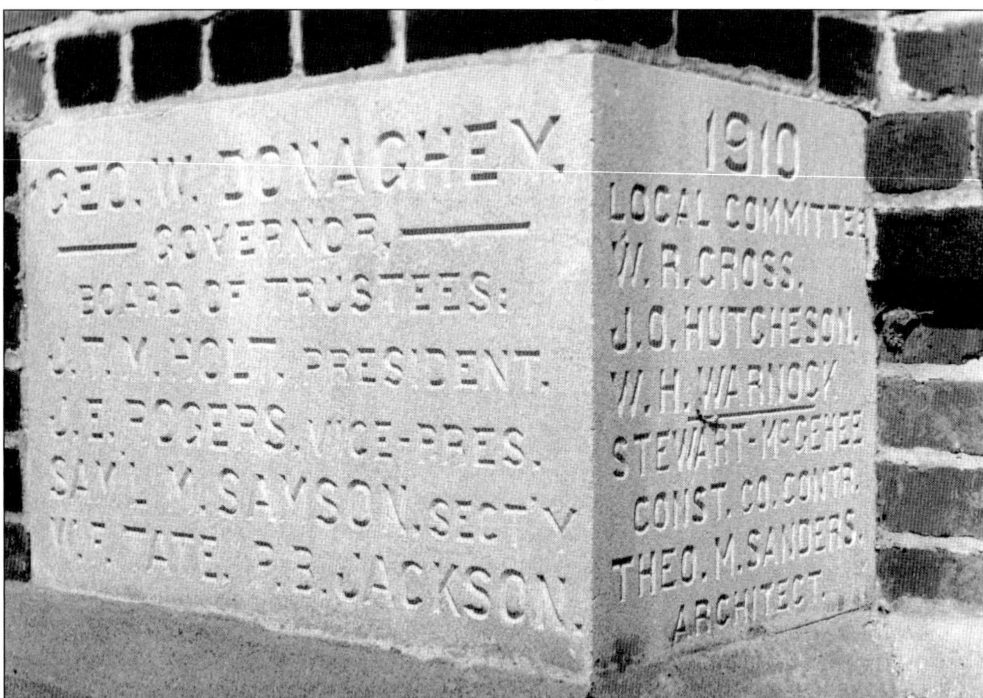

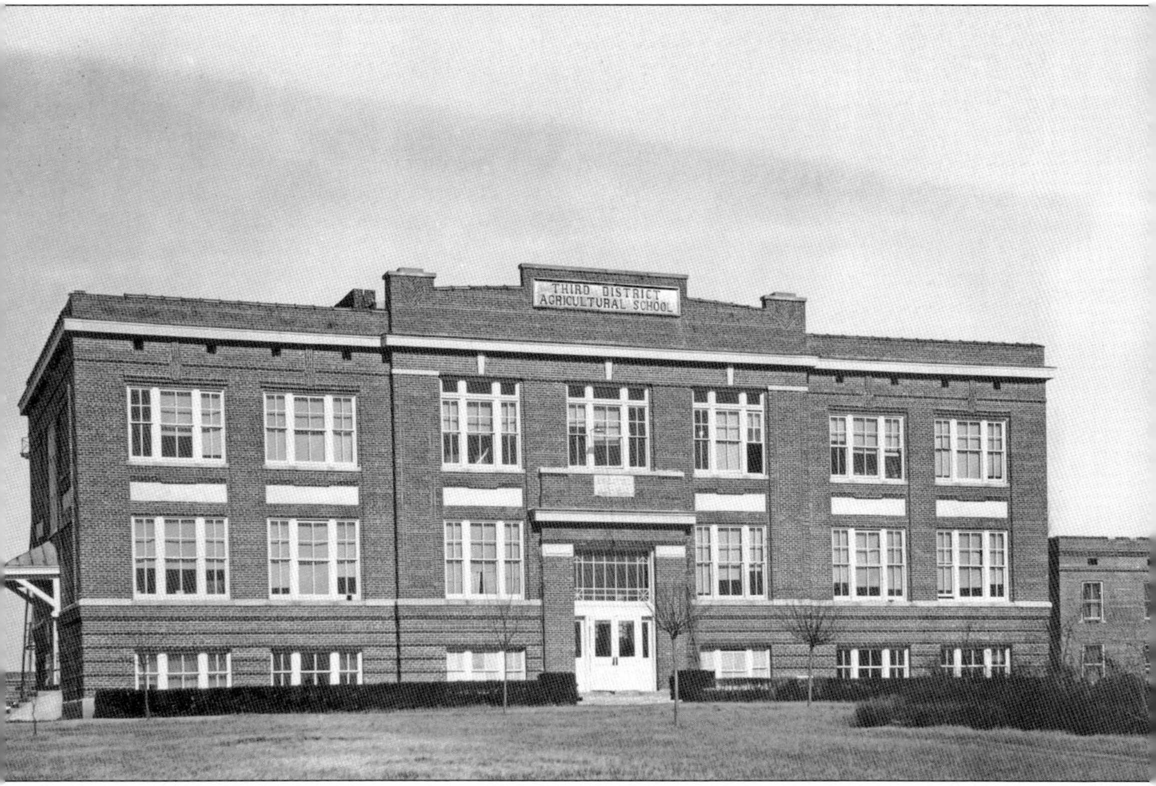

Generations of students were taught in the classrooms of Old Main from 1911 to 1975. The three-story brick building had a wooden interior. Students climbing its stairs eventually wore the steps into irregular curves. Originally, the first floor, partially underground, had facilities for teaching home economics; it also housed science laboratories. The second floor held regular classrooms, a library, the principal's office, and a business/post office. The third floor had larger classrooms. The largest room, running almost the length of the building, served as an auditorium for required daily student assemblies. In June 1912, Old Main served as a chapel for the wedding of coach and history teacher Ruford Turrentine and home economics teacher Lucille Benoit.

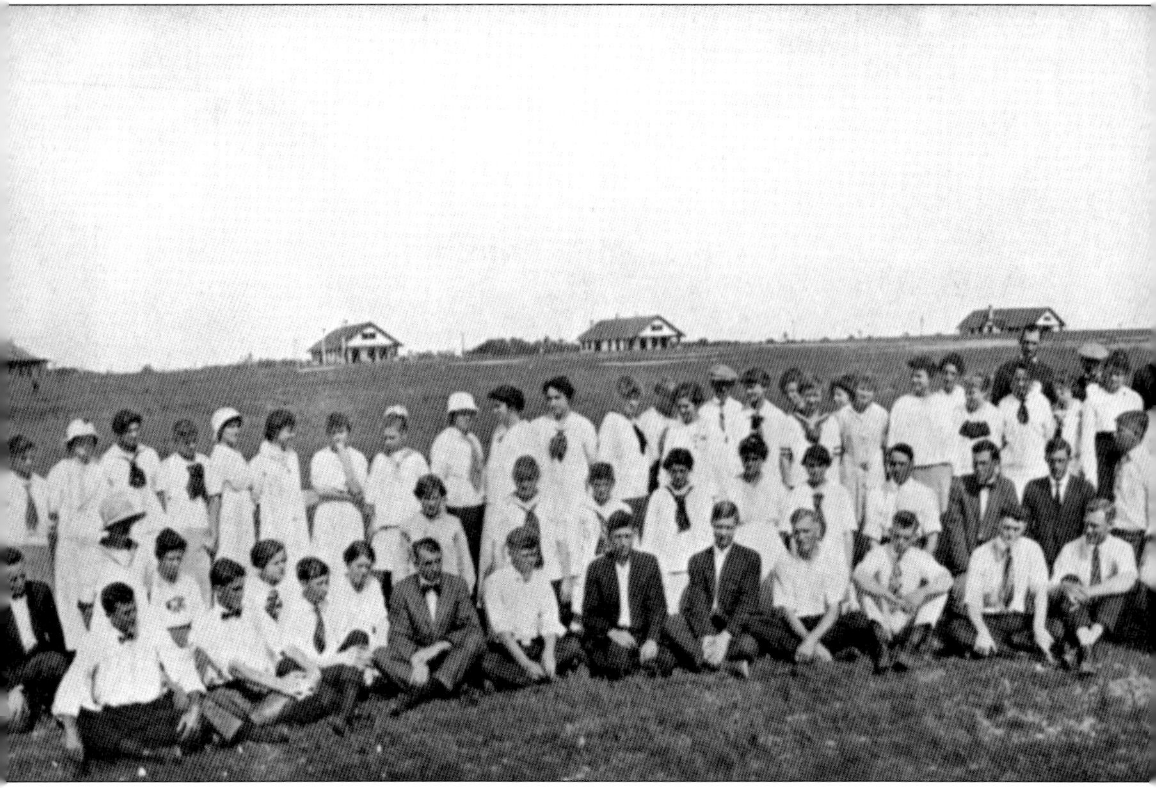

TDAS students named the rising ground of the campus "Aggie Hill." By 1916, when these students and faculty members were photographed, the building of the school was complete. Instruction had begun four and a half years earlier. The houses in the distance on the left were faculty residences. Eventually, nine additional faculty houses were added to the original

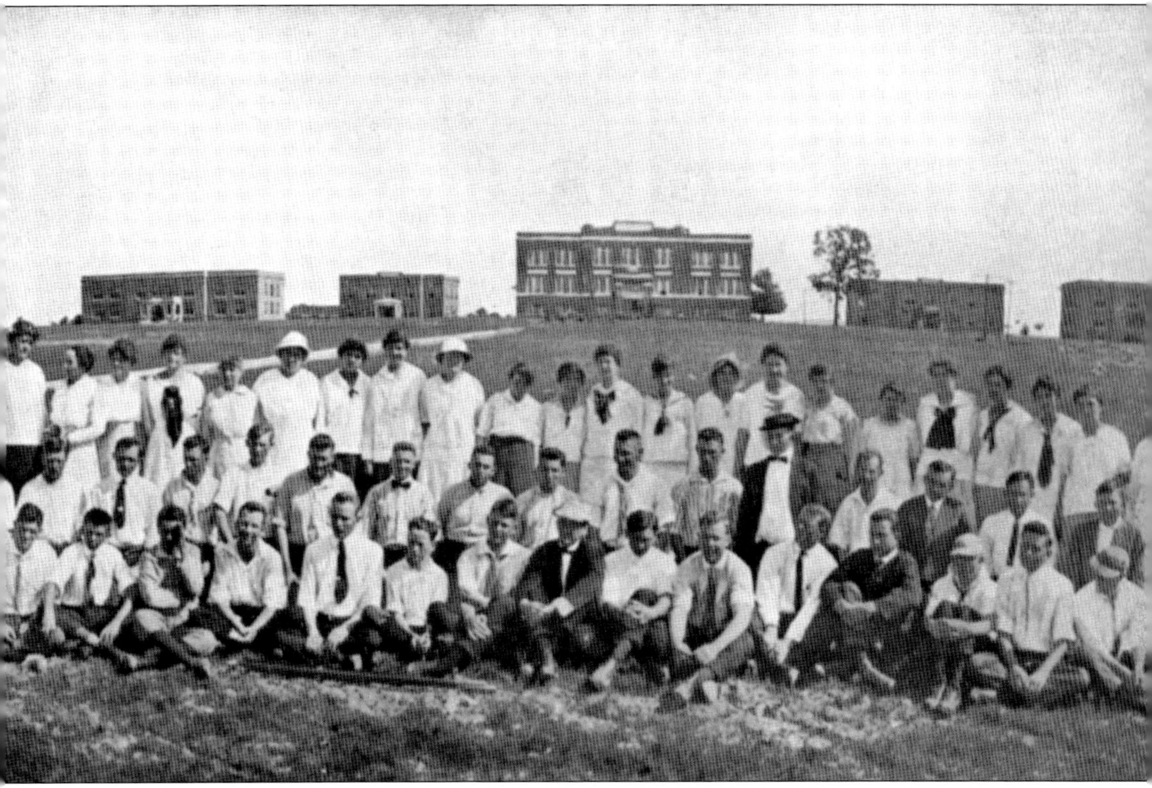

three. On the right stood Old Main with residence halls on either side. Behind Old Main stood a small brick building used for various purposes, and a large dining hall. Beyond the faculty houses lay several barns. Surrounding the campus on three sides was farmland.

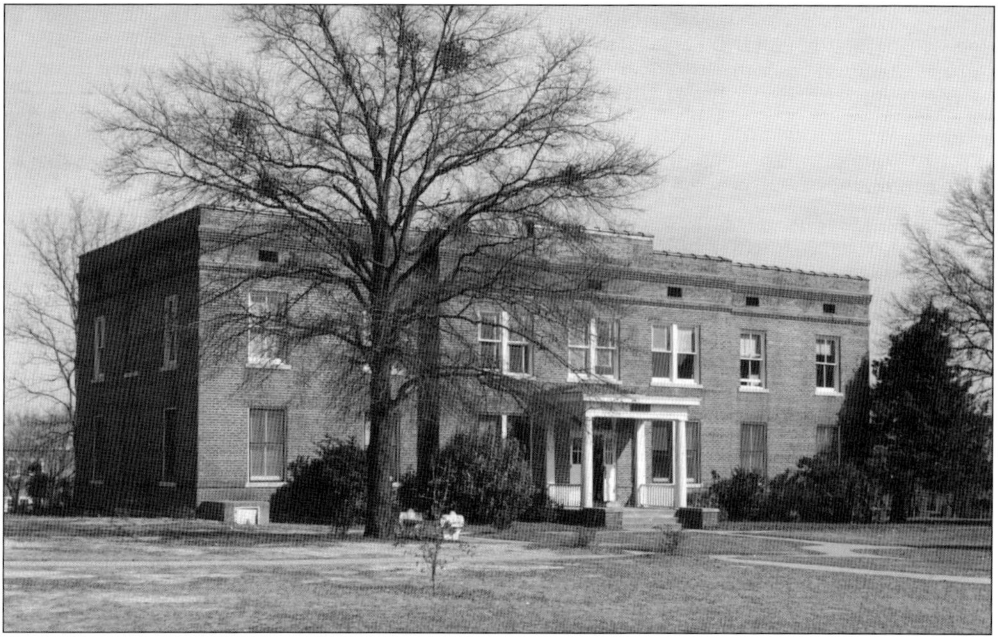

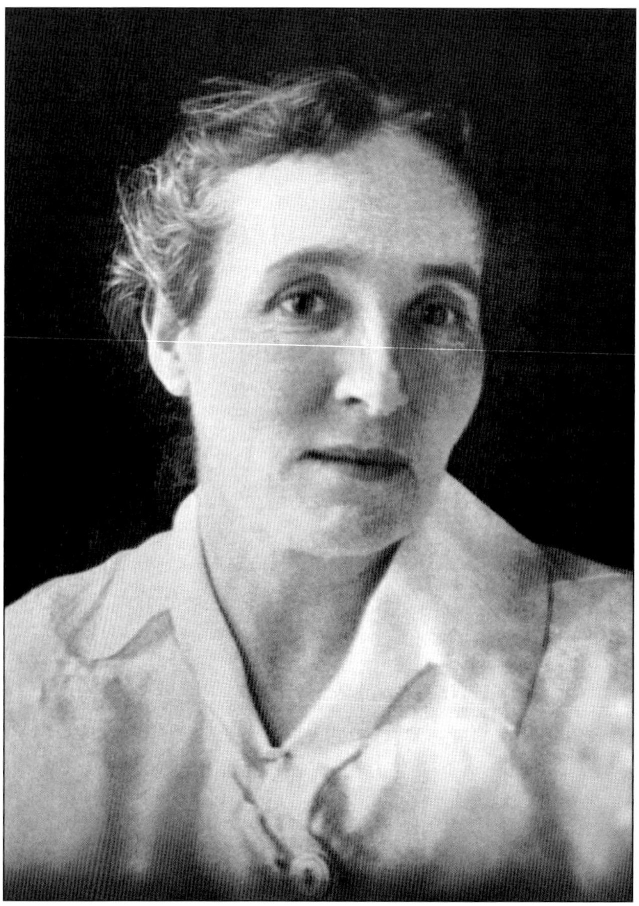

When first opened in January 1911, this dorm, which would become Jackson Hall, housed young men. A year later, it became a women's hall called Girls Dorm. This change was to keep the sexes separated, with men on the west side of campus and women on the east. On Sundays, men and women were allowed to walk together about campus, but only under the watchful eyes of faculty chaperones.

In 1935, to honor its original "house mother," Girls Dorm was named for Laura M. Jackson. A beloved presence, Jackson lived with her young women from 1911 to 1917, first in what would become Holt Hall and later in Girls Dorm. She enforced strict rules, but in a kind way. Beds were to be made and rooms swept by 7:30 a.m. Studying in rooms from 6:45 to 9:00 p.m. was required. Lights were then turned off for sleep.

Opened in January 1911, Boys Dorm became a men's residence in 1913 to move the young men closer to the farm and barns where they worked. The women who had lived there in 1911–1912 moved to Girls Dorm, later Jackson Hall. In 1935, the men's residence hall was named for James T.M. Holt, president of the board of trustees from 1909 to 1921.

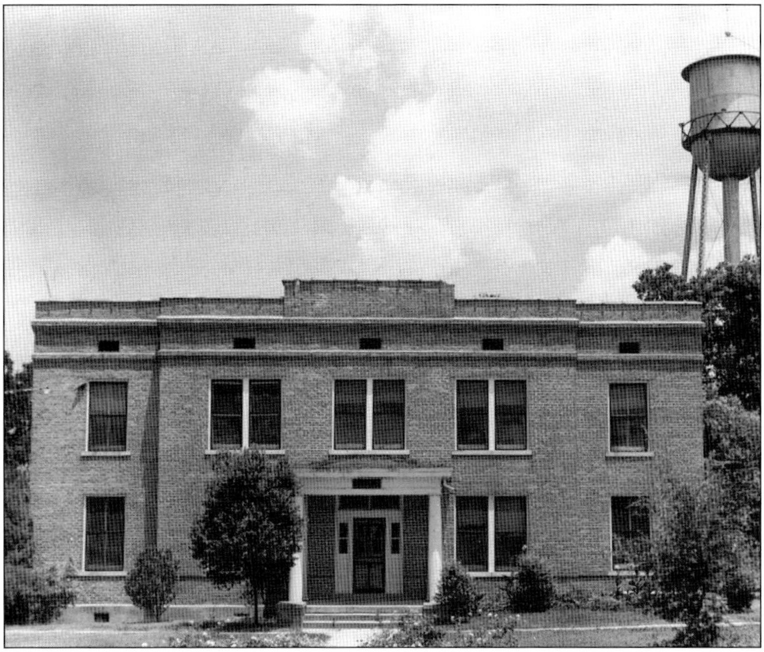

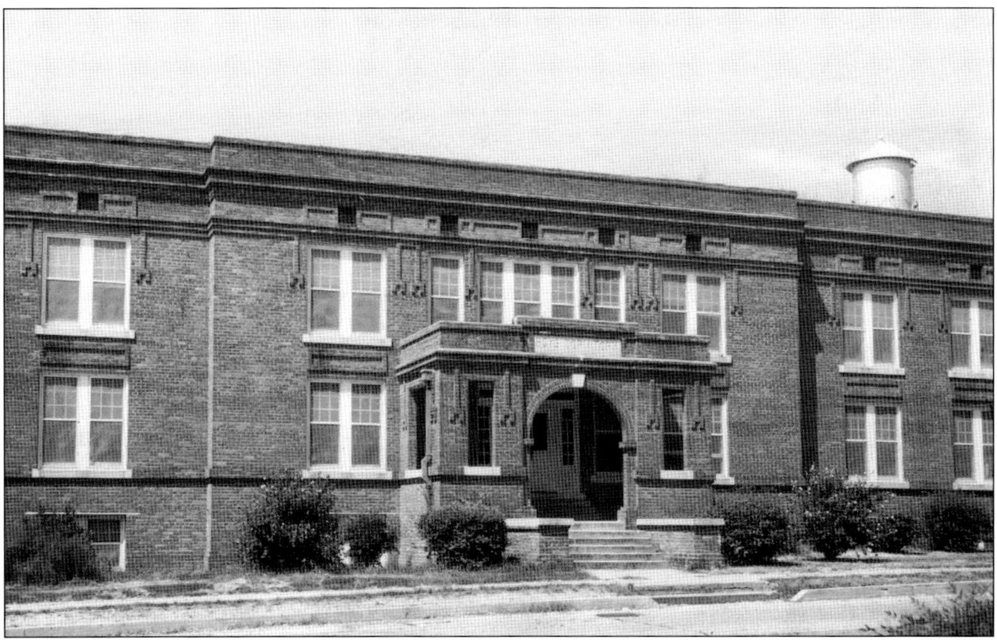

New Boys Dorm, later McCrary Hall, was built in 1913–1914 for men. Usually, residence halls had two students in each room, but sometimes might house three or four to accommodate large enrollments. Like all traditional dormitories, all TDAS halls had only one common bathroom and shower room for each floor. In 1935, the building was named for N.C. McCrary, president of the board of trustees from 1924 to 1934.

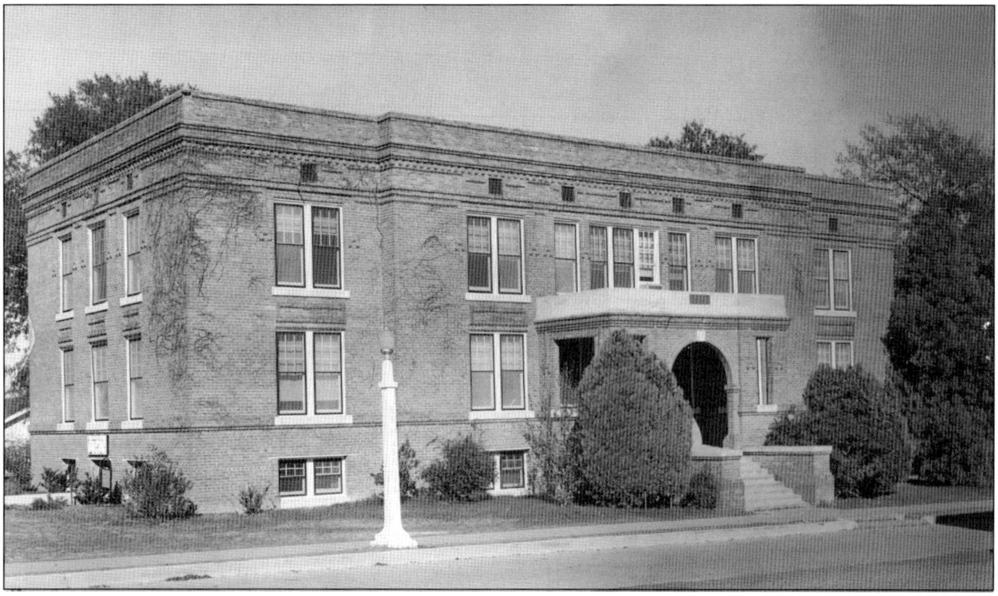

New Girls Dorm, later Caraway Hall, was built in 1913–1914 as a women's residence hall. It was named in 1935 to honor Senator Hattie Caraway, the first woman elected to the US Senate. First appointed to succeed her husband after his unexpected death, Caraway in 1932 became the first woman to run for and win a Senate seat. She helped the school obtain federal funds and grants during the Great Depression.

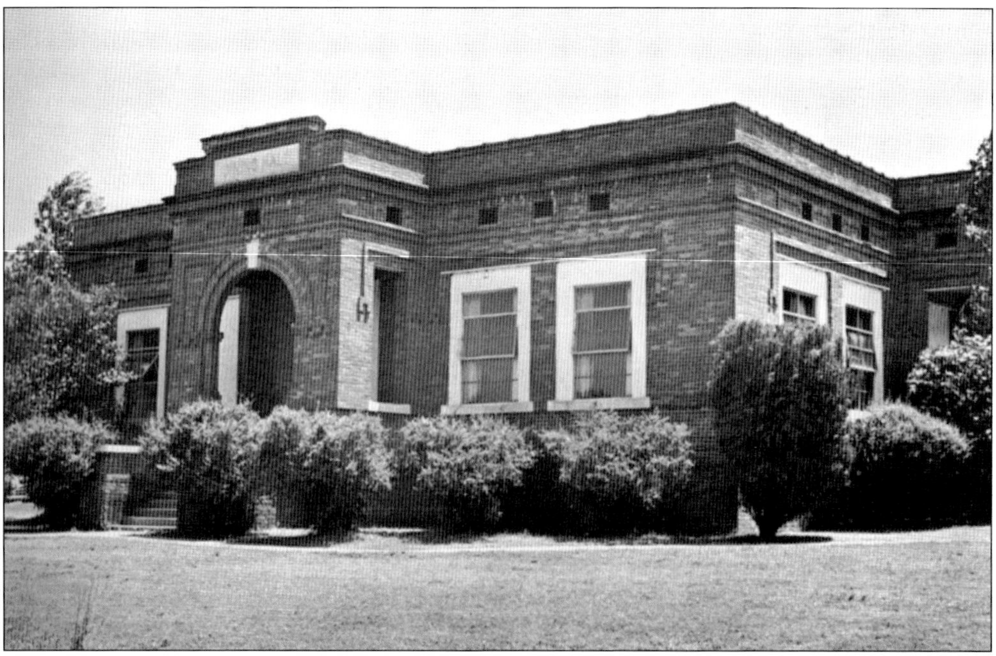

This dining hall, built in 1913, stood 50 yards behind Old Main. It replaced a smaller original dining hall. During the TDAS years, almost all of the food preparation was done by student labor, particularly young women who earned enough in the kitchen to pay for their own education. Young men grew the food, from meat to milk to vegetables, on the school's 390-acre farm.

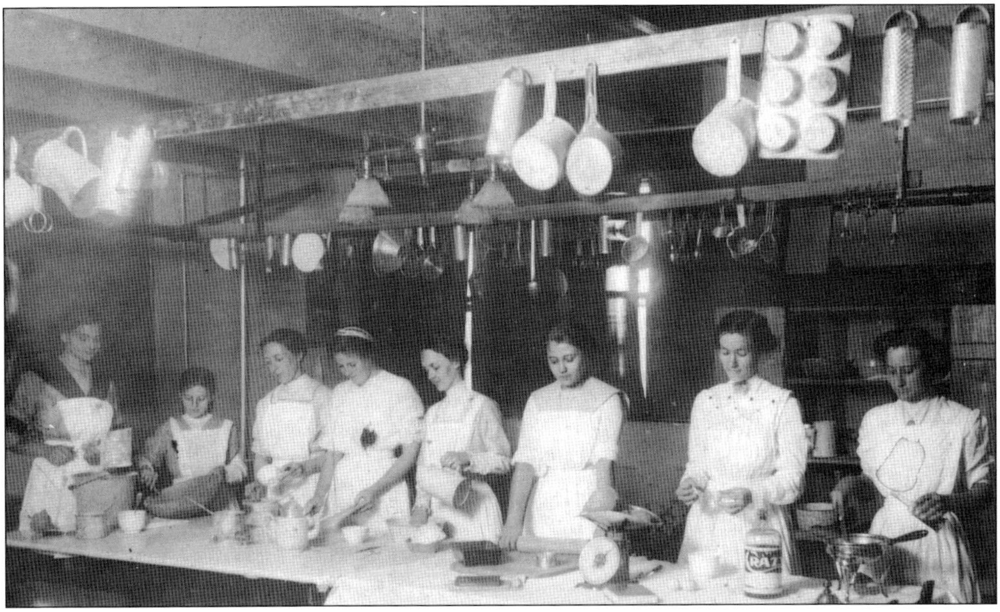

Generally, only young women worked in the kitchen of the TDAS dining hall. With almost all food grown on the campus farm, there was plenty to do to turn freshly gathered vegetables, milk, and meat into table-ready food three times each day. The men sometimes worked as butchers to cut meat.

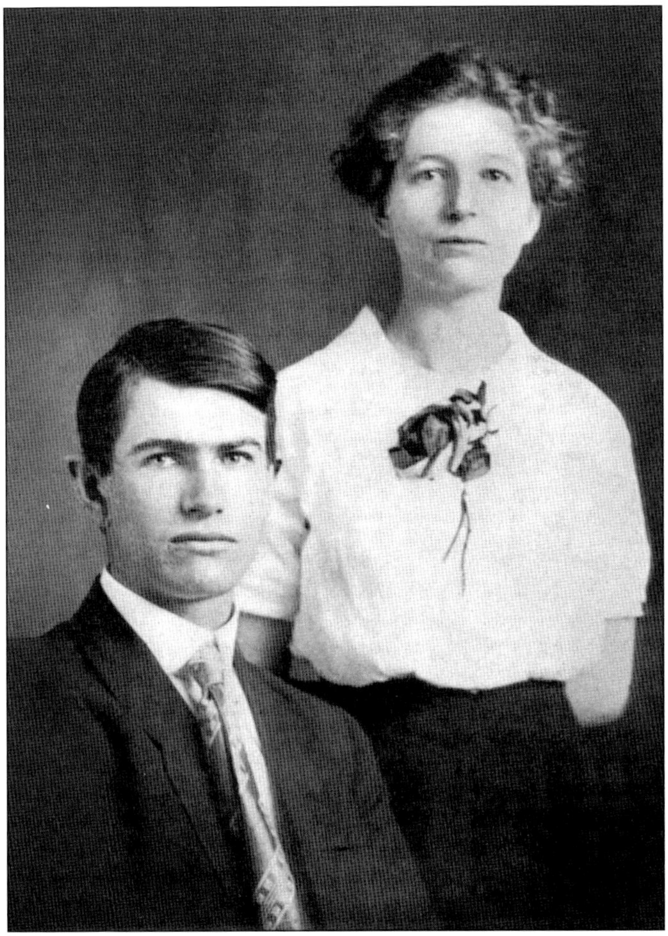

Jesse and Caro Bussey were hired to manage TDAS's food service in 1913. They were a team for decades, with Mrs. Bussey planning menus and monitoring students as they ate and Mr. Bussey supervising the kitchen cooks. Jesse Bussey fell ill in the late 1930s, but Caro continued to provide healthy and tasty food for thousands of students until her retirement in 1955.

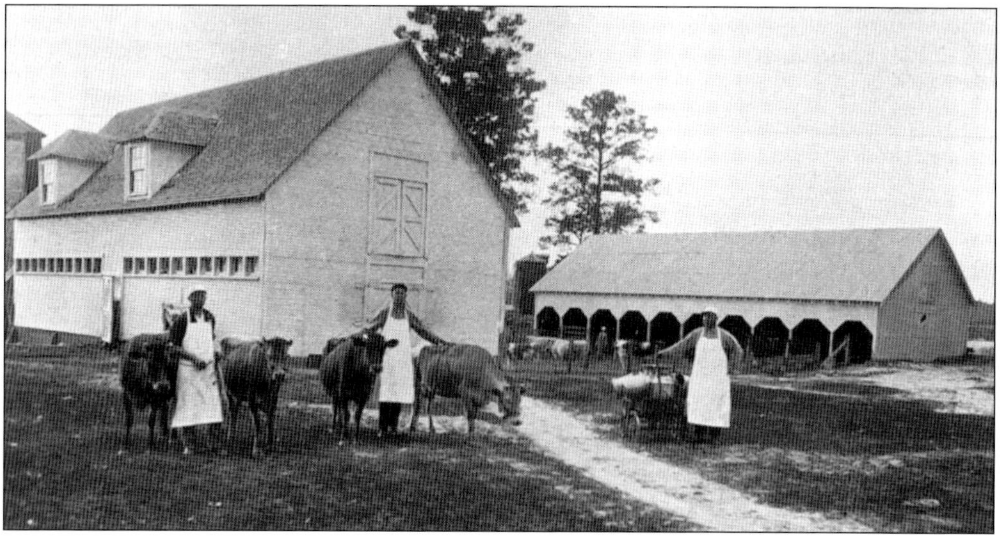

Barns for milk cows, beef cattle, chickens, pigs, and work mules were on the campus's west side. These young men have milked the cows and loaded milk barrels onto a cart to take to the dining hall. Tuition was free; however, a majority of students, both men and women, had to work 25 hours per week at 10¢ an hour to pay the $10 cost of room and board per month.

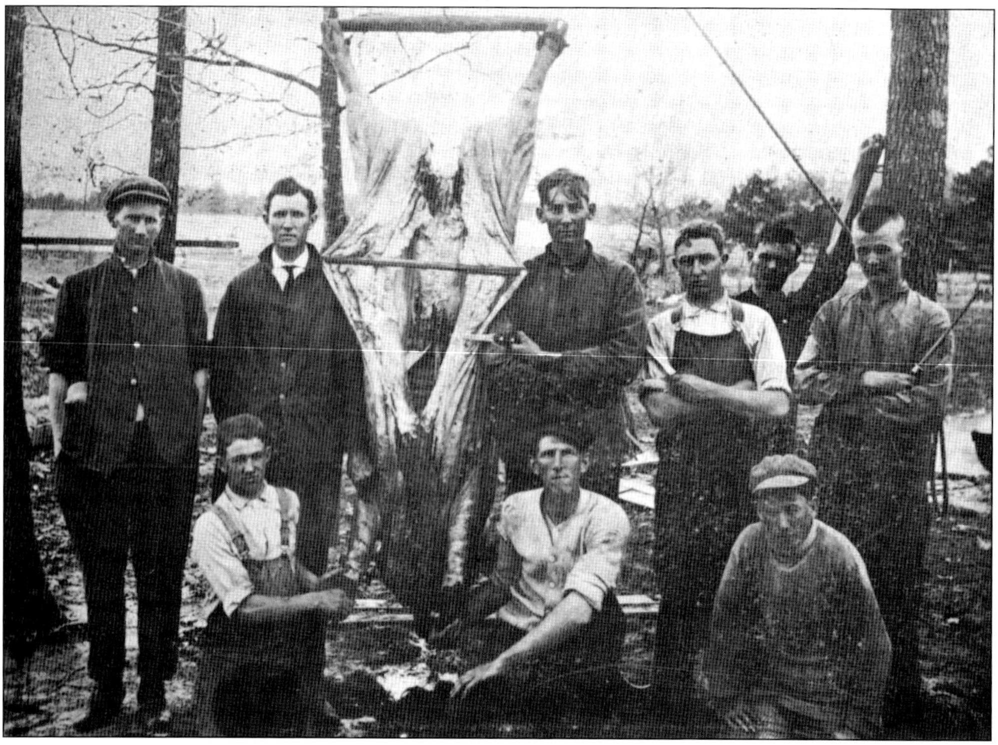

Even youth who had grown up on a farm might need direction to butcher a large hog. Agriculture instructor Hainan Holtzclaw, standing to the immediate left of the hog wearing a tie and protective clothing, instructed these students. Holtzclaw was among the University of Arkansas's earliest agricultural graduates (the first were in 1908). He had earned a bachelor's degree in agriculture and a master's in animal husbandry.

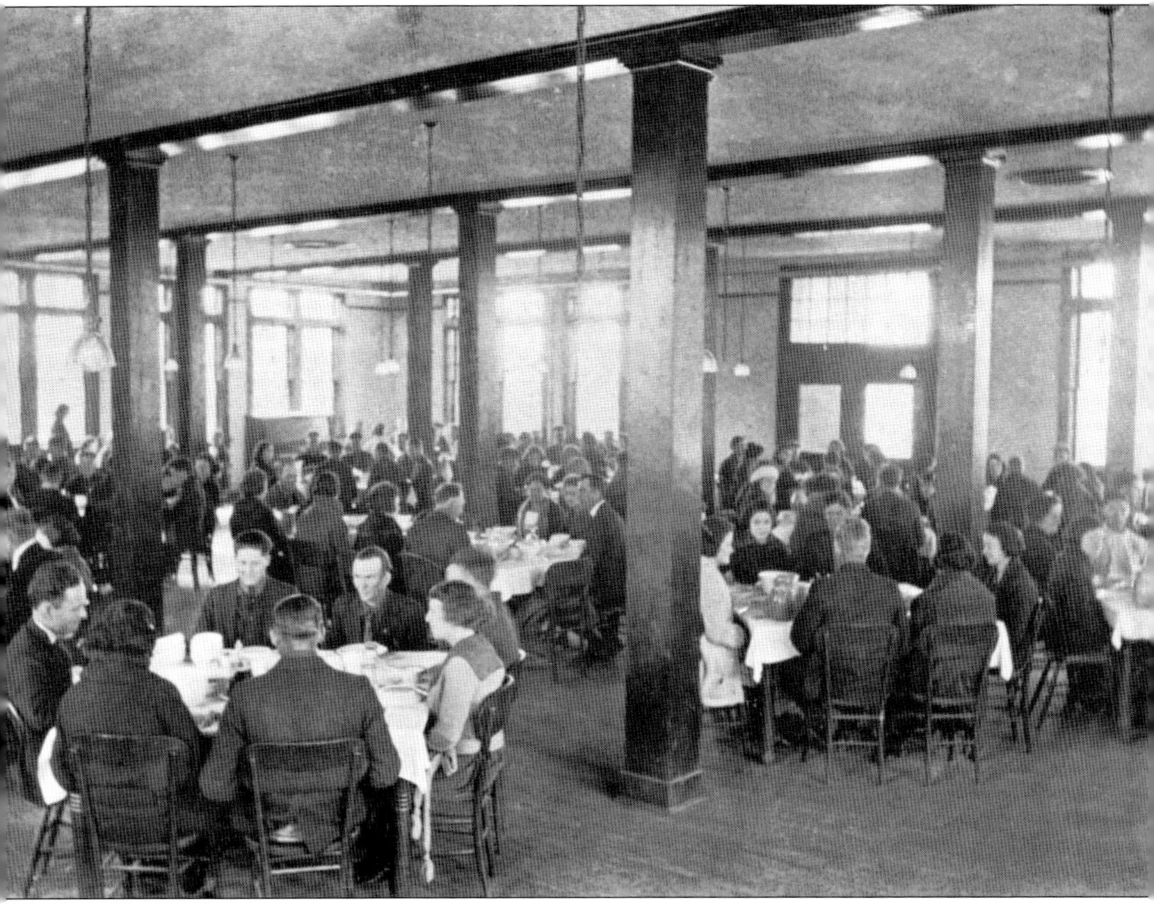

This dining hall was used from 1913 to 1936. It accommodated 250 diners at a time. Home economics teachers and Caro Bussey used the meals to teach table manners and social graces to rural students, who had not learned such behavior at home. Males and females in balanced numbers had assigned places at tables seating eight. One girl at each table brought the food from the kitchen in large bowls and platters and served it home-style. After meals ended, all diners were supposed to remain seated, engaged in quiet conversation, until a bell permitted them to leave. Teachers moved the students every few weeks so that they would become more widely acquainted with each other. After remodeling in 1937, the dining hall became the school's library until 1953.

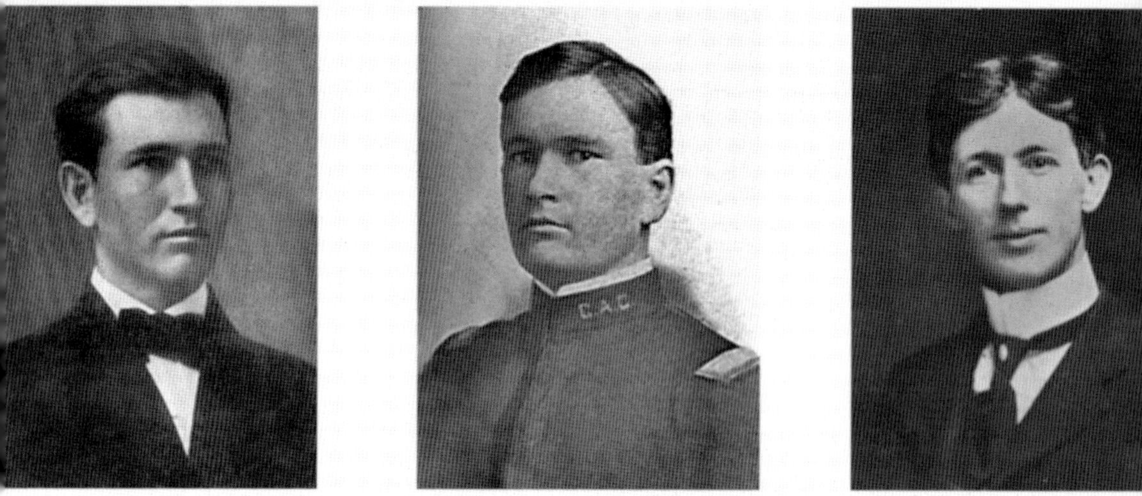

Between 1911 and 1914, TDAS had three principals in quick succession (from left to right): David Burleson, Harper K. Sanders, and Dr. William S. Johnson. The school hired out-of-state agriculture graduates as its first two principals. Burleson was a graduate of Alabama Polytechnic Institute, and Sanders came from Clemson Agricultural College in South Carolina. Both young men had only recently graduated and never gained the confidence of the board of trustees. Dr. Johnson, however, had a long and distinguished academic career, graduating from Ouachita Baptist College in Arkadelphia, Arkansas, earning a PhD from Yale University, and teaching at the University of Arkansas. He also had to leave after only one year, as he did not have an agricultural degree, an explicit requirement of the legislative act that created TDAS. The board of trustees had apparently tried to ignore that provision.

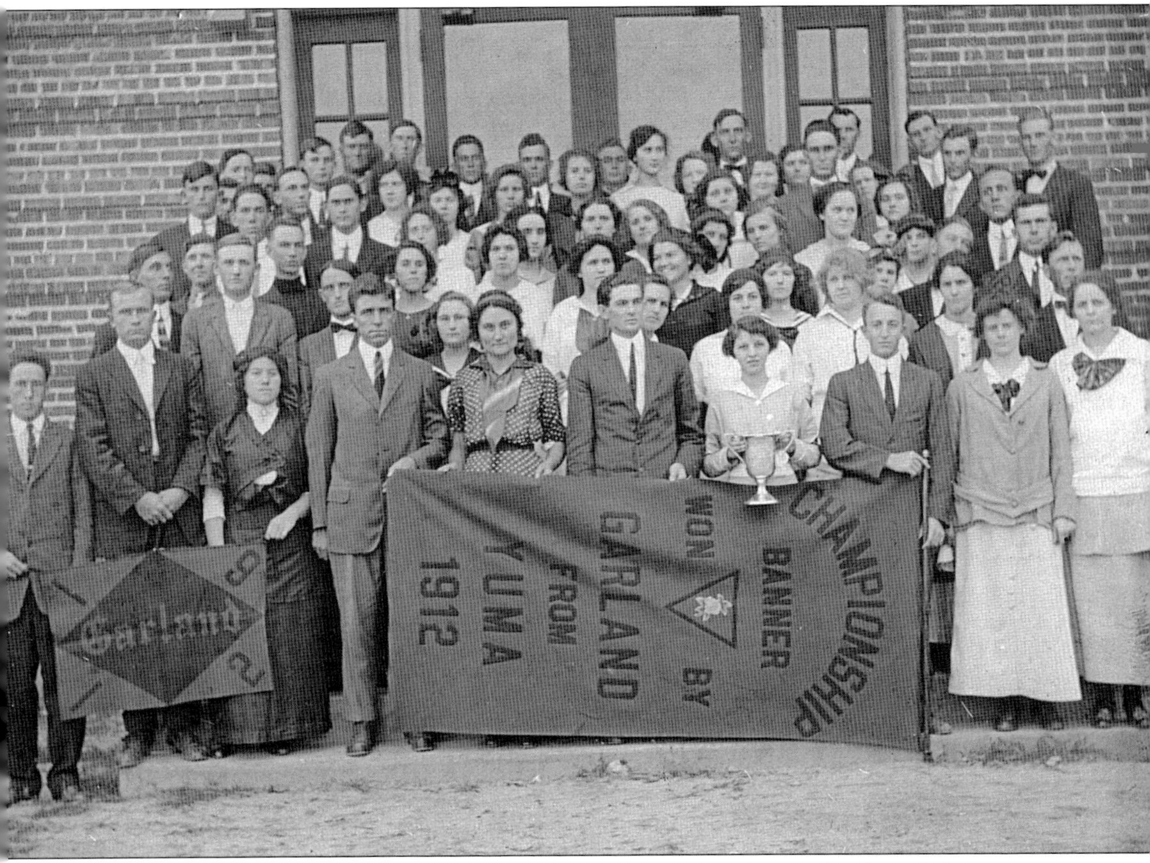

These students in 1912 were members of two literary clubs, the Garlands and the Yumas. Speeches, literary readings, and debates on public issues were considered an essential part of the education that TDAS provided to give students skills they might practice as citizens. However, these were largely extracurricular activities of the clubs. On Friday and Saturday nights, students met in debate, oratory, parliamentary practice, and for entertainments. The clubs also served as social organizations and held parties, as well as producing theatrical plays and musical recitals. Near the school year's end, the clubs competed to claim a championship banner and cup, like the ones held by the Garlands.

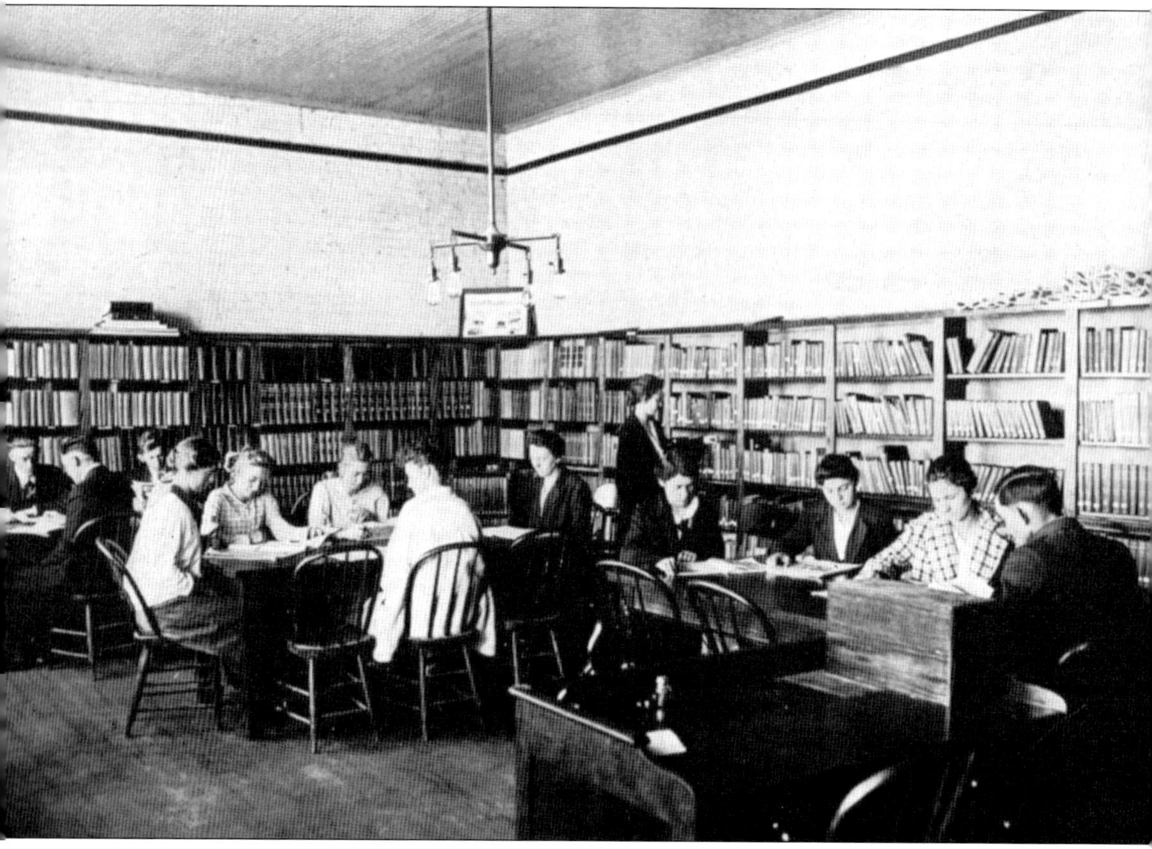

The TDAS library was located in one large room on the second floor of Old Main. At first, books were scattered across the campus in rooms assigned to various departments. James Peace, a recent Hendrix College graduate hired in 1914 to teach English, organized the first library by gathering all the books into Old Main. The library was not then a high priority, perhaps because of the school's emphasis on vocational training. Most library materials were reference books, dictionaries, and US Department of Agriculture publications. However, there were numerous subscriptions to magazines, ranging from *The Progressive Farmer* and *Good Housekeeping* to *The New Republic*, *Outlook*, and *The Literary Digest*. The last three magazines were leading publications focusing on current events, especially on progressive politics and government. The faculty wanted students to be acquainted with and able to discuss and debate public issues so that they might become leaders in rural Arkansas.

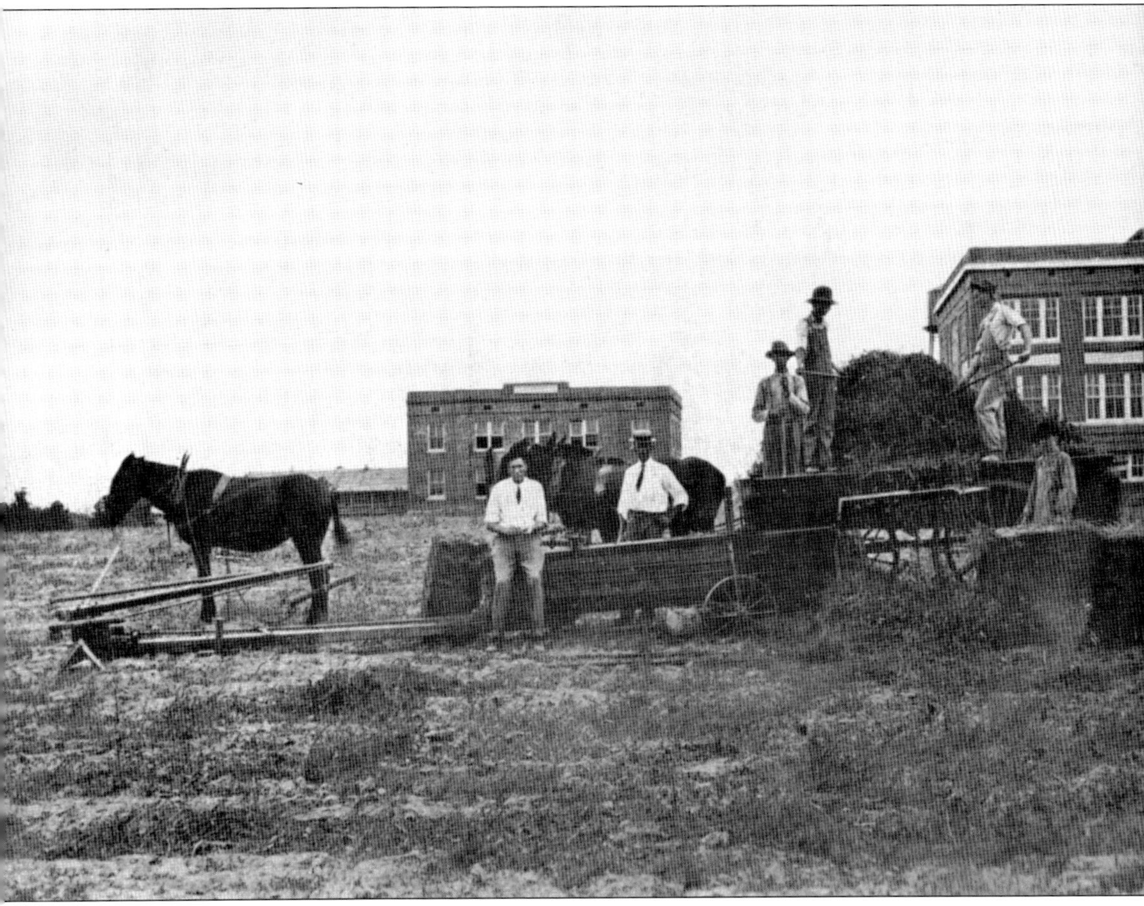

During TDAS's first two years, the land near campus buildings was used to grow crops. In 1912, hay was harvested in the area immediately in front of Old Main and Holt Hall. The two men wearing ties must have been faculty supervisors, dressed perhaps to pose for the photograph. The men in overalls were student workers. Some work in the fields was related to agricultural classes, and students did not receive compensation for their efforts. Other work allowed students to earn money to pay for room and board. Act 100 establishing the agricultural schools specified that all work be performed by students. For several decades, the school hired almost no full-time physical plant employees, relying on student workers to maintain the campus and to raise crops and animals.

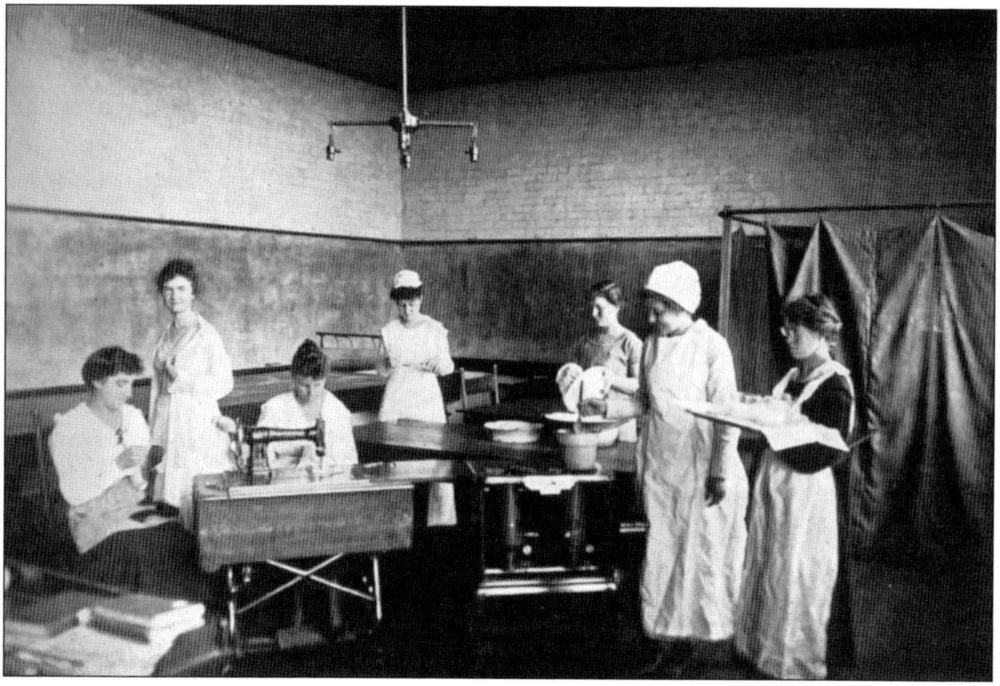

The only path of study open to young women at TDAS was home economics. Students learned the skills of sewing, cooking, interior decoration, childcare, and simple medical treatment. Students also enrolled in a full regimen of history, English, mathematics, and the sciences for a high school diploma.

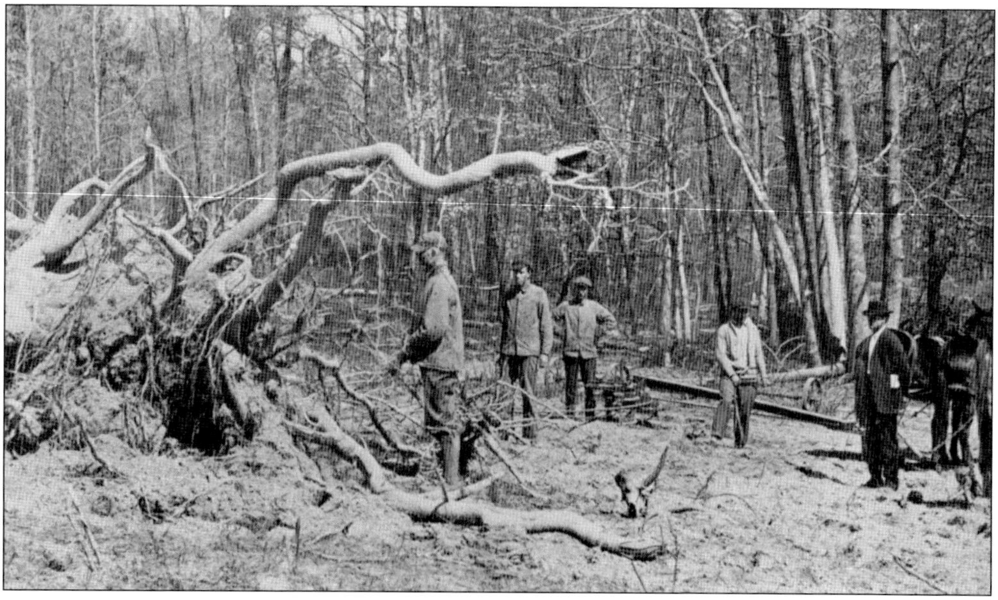

TDAS had 390 acres for farming and 20 acres for the campus. Approximately 150 acres were first cultivated. The previous owners had exhausted the land by repeatedly planting cotton without crop rotation. To get new farm land, students cut down trees and learned how to remove stumps with a stump puller, partially shown here, using mules pulling a long beam with chains attached to a pivot point to extract the roots.

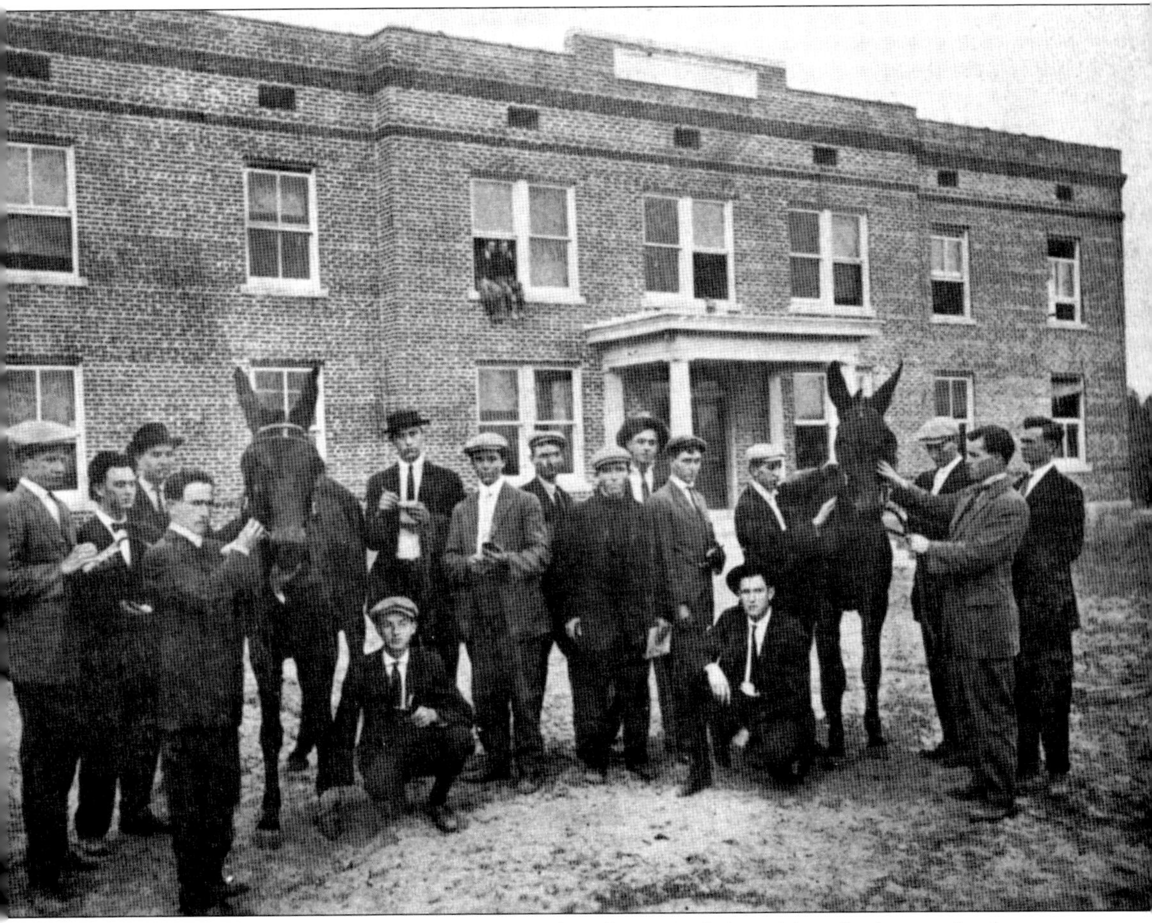

TDAS's agricultural curriculum was vocational and practical. Acquiring the best animals was crucial for a successful farmer. Mules like the two in this picture were the principal work and plow animals, rather than horses, in Southern agriculture. Students learned to pick the best mules and other animals by participating in stock judging competitions at county and state fairs. Most TDAS students came from poor families; when their earnings were inadequate to cover the expense of going to a fair, faculty often stepped in to help. Agricultural instructor Hainan Holtzclaw, kneeling at right, took Marvin Williams, far right, into his home for a semester when the young man ran out of money. The full story was not revealed for five decades until Williams, by then a long-serving state senator in Mississippi, wrote an unpublished memoir for his children and grandchildren. The tradition of faculty and staff making special efforts to help students continued through the decades to the present.

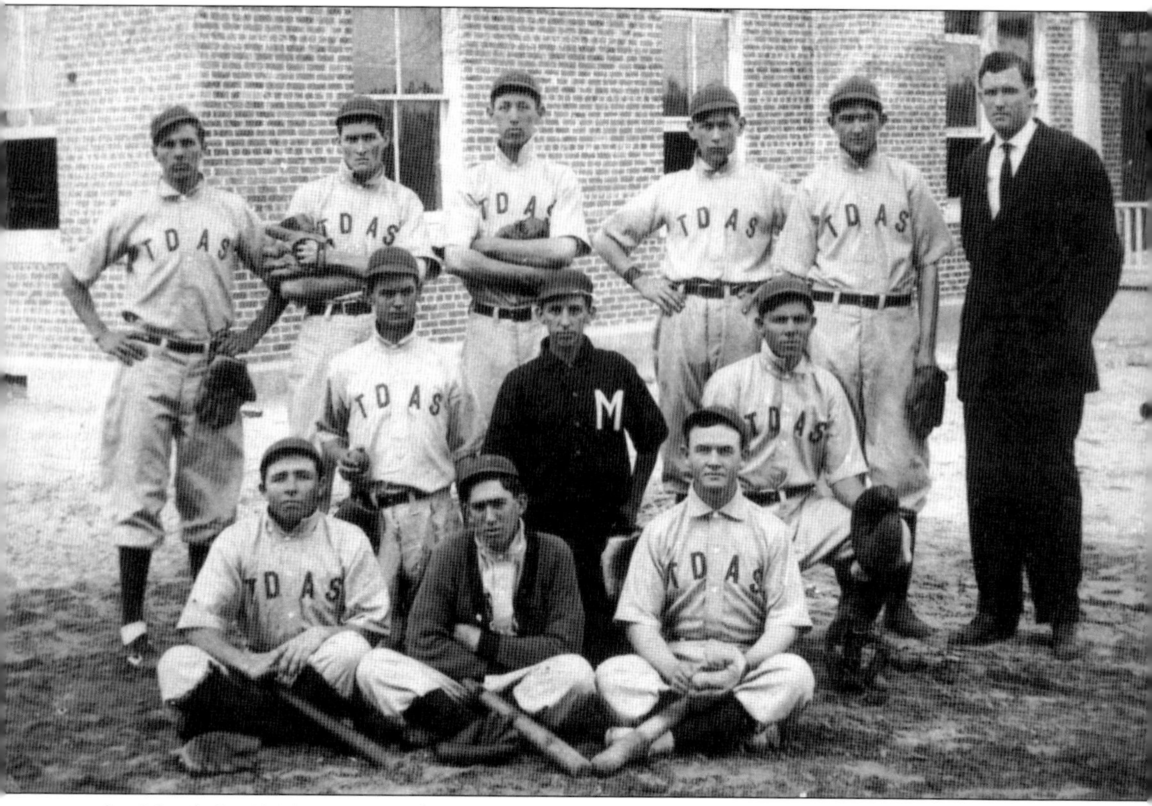

On March 3, 1911, two months into the school's opening semester, the board of trustees authorized $70 for baseball uniforms bearing the school's initials. That spring, the team played ball for the first time. This early start gave baseball the honor of being SAU's oldest continuous athletic program, predating Mulerider football, which began the following fall. Agriculture instructor Hainan Holtzclaw coached the team in the early games. A baseball diamond in a cleared field at J.W. Witt's cotton farm (west of present-day Peace Shopping Center in Magnolia) was marked off for these contests, all between TDAS and Magnolia High School. Team members included, in unknown order, Fred Baskin, Horace L. Buffington, John W. Dawson, Marvin Dudney, Irwin Heath, Thomas M. Holt, Conrad Lewis, William C. Peace, N. Alton Sawyer, Robert Smith, and Lewis Tate.

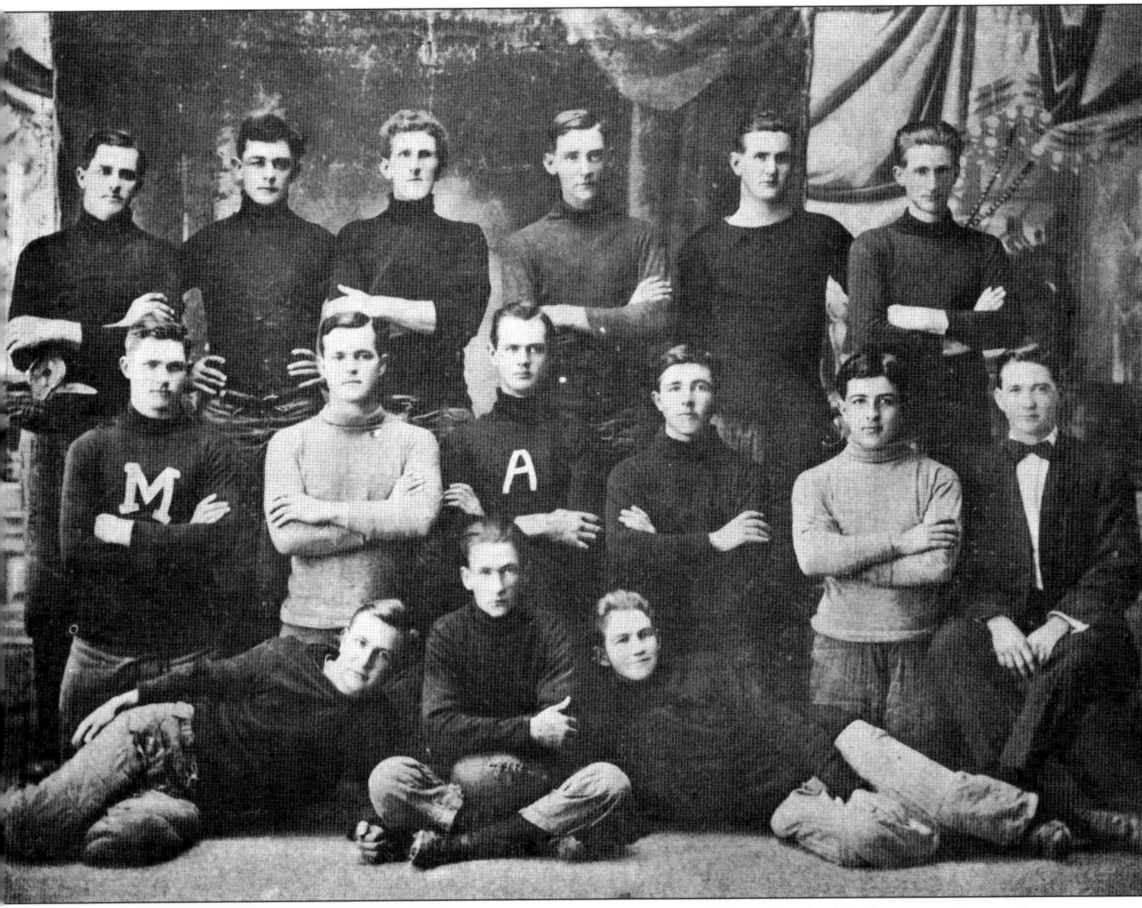

In 1912, TDAS's first coach, George Ruford Turrentine, and his football players chose the team name Mule Riders at the end of the season. However, the name Aggies was often used until Muleriders was officially adopted in the early 1920s. A mule with a rider then began to appear on the sidelines at games. There are numerous stories about the origin of the name, including the most likely one, that it imitated Rough Riders, the heroic cavalry unit led by Theodore Roosevelt in the Spanish-American War. Alternate stories claim it came from teams riding mules to McNeil, five miles away, to catch trains to travel to football games elsewhere, or that early TDAS players, like all poor farm boys in the South, more often rode mules than horses. Whatever its origin, Muleriders remains unique; no other university or college in the world uses that name.

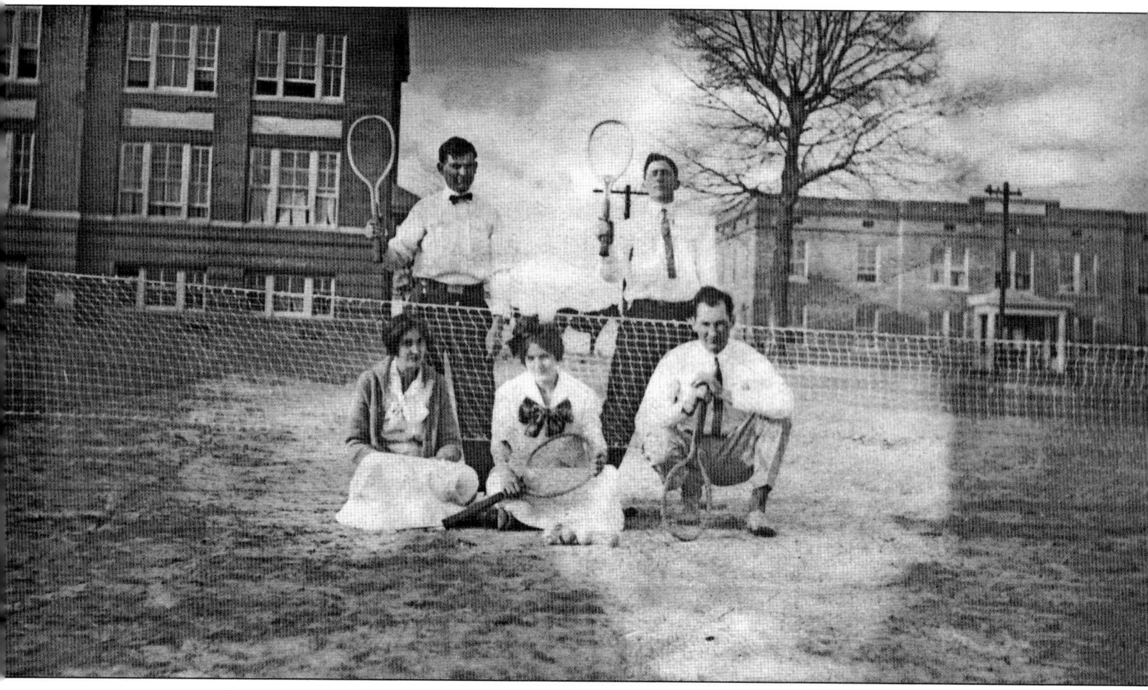

Recreational opportunities for TDAS faculty before World War I were few. Most faculty members lived in campus housing. Magnolia was more than a mile away, and walking, riding a horse or mule, or riding in a buggy were the only means of transport. When TDAS opened, there was only one automobile in Columbia County. Duke Emerson, who ran a livery stable just off the square, bought the county's first automobile in 1910, a Cadillac in which he gave quick rides around the square to curious farmers and townsmen. Other attractions were few. There were frequent church and tent revivals, and an annual lyceum with a mixture of educational lectures and vaudeville acts. The city's first silent picture show opened only shortly before TDAS was built. On campus, faculty lawn tennis was popular. Holding rackets in front are Mrs. Prentice and Mr. Bishop; standing behind are James M. Peace and Harry Goodson. With no racket, Mayfred Stoughton must have come to watch, or perhaps to referee.

Our Soldier and Sailor Boys

April 1st of last year found not a single student of our school in a training camp. Now we can say with pride that we have a hundred and twelve boys in the training camps, and some of that number are already in France fighting for the liberties of the world. We regret very much to lose these boys but are proud of them and the record they are making.

In the 1918 TDAS yearbook, heartfelt tribute was paid to the young men who volunteered for war against Germany in 1917. Approximately 100 young men from TDAS joined a hastily formed company of the Arkansas National Guard, and most were incorporated into the 39th Division of the US Army. Others joined the Navy. After the United States entered the war, students and faculty left behind enthusiastically joined local citizens to buy war bonds, knit scarves, make bandages for the wounded, and grow more food. Some soldiers from TDAS fought in the victorious Battle of Saint-Mihiel, the first major engagement of American forces against Germany. Altogether, six former TDAS students died during the war. Two of the 1917 volunteers who were killed in France were specially recognized in the 1918 yearbook.

In Sacred Memory of

Our Deceased Soldier Boys

Fate Camp

and

Floyd Chaffin

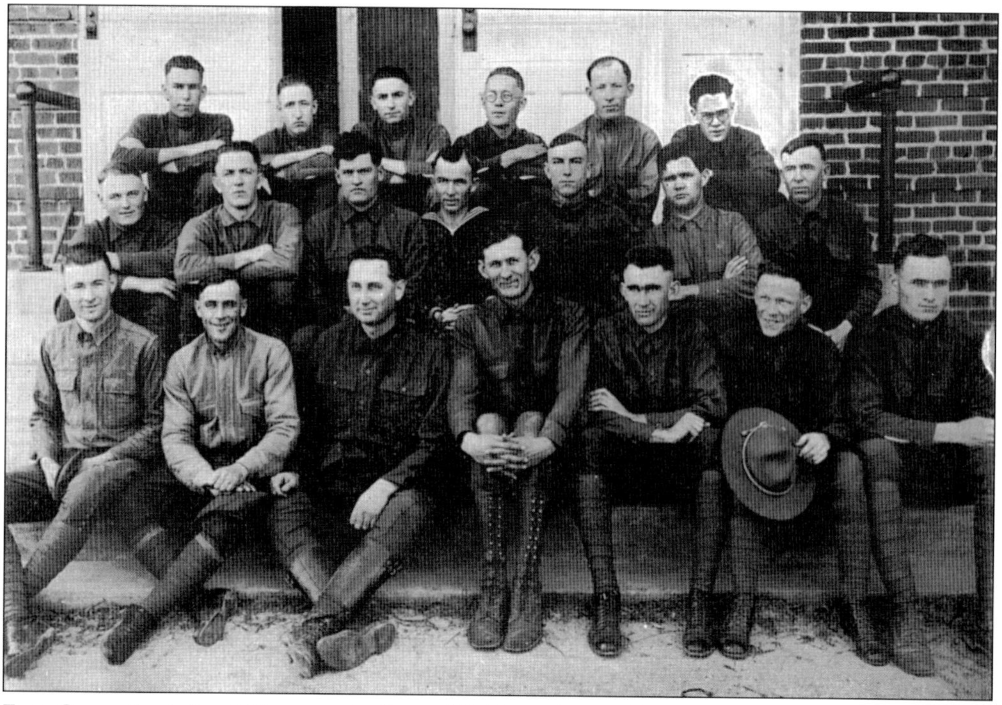

Fate Camp Post No. 108, named after a TDAS student killed in World War I, was the first American Legion unit established in Magnolia. It held meetings at TDAS, for most members were former TDAS students. The veteran in the first row with hands clasped around his knees is Earle E. Graham, a new agriculture teacher at TDAS in 1919, who would later become a long-serving academic dean.

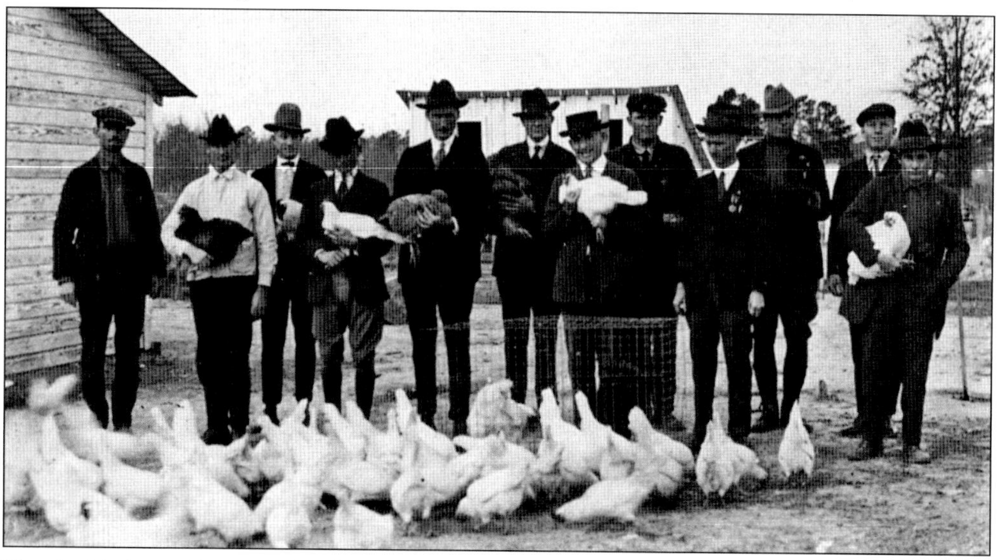

The Smith-Sears Veterans Rehabilitation Act of 1918 provided vocational rehabilitation for permanently injured soldiers. From 1919 to 1924, scores of veterans, including these men, enrolled in a poultry-raising program at TDAS. The program included two years of course work and projects, plus business record keeping and marketing, aimed at turning veterans into full-time poultry farmers. Rental homes west of campus housed the men and their families.

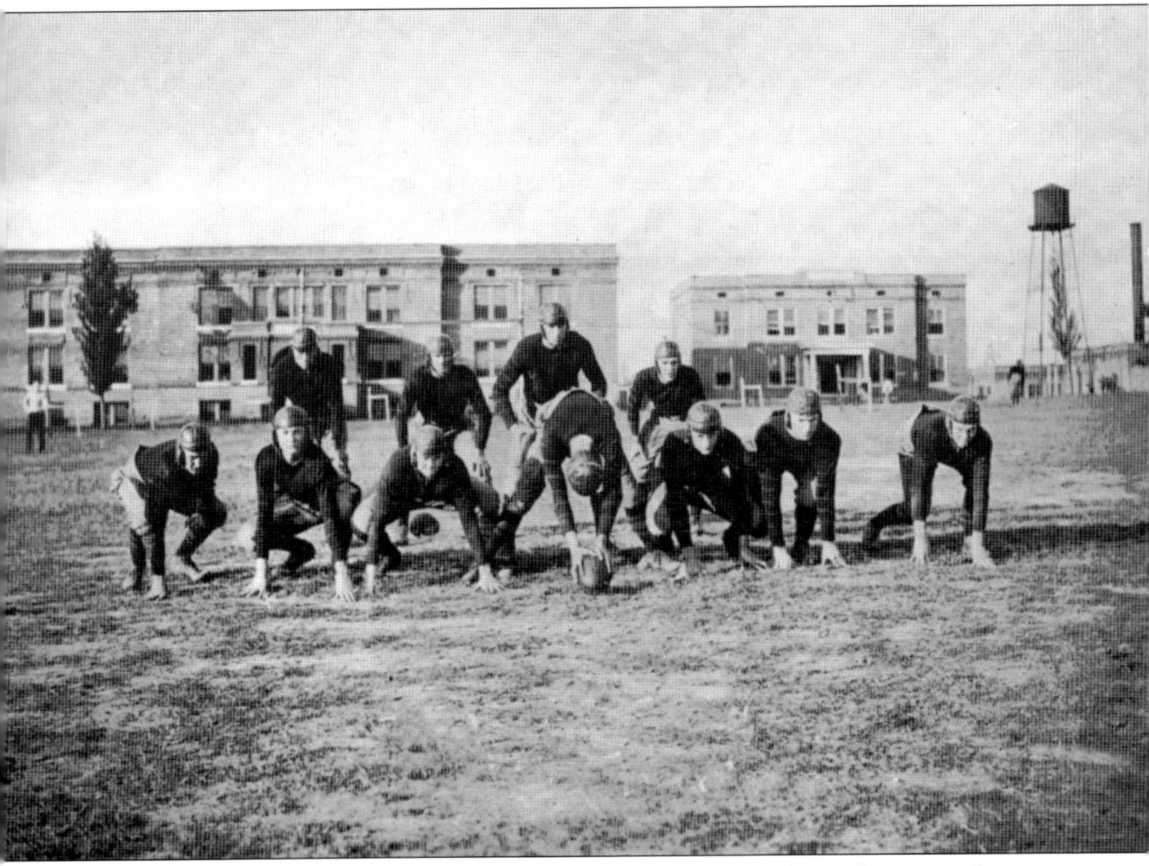

Tough veterans of World War I played on the 1919 Mule Rider football team and gave the school its only undefeated season. Quarterback Ves Godley, an underage US Navy veteran, ran the team because its nominal coach, an agriculture teacher, knew nothing about football. Carl McCollum, a utility back, often took the 13 players to games in his Model T Ford truck. They made quick work of five high school teams and then won against Monticello's agricultural school and Henderson-Brown College in Arkadelphia. The final game on Thanksgiving Day in Magnolia was against the Louisiana Industrial Institute of Ruston (later Louisiana Tech University). The winning play occurred at game's end when center Dolph Camp, later president of Southern State College, snapped the ball to Godley, later a Magnolia A&M College instructor, who threw a 30-yard pass to right end Fonzie Moses for a touchdown. The Arkansas State Athletic Association, composed of both high schools and colleges, decided the undefeated team could not claim a championship since it had not played enough games against high schools or colleges to claim either title.

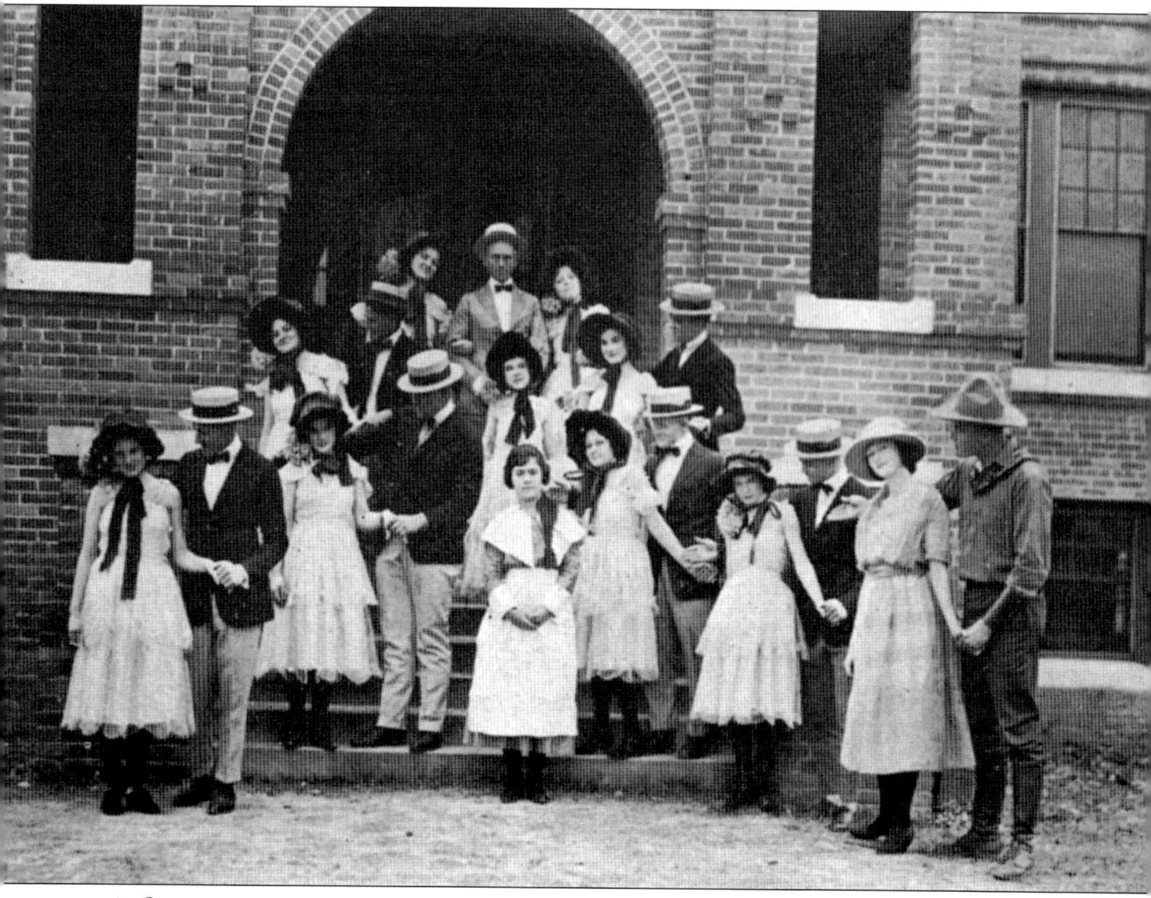

At first, opportunities at TDAS for young women outside the classroom and kitchen were few. However, after World War I, women were regularly featured in theatrical productions during the school year. *The Arrival of Kitty* was staged at TDAS in May 1922. This play, originally appearing on Broadway in 1906 at the West End Theater, was a farce of romances and marriages in the offing, all of them confused by mistaken identities. The play was staged during graduation week. During that week each year, former students returned to campus to visit, and parents of graduates and local citizens came to campus to see displays of agricultural produce, admire dresses and embroidery and other sewing work of the home economics department, and attend special events, such as a theatrical production. The week ended with a baccalaureate service at a local church and commencement at TDAS, during which students received their diplomas.

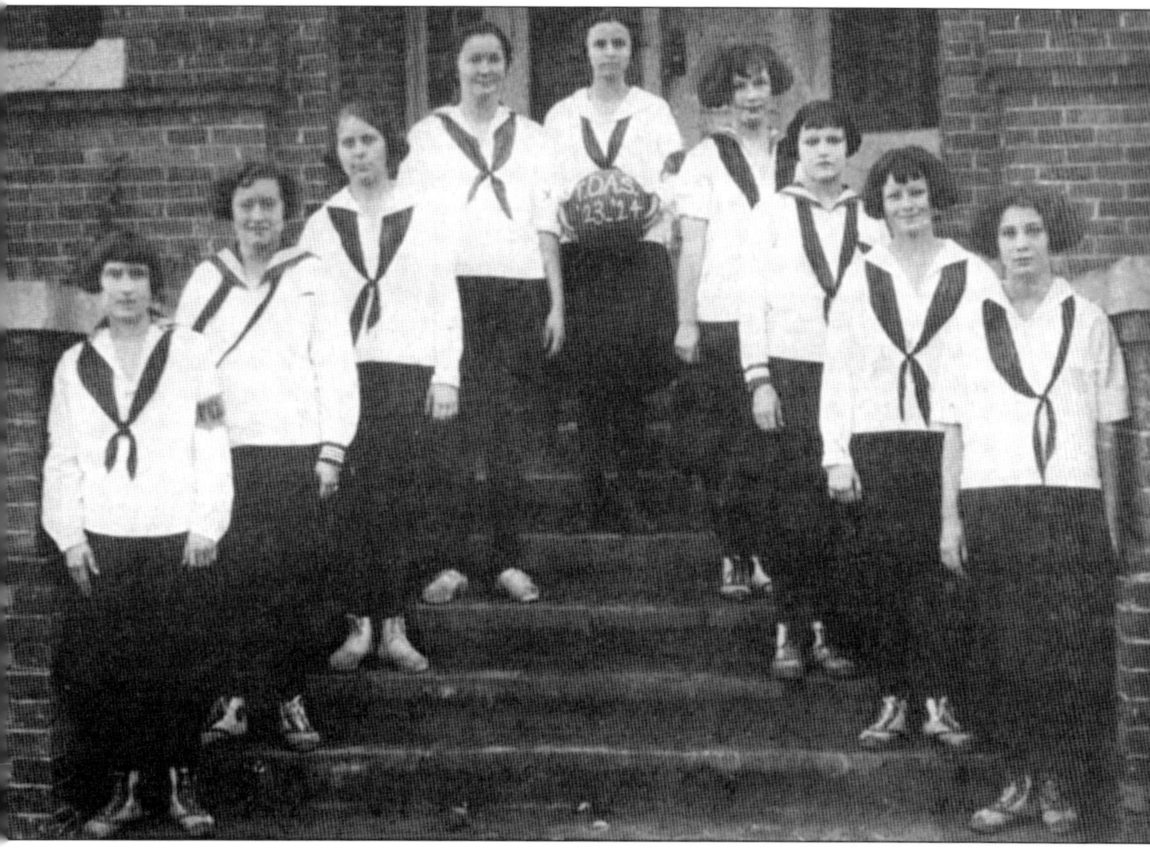

Over time, opportunities for female students included athletics. A women's basketball team began in 1923. Across the nation, there were always those who believed women's competitive sports in general were both unladylike and unhealthy for females. Within a decade, a new female coach from out of state who advocated this viewpoint came to TDAS's successor school, Magnolia A&M College, and ended the basketball program in favor of intramural sports until after World War II. As this photograph reveals, the players at the beginning remained well covered in bloomers, a pants-like costume that reached below the knee, and a full blouse. However, before women's competitive basketball ended in the late 1920s, A&M women's teams were wearing uniforms much like those of late-20th-century players.

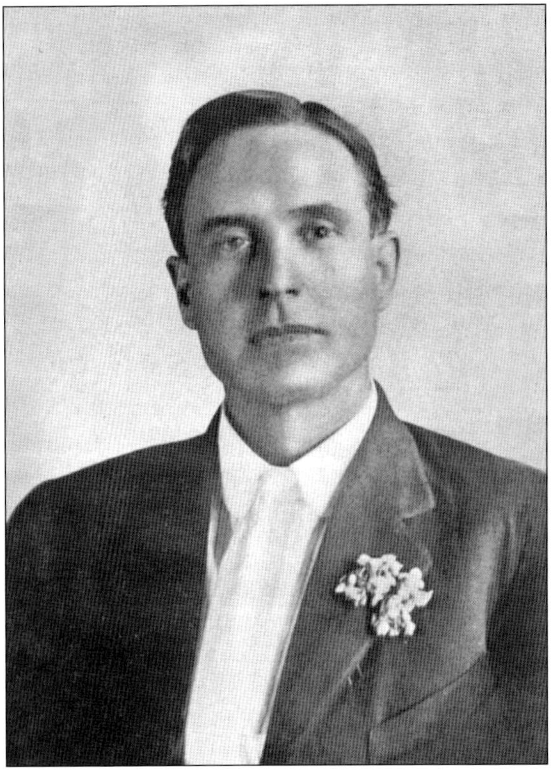

In 1915, Elbert E. Austin became TDAS's fourth principal. He was unfairly dismissed in 1921. Loss of enrollment during World War I created financial difficulties that Austin, without adequate board of trustees support, failed to overcome. He also was a casualty of a larger confrontation between the board, faculty, and students over the school's progress. The board dismissed most of the faculty at the same time as Austin.

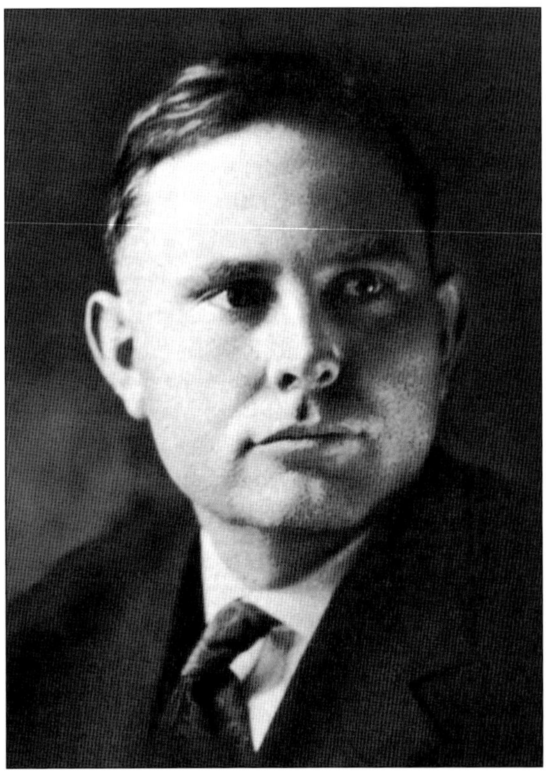

Charles A. Overstreet became the TDAS principal in 1921. Beginning in 1923, he and a largely new faculty transformed TDAS into a two-year junior college and achieved accreditation in 1929. Overstreet was autocratic, but students affectionately called the large man "Big Charlie" behind his back. He saved the school during the Great Depression and again during a severe decline in enrollment during World War II. He retired in 1945.

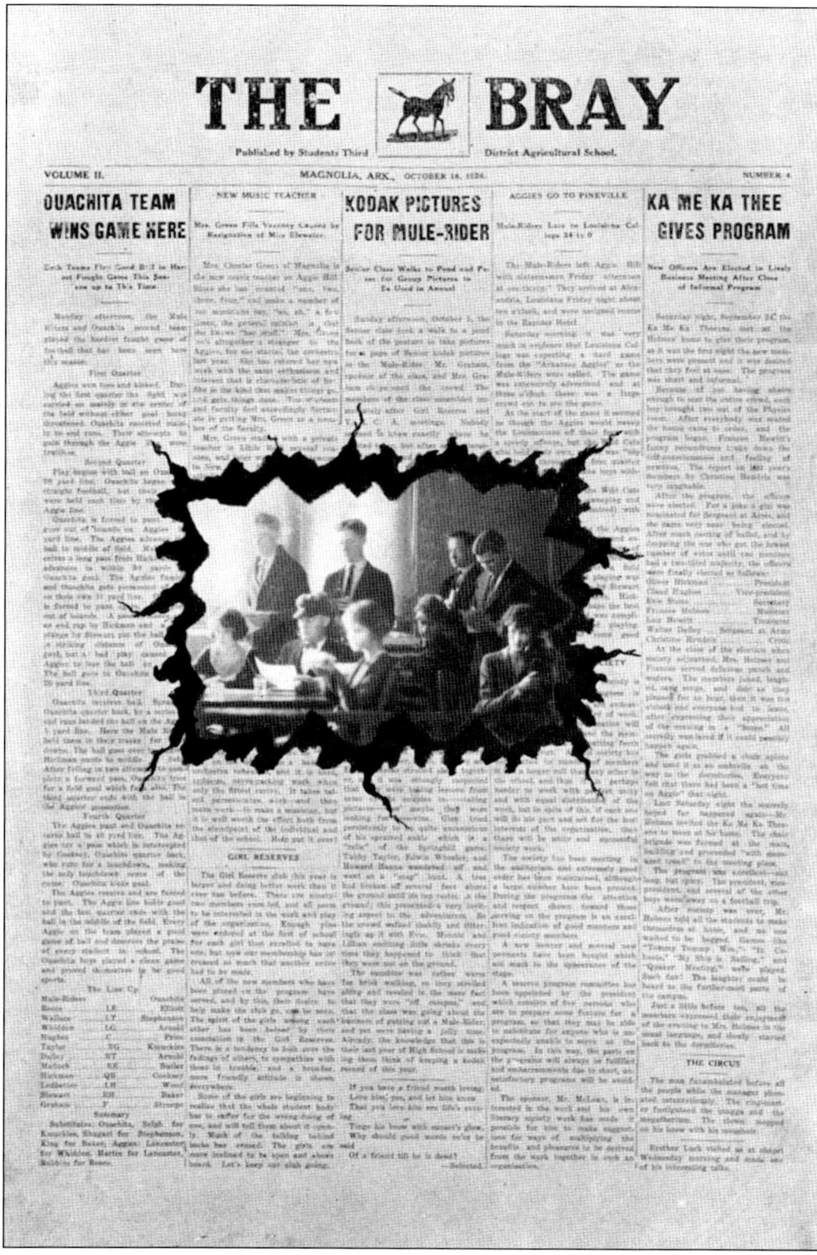
THE BRAY
Published by Students Third District Agricultural School.
VOLUME II. MAGNOLIA, ARK., OCTOBER 14, 1924 NUMBER 4
OUACHITA TEAM WINS GAME HERE
NEW MUSIC TEACHER
KODAK PICTURES FOR MULE-RIDER
AGGIES GO TO PINEVILLE
KA ME KA THEE GIVES PROGRAM
GIRL RESERVES
THE CIRCUS

A school newspaper, *The Bray*, printed its first issue on September 25, 1923. Named after the sound a mule makes, the title matched the football team's name and that of the yearbook, whose title changed from the *Monitor* to the *Mule Rider* in 1922. According to school tradition, agriculture instructor Earle E. Graham persuaded students to adopt the parallel titles. The first *Bray* editor was Naida Northum, who served four years until she completed a high school and associate of arts degree. She managed a staff of 27 reporters who covered every school organization and event, no matter how small. Northum represented a part of the transition from a vocational high school to a liberal arts junior college. Her talents were so outstanding that, contrary to the prevailing custom at TDAS that kept young women in secondary positions, no male challenged her for the editorship.

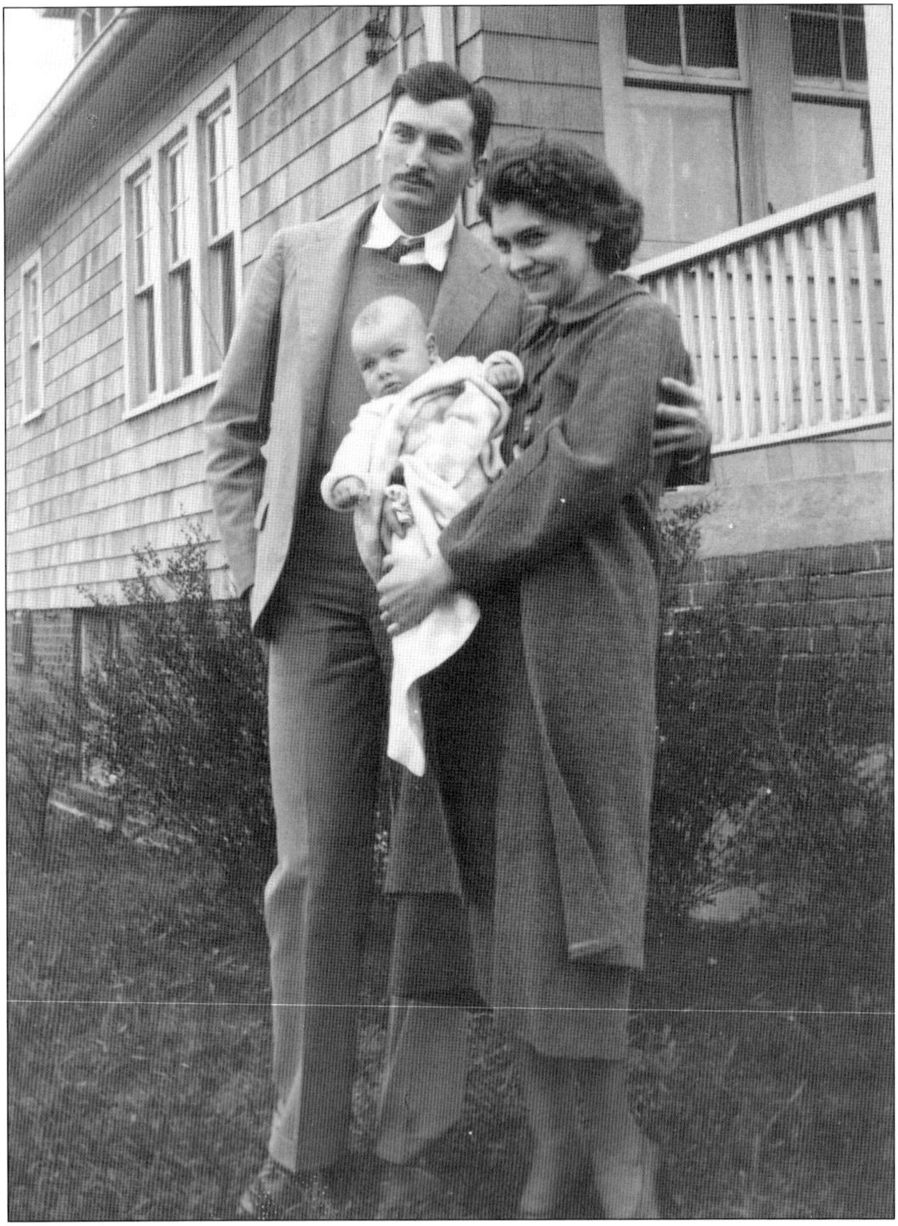

John P. McCollum, pictured here with his wife, Vashti, and son James, was among several distinguished graduates of TDAS. Born and raised on a family farm at Walkersville, a short distance from Magnolia, McCollum graduated from TDAS in 1924, earned a bachelor of science degree from Oklahoma A&M College in 1927, and a PhD from Cornell University in 1930. He served as a professor of animal husbandry during four decades at the University of Illinois. At some risk to his career, McCollum supported his wife as she fought a controversial lawsuit against Champaign-Urbana, Illinois, public schools from 1946 to 1948. The US Supreme Court in *McCollum v. Board of Education* issued a landmark decision in 1948 declaring that religious instruction in a tax-supported school was a violation of the First Amendment's Establishment Clause guaranteeing religious freedom through separation of church and state.

Two

State Agricultural and Mechanical College, Third District

In spring 1925, Glenn Martel, history instructor and band director, took his orchestra on a week-long tour through Southwest Arkansas and Northwest Louisiana. The purpose was to advertise and celebrate the new Arkansas State Agricultural and Mechanical College, Third District. Everywhere, the group announced the establishment of Magnolia A&M College rather than the school's official but awkward-sounding name. Magnolia residents often shortened the name to A&M.

Magnolia A&M built a four-room teacher training school in 1927 and established a teacher education program. Until World War II, public school students in grades one through eight were brought to college, where student practice teachers preparing for rural school positions taught them guided by supervising faculty.

In addition to a new junior college–level associate of arts degree, Magnolia A&M continued to offer high school diplomas until 1937. High school classes served in part as remedial instruction for ill-prepared students. Large numbers of Magnolia A&M graduates continued their education at bachelor degree–granting institutions.

In 1926, the state of Arkansas placed a National Guard armory on the campus. Many male students at the college joined the guard company to earn money to pay for their education. The unit was mobilized in 1941 and served throughout World War II.

Pres. Charles A. Overstreet led Magnolia A&M through three decades, from the flourishing 1920s to the 1930s and 1940s, decades of depression and war. The largest change to Magnolia A&M occurred after World War II, when hundreds of veterans took advantage of GI Bill funding to seek degrees. A new president, Col. Charles Wilkins, met their needs and directed the school toward becoming a four-year college.

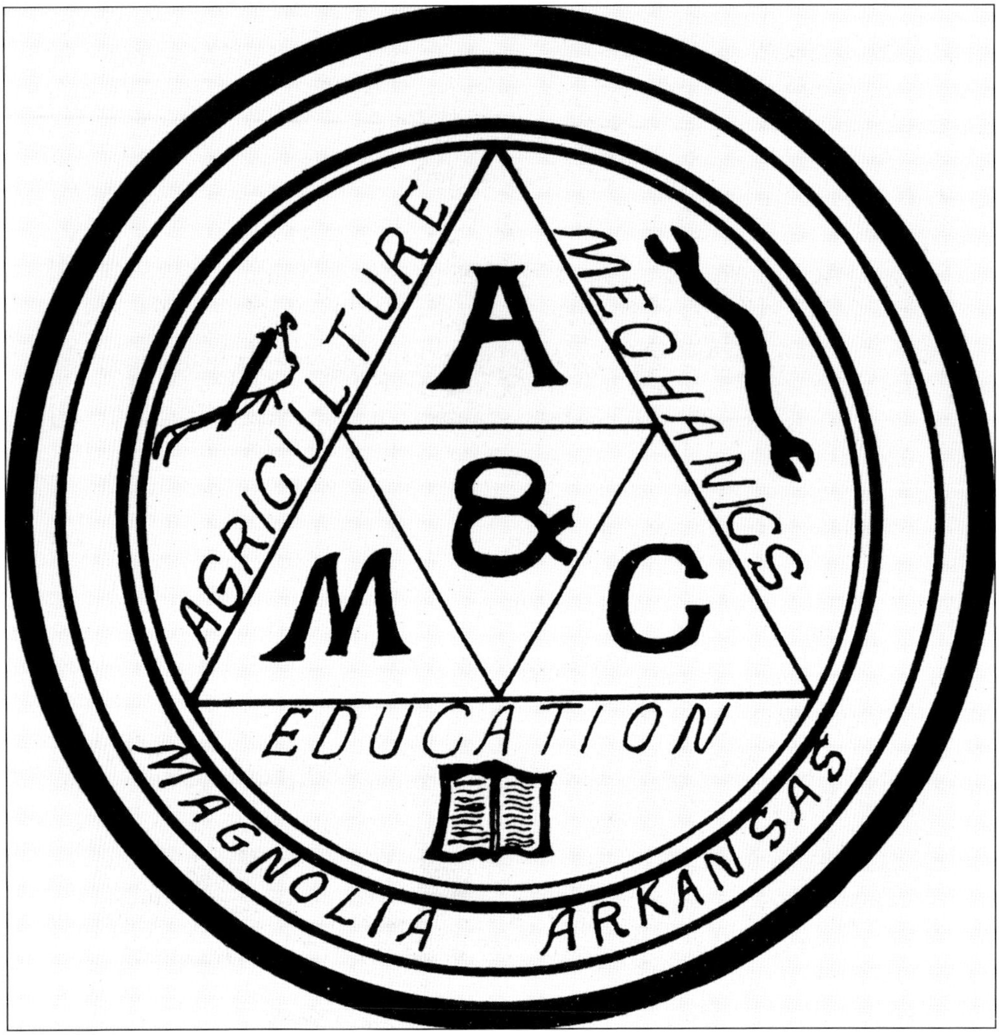

When the Third District Agricultural School was renamed the Arkansas State Agricultural and Mechanical College, Third District, a seal was created for the new college. The seal expressed the school's missions to teach agriculture, mechanics, and education on a collegiate level. In 1923, in Special Act 229, the legislature had instructed the agricultural schools to establish departments "for the training of Rural School Teachers." During that same year, the University of Arkansas and the schools issued a joint statement recognizing the institutions as de facto junior colleges. The schools would upgrade their curriculum and faculty; the university would accept their degrees as "equivalent to two years of work in a junior college or the freshman and sophomore years in a standard college." The schools created college-level curricula, employed new faculty with master's degrees, and required older faculty to take graduate courses during summers until they, too, had advanced degrees.

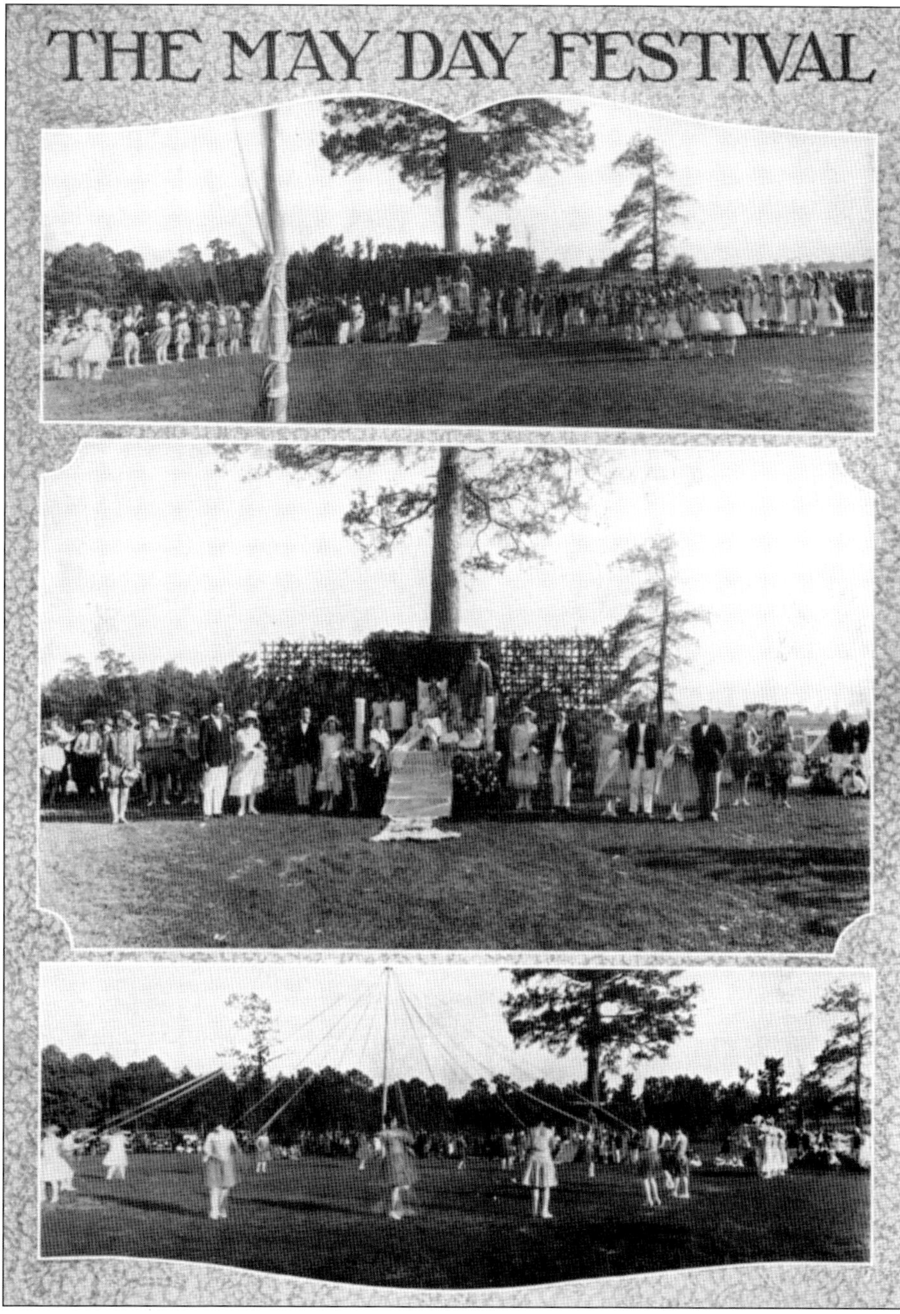

On May 2, 1925, to celebrate the new Magnolia A&M College, several thousand visitors and students witnessed a remarkable May Day Festival staged by music director Glenn Martel and speech and theater instructor Jewell Stevens. A May Queen, Monnie Kent, accompanied by beautiful young women in costume, arrived on a palanquin carried by 10 young men, also in costume, to a throne in front of the Lone Pine Tree. As the school orchestra played, 16 Merry Maids wrapped the nearby May Pole in ribbons. The orchestra then performed a spring concert. Many colleges across the United States performed a similar ritual each spring during this era. Magnolia A&M continued the tradition in one form or another until World War II.

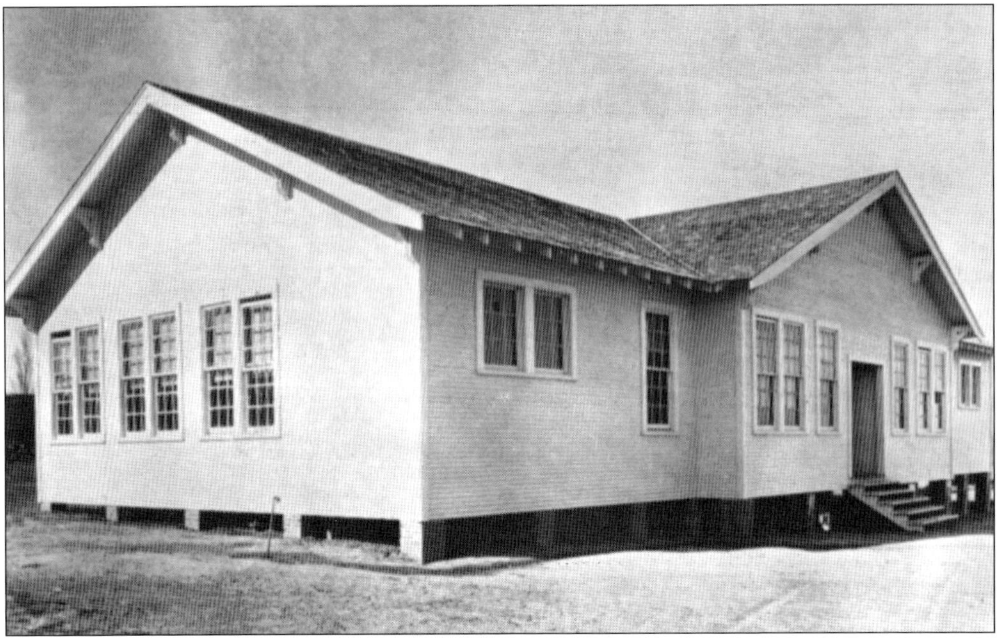

To implement its mission to train rural schoolteachers, Magnolia A&M built a four-room schoolhouse to teach children from grades one to eight. Merrit O. Alcorn, with a master's degree from the George Peabody College for Teachers in Nashville, Tennessee, headed the education department. Student teachers in training, under close supervision of faculty, taught the children. This type of teacher training continued until World War II.

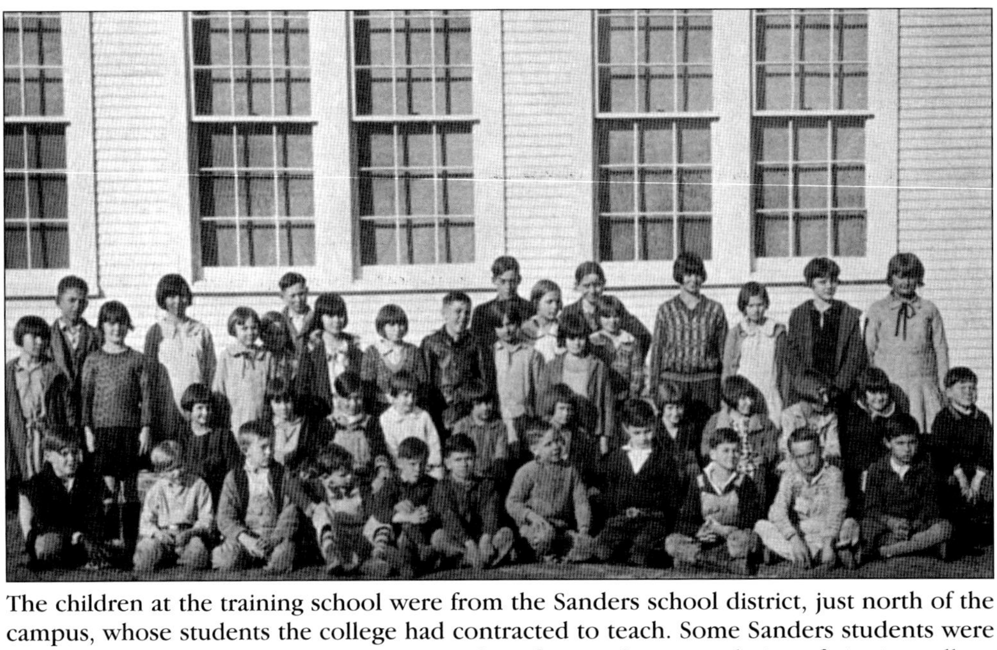

The children at the training school were from the Sanders school district, just north of the campus, whose students the college had contracted to teach. Some Sanders students were able to continue their education on campus from first grade to completion of a junior college degree. The high school department of TDAS continued until 1937, in part to provide some college students with needed remedial courses.

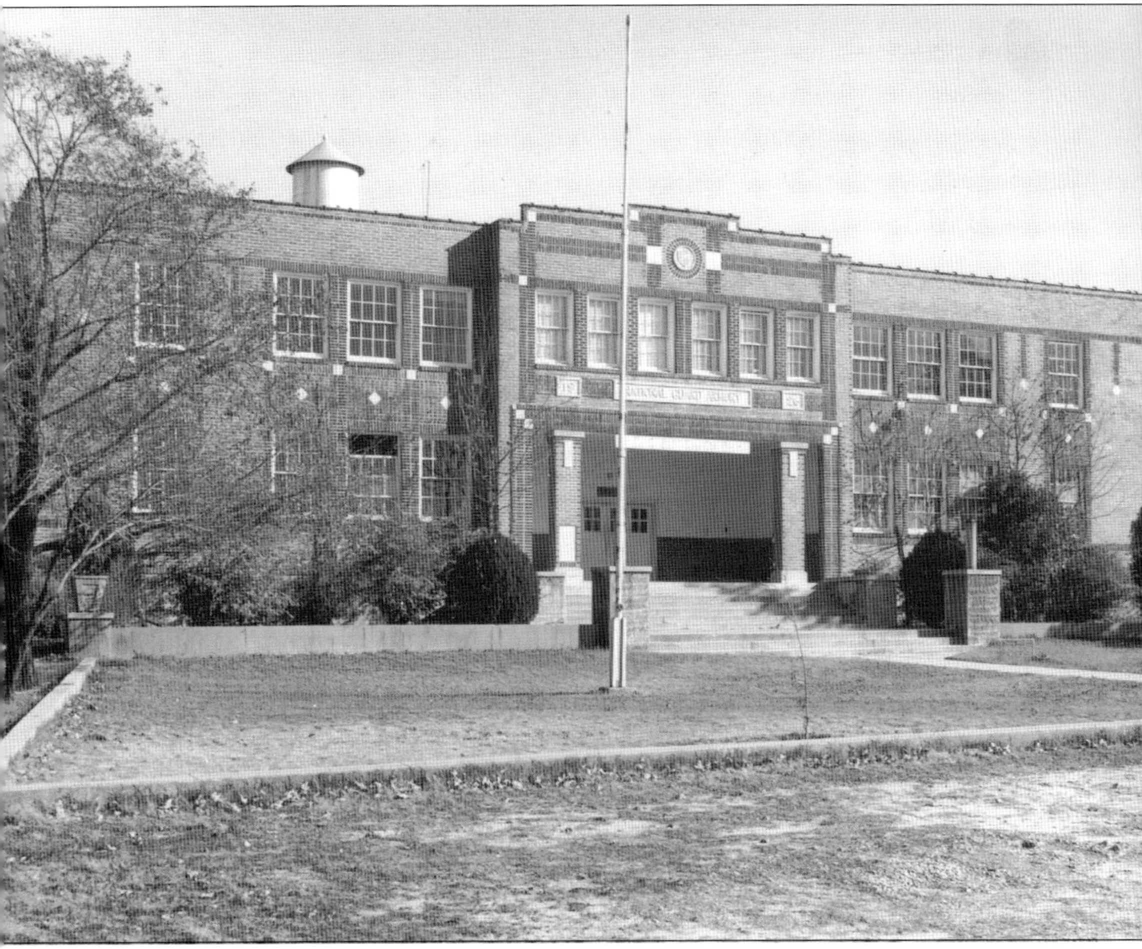

In 1925–1926, a National Guard armory was constructed on the A&M campus. It housed Arkansas National Guard, Company B and Company D of the 153rd Infantry. Its officers were A&M instructors, and the soldiers were their own college students. Students could earn from $24 to $75 every three months, depending on their rank, to pay for school expenses. Guardsmen had to attend two early morning training drills each week and an annual encampment at Camp Pike (later renamed Camp Robinson) in North Little Rock. The armory's facilities doubled the number of classrooms, and its open space for guard assemblies gave the college an interior basketball court and a stage for A&M's theater. Before the men of Company B and Company D were called to serve in World War II, their most exciting and important duty occurred during the Great Flood of 1927. The Mississippi River and its tributaries, including those in Arkansas, inundated large parts of the state. The guardsmen were called to action to protect levees and help some of the 150,000 refugees forced from their homes.

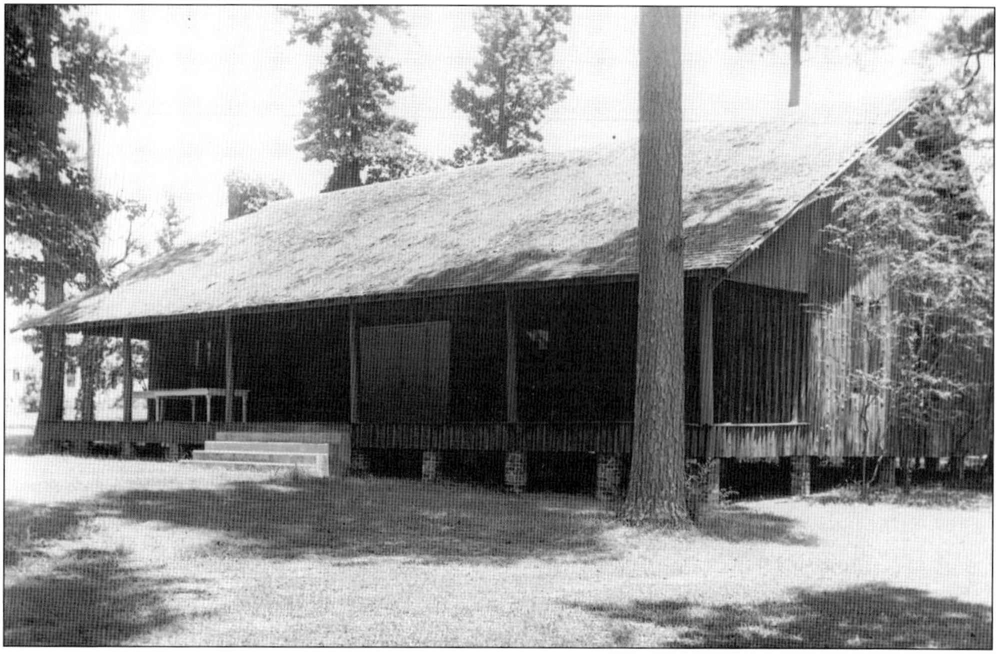

Seniors in three classes, 1931 through 1933, contributed money and labor to construct this rustic club house. It sat in a pine grove on the campus's southeast corner. It held the school's first dance, on October 6, 1934, a significant concession to student demands to overturn the school's compliance with local religious objections to dancing, then enforced at small colleges throughout Arkansas.

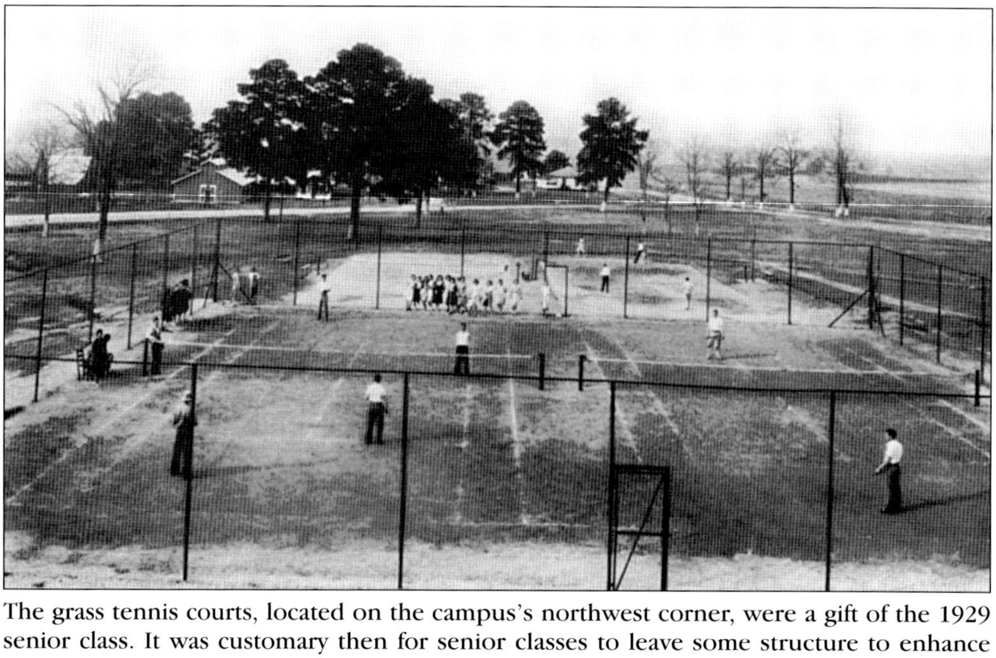

The grass tennis courts, located on the campus's northwest corner, were a gift of the 1929 senior class. It was customary then for senior classes to leave some structure to enhance the school. Tennis matches were intramural or recreational, as A&M did not participate in intercollegiate competition in tennis. Football and basketball were the only competitive sports played against other teams of the Arkansas Intercollegiate Conference (AIC).

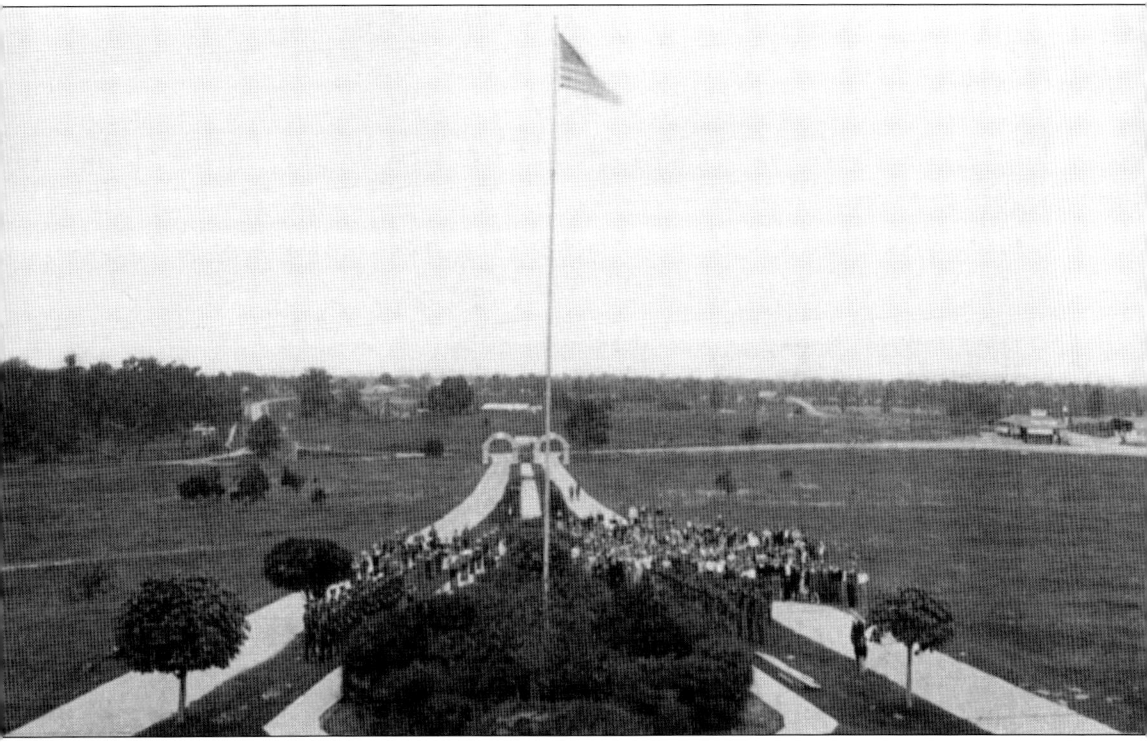

It was a grand day in 1930 when the Stars and Stripes were raised atop an enormous flagpole in front of Old Main. Like other structures donated by senior classes, this gift added to the campus's appearance. This photograph, taken from the roof of Old Main, shows the largely empty countryside that lay between A&M and the city of Magnolia, whose limits ended at present day East Columbia Street. The small structure in the distance on the right was a bus stop and service station named the Blue and Gold. The college's colors were painted in bright colors on the building's large sign. Students could buy freshly cooked hamburgers at a small grill there.

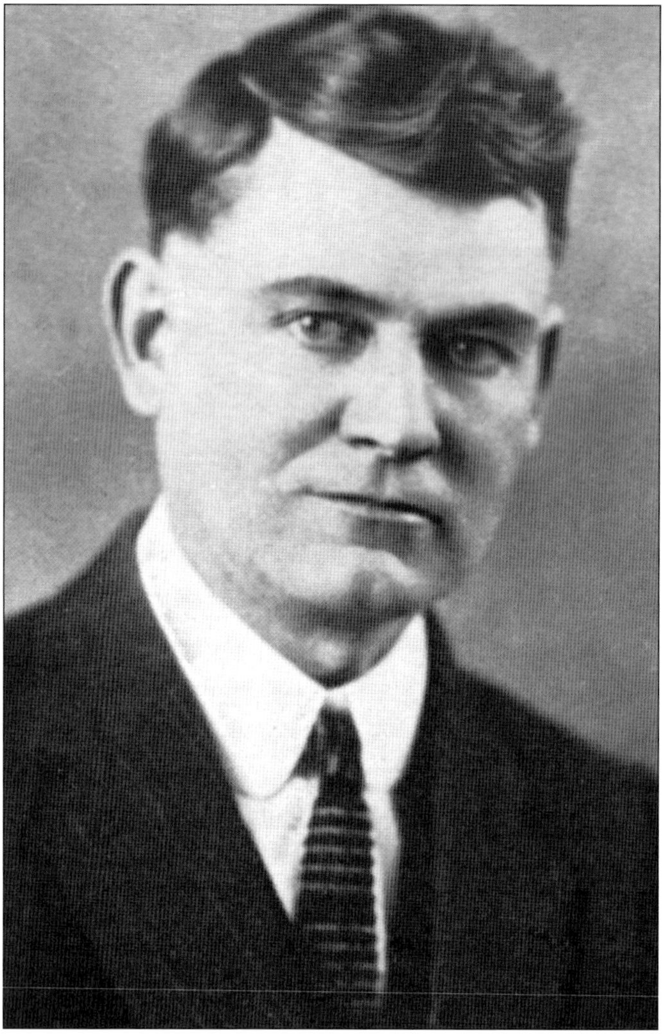

With the added classroom space in the new armory, the A&M library could be expanded in Old Main from one to three large rooms. James M. Peace, who had served as unofficial librarian since 1914, was named librarian in 1928. He attended summer courses in library science at the University of Wisconsin, and made improvements needed to secure accreditation at A&M. A minimum of 5,000 volumes was required to meet the junior college standards of the North Central Association of Colleges and Secondary Schools. In 1927–1928, aided by an assistant librarian, Martha K. Machen, Peace added 2,000 books to the collection and another 2,800 in 1929–1930. With grants from the Carnegie Corporation of New York, 10,000 more volumes were added during the 1930s. The library moved to the remodeled 1913 dining hall in 1937. Peace served as librarian until 1949.

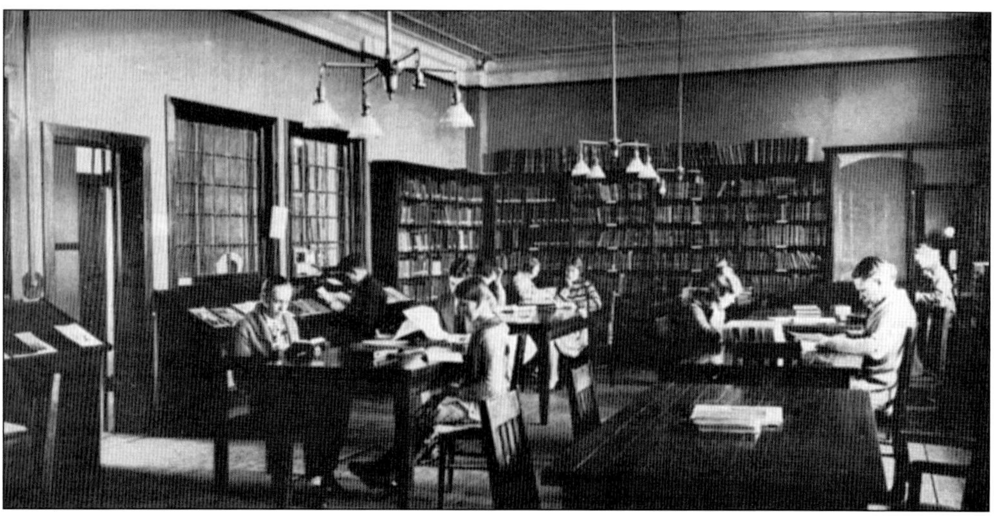

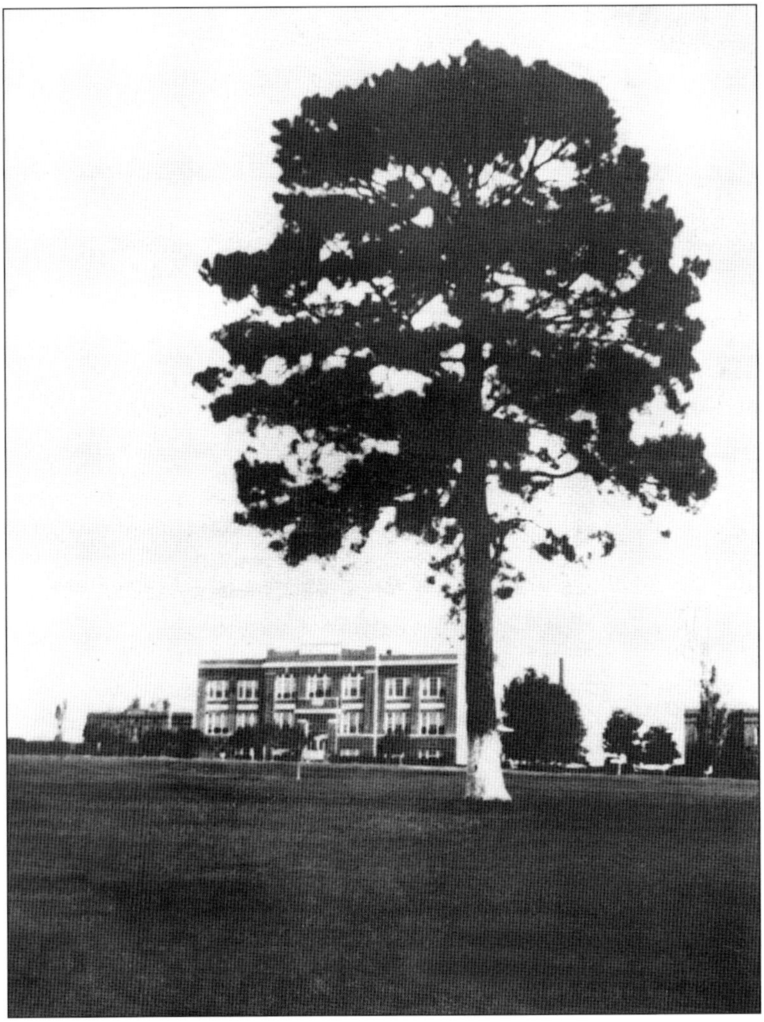

Of many trees planted when TDAS opened, only one survived. A student tradition developed that love declared under that tree would last, just as the tree had. For the next half-century, students pledged devotion and proposed marriage under the "Trysting Tree." Student poet Rufus C. Sparks penned a long ode in 1929 to celebrate the tree. Three of its stanzas were:

You say that I am lonely?
You know not what you say!
I think I shall be happy until my dying day.

Just twenty years have wafted
The school has grown by bounds,
And I'm the only pioneer
That still stands on the grounds.

I've made so many matches
For couples young and gay,
I think I shall be happy
Until my dying day.

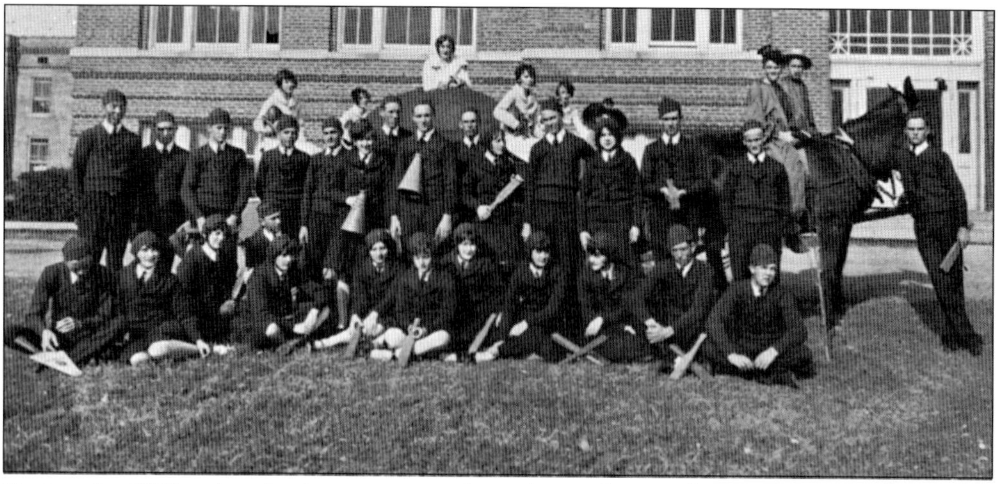

During the 1920s, cheerleaders, pep squads, and a student Mule Rider whipped up yelling fans and the team at A&M football games. Alumnus Arie Dwight Mackey recalled: "What a wonderful memory on a beautiful autumn afternoon. . . . Just before the game, the Muleriders coming on to the field and the Mascot, the Mule, with his rider upon him, running up the sidelines at full speed and braying."

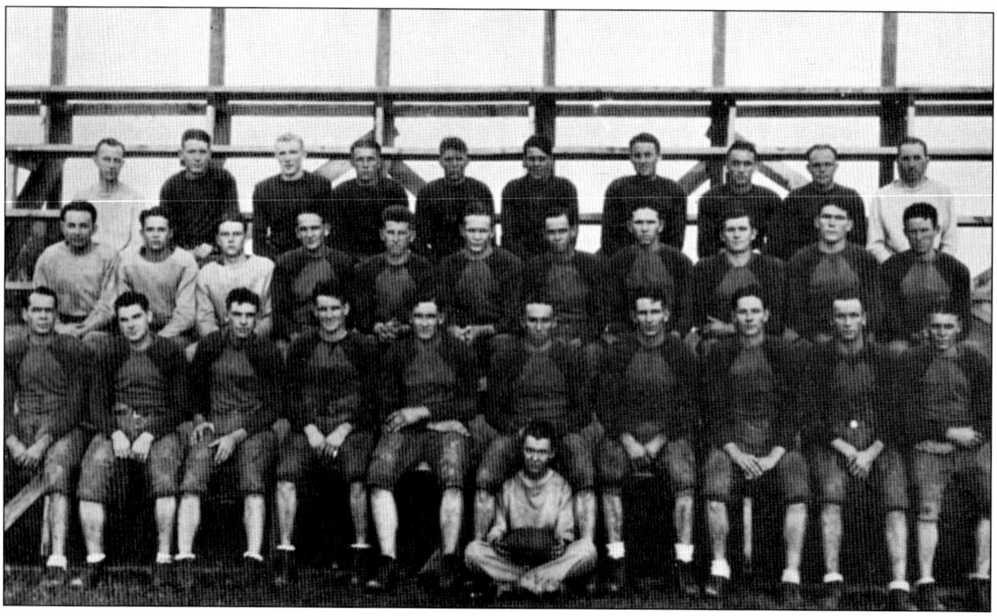

The 1929 Mulerider football team won the school's third AIC championship during the 1920s. Many players in the golden years of A&M football went on to larger schools. Mulerider center Claude H. Hughes played at the US Naval Academy and won Navy's coveted Thompson Trophy Cup in 1930. However, A&M president Charles A. Overstreet suspended football in 1937. The board of trustees renewed it in 1940.

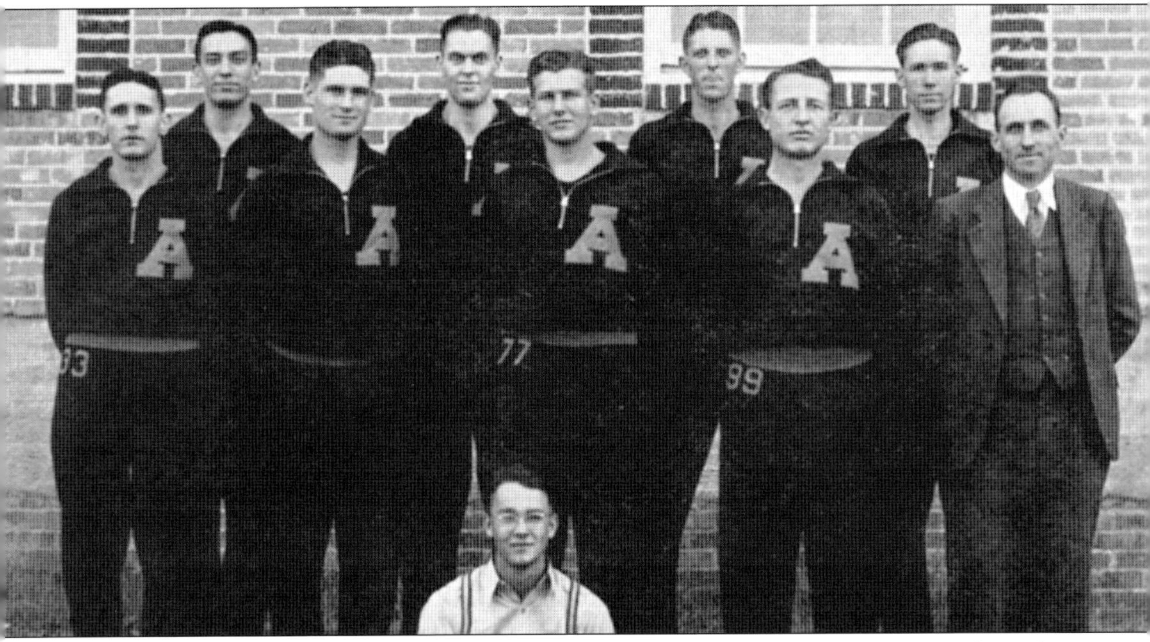

After Ves Godley earned a bachelor's degree in agriculture from Oklahoma A&M College, he returned to his alma mater, Magnolia A&M, in 1926 to teach animal husbandry and to coach basketball. His basketball teams won back-to-back AIC championships in 1934 and 1935. His teams stood out for their talented play and for their uniforms in reverse school colors, vivid gold-colored suits with large blue numerals. The 1934 team posted 17 victories in 18 contests, scoring 952 points to 557 for opponents. In an era of low-scoring, defensive play, the team averaged 52.8 points per game compared to their opponents' 30.9 points. The stars of the teams included forward Elmo Bellamy, guard Cleo Moody, and center Otho Goodman.

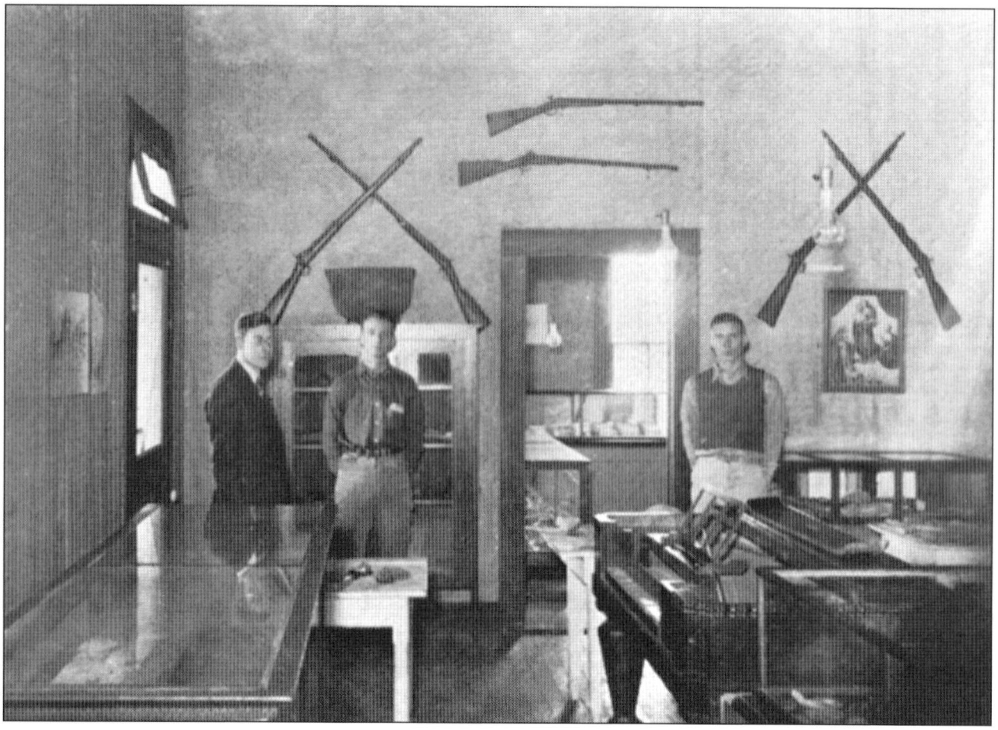

Magnolia A&M established the South Arkansas Museum in 1934. Samuel Dorris Dickinson, left, a Prescott, Arkansas, native son, who had earned a bachelor's degree in anthropology from the University of Arizona and studied at Mexico's National University, managed the museum and taught classes. His digs, the first professional excavations undertaken in the state, along with his publications, later gave him a claim to the informal title "Father of Arkansas Archeology."

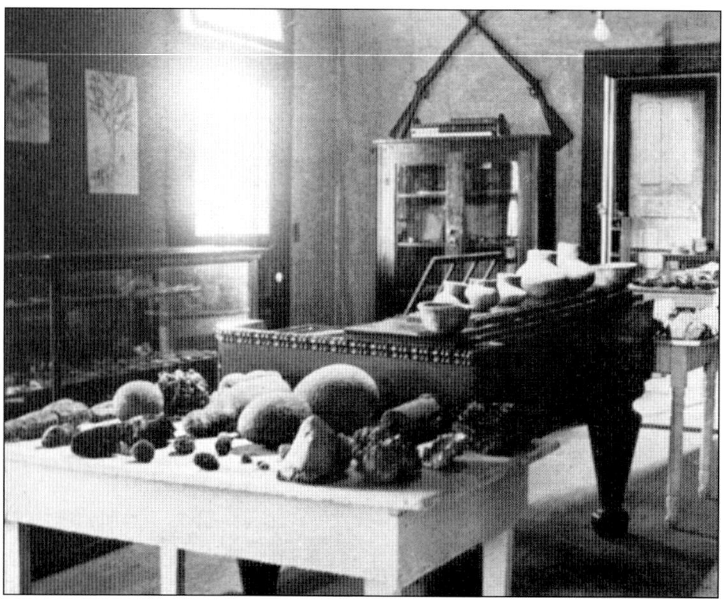

The small museum contained an assortment of fossils, prehistoric and Indian implements, and donated items from the Civil War era. Dickinson was a young man of broad tastes who also taught history and art classes along with directing serious plays, including *Antigone*, *Salome*, and a *Midsummer Night's Dream*. Unfortunately, the museum did not long survive his departure in 1938.

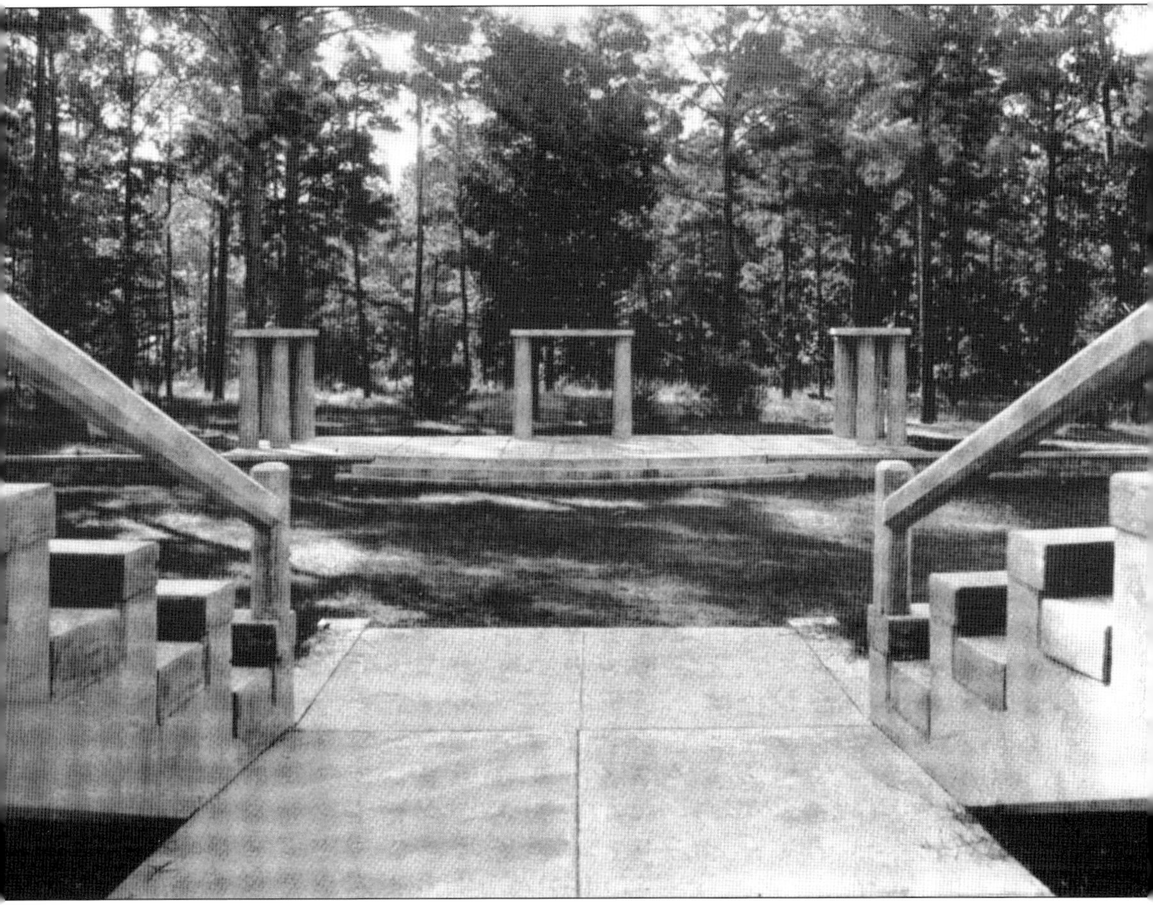

During the 1936 spring semester, students studying Greek and Roman history, inspired by instructor Samuel Dorris Dickinson, decided to perform a Greek play as the course's capstone; moreover, they decided to build a Greek theater for its staging. This effort symbolized changes at A&M. Fewer students studied agriculture. The school increasingly tilted toward the liberal arts, focusing more on students planning to earn a bachelor's degree elsewhere. Dickinson's history students persuaded the 1936 senior class to donate the $200 they had raised for a gift to the college to go toward the theater. National Youth Administration (NYA) vocational students helped history students cast columns and build a stage. Time ran out to place cornices atop the slabs that served as capitals. A performance of *Antigone* was held on May 14 before a large crowd of parents, alumni, and townspeople. The next year, the NYA vocational students constructed the semicircular, concrete bleachers facing the stage. The Greek Theater is one of only two such structures in Arkansas. It is listed in the National Register of Historic Places.

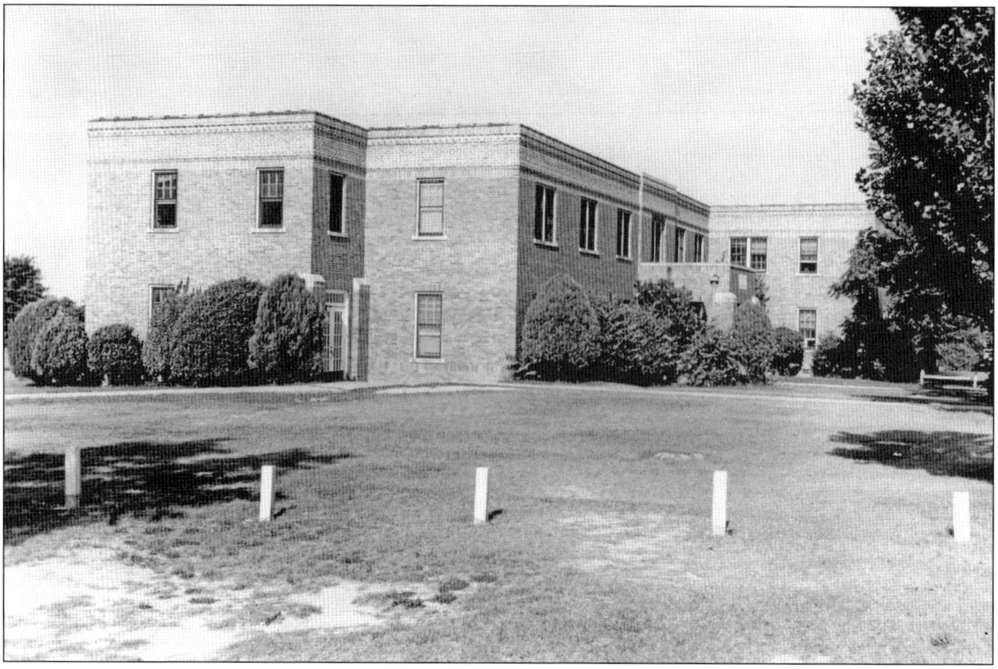

During the Great Depression, the New Deal program that most benefitted Magnolia A&M was funding from the Works Progress Administration (WPA) that partially paid for new campus buildings. Cross Hall, a residence hall for men located across the street from McCrary Hall, was built in 1935–1936.

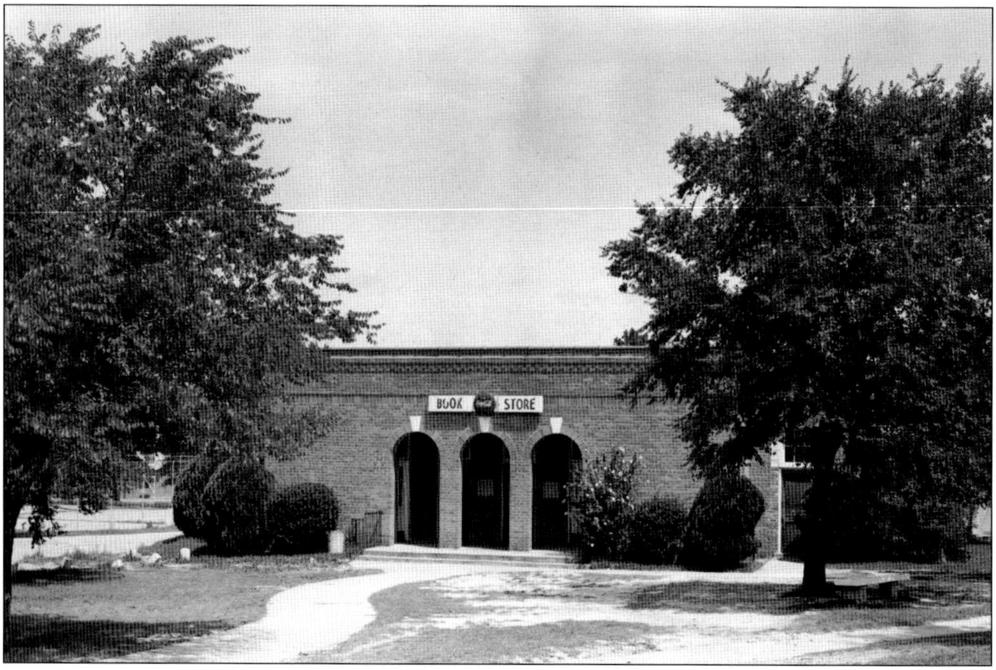

In 1939, vocational youth of the NYA built a college bookstore and confectionery. Located on the campus's northwest corner next to the library, it contained a small bookstore, snack bar, post office, and lounge.

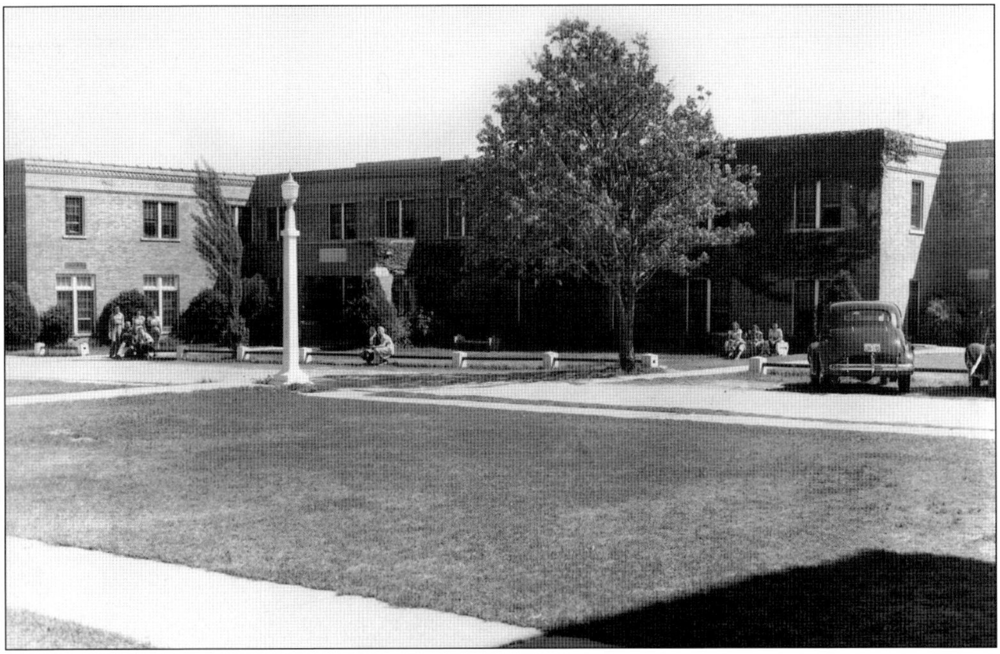

In 1936, Nelson Hall was built with the same WPA funding and at the same time as Cross Hall. It housed women for many decades. The street lamp in front, a senior class gift, was one of many that lit the east-west road that ran in front of the college's residence halls. The building was named for Mary H. Nelson, the first Magnolia A&M College dean of women.

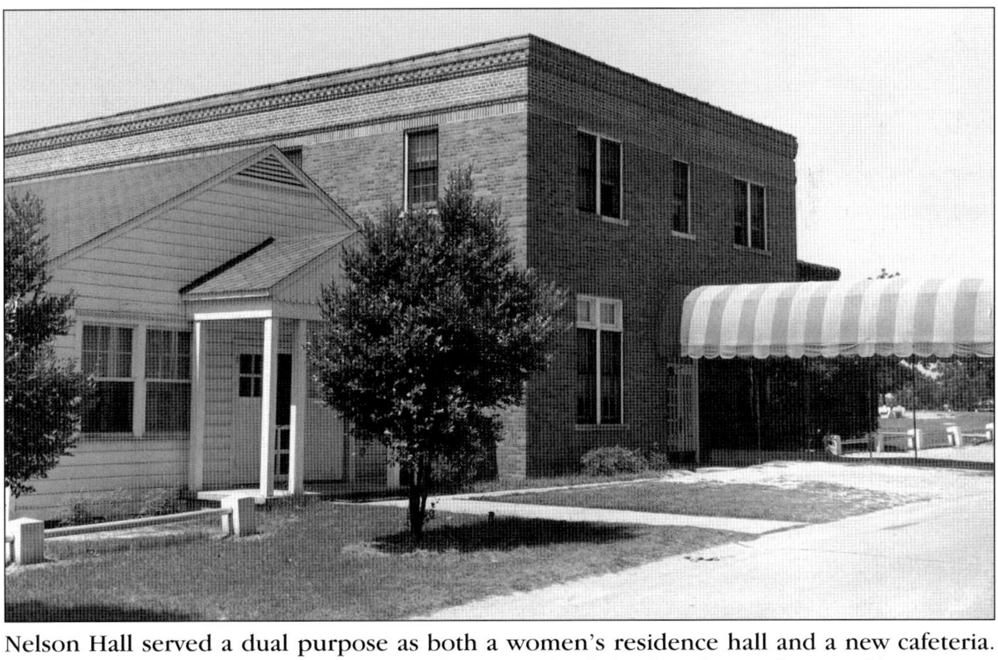

Nelson Hall served a dual purpose as both a women's residence hall and a new cafeteria. Originally, the cafeteria and kitchen took up much of the first floor. After World War II, to feed increasing numbers of students, a military surplus metal building was added to the east side of Nelson Hall for additional seating. Students entered the cafeteria from beneath the canopy, where a line formed.

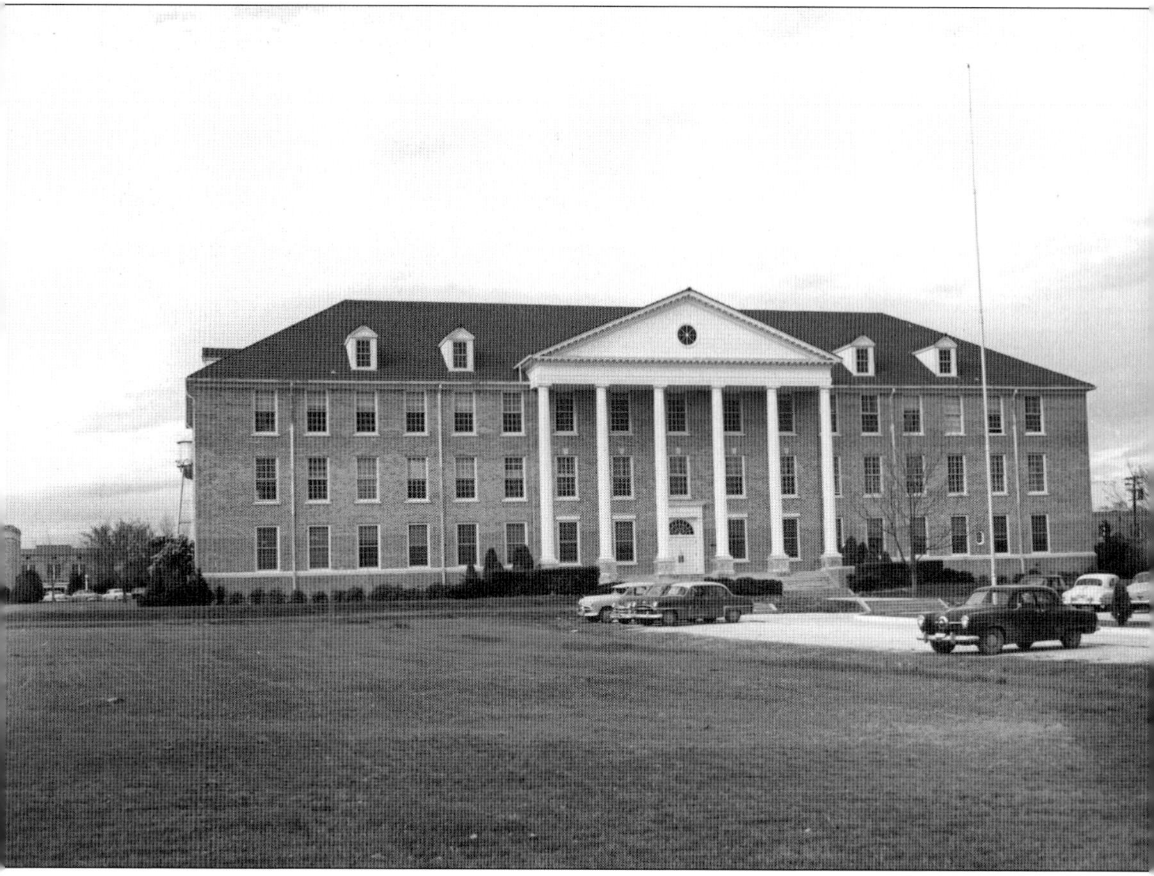

Overstreet Hall was the largest A&M project supported by New Deal programs. In 1939–1940, a grant and loan totaling $300,000 began its construction. World War II delayed its completion until 1945. For more than half a century, it housed the biology and chemistry departments on the upper floors. With a traditional auditorium, it also was the home of the speech and theater department. For many years, the English department and classrooms shared the first floor with the president and administrative offices. Overstreet Hall was remodeled numerous times during its first 70 years. Among notable changes were the addition of new heating and cooling systems, a modern theater, and a board of trustees' room. When the science departments obtained their own building, almost all campus administrative offices were consolidated in a major refurbishment of Overstreet Hall. In 1950, the building was named for Charles A. Overstreet, the former principal of TDAS and president of Magnolia A&M College.

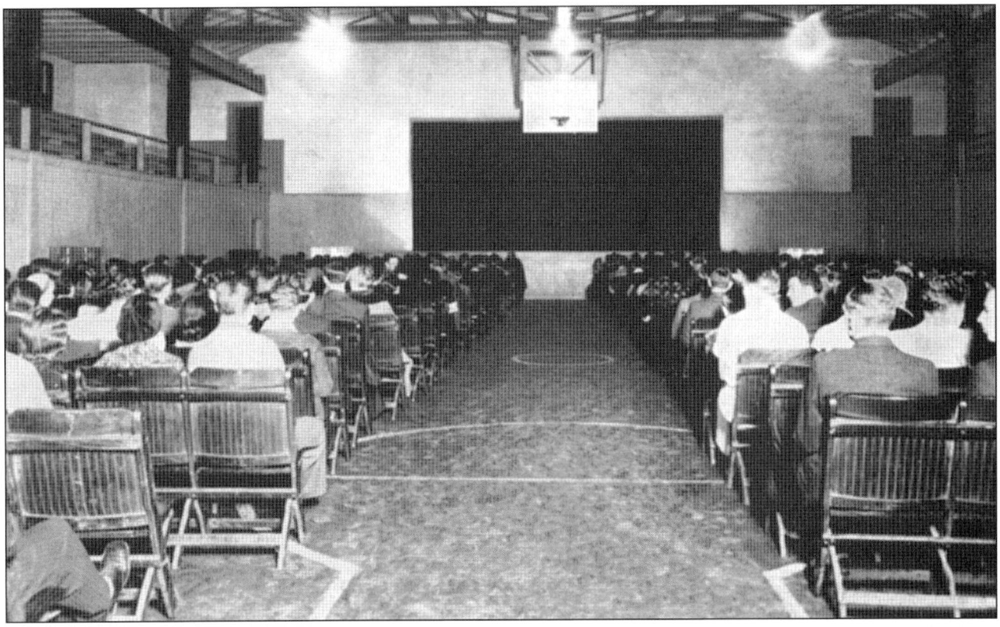

Touring speakers and musicians appeared once a month on A&M's Armory Stage before audiences of students and Magnolia citizens. A Dallas, Texas, booking agency that served most colleges in the southwestern United States organized the tours, and A&M secured many acts that were on their way to larger institutions. With chairs removed, the floor became the school's basketball court.

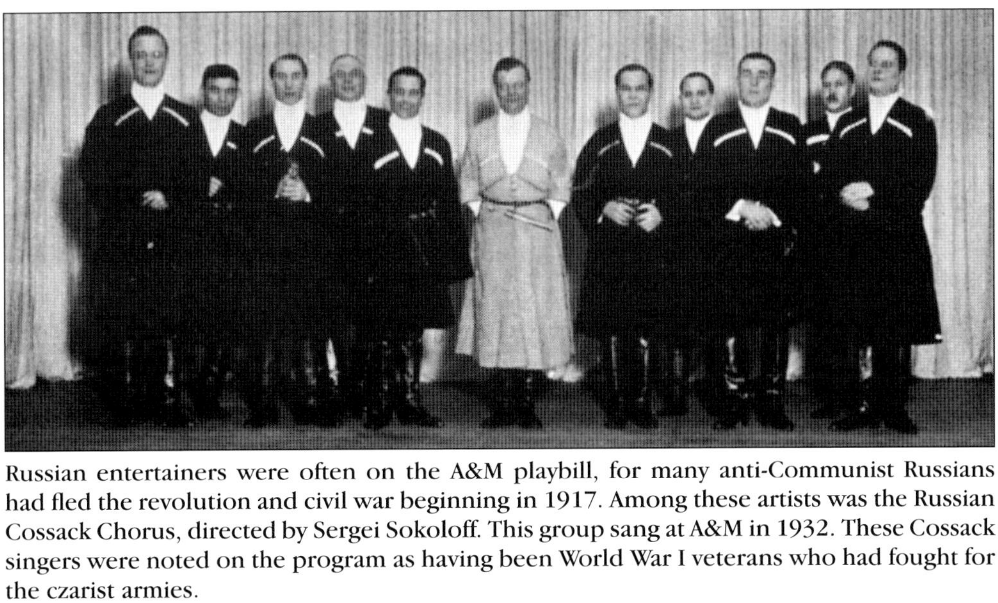

Russian entertainers were often on the A&M playbill, for many anti-Communist Russians had fled the revolution and civil war beginning in 1917. Among these artists was the Russian Cossack Chorus, directed by Sergei Sokoloff. This group sang at A&M in 1932. These Cossack singers were noted on the program as having been World War I veterans who had fought for the czarist armies.

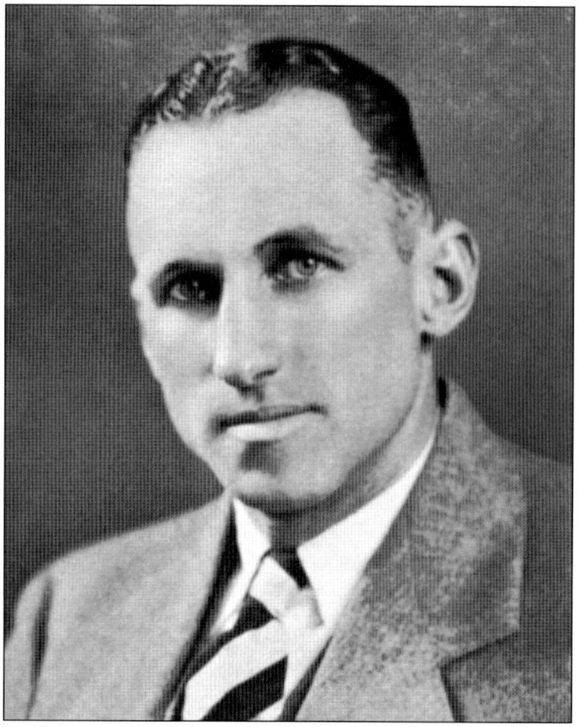

The event that attracted the most attention to Magnolia A&M College during the 1930s featured agriculture instructor Ves Godley's prized milk cow Sultane's Magnolia Belle. Starting in 1933, Godley sought to produce a national championship animal and a prize-winning dairy herd. He succeeded when Magnolia Belle was named the American Jersey Cattle Club's 1936 winner. A grand celebration took place on February 11, 1937, when representatives from the New York office came to present awards. Under careful testing, Magnolia Belle scored a national record for one year's production of 1,043 pounds of butterfat and 14,247 pounds of milk. One cow from Godley's herd was one of only 30 shown at Borden Milk Company's exhibit hall, the Dairy of Tomorrow, at the 1939 New York World's Fair.

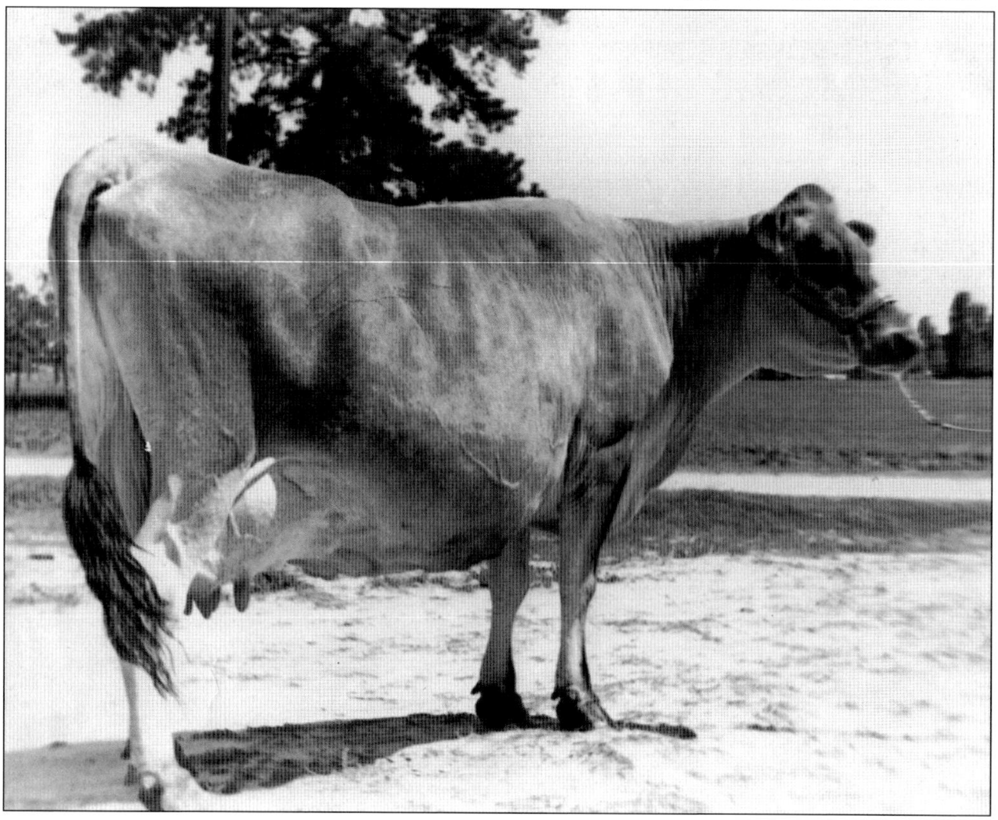

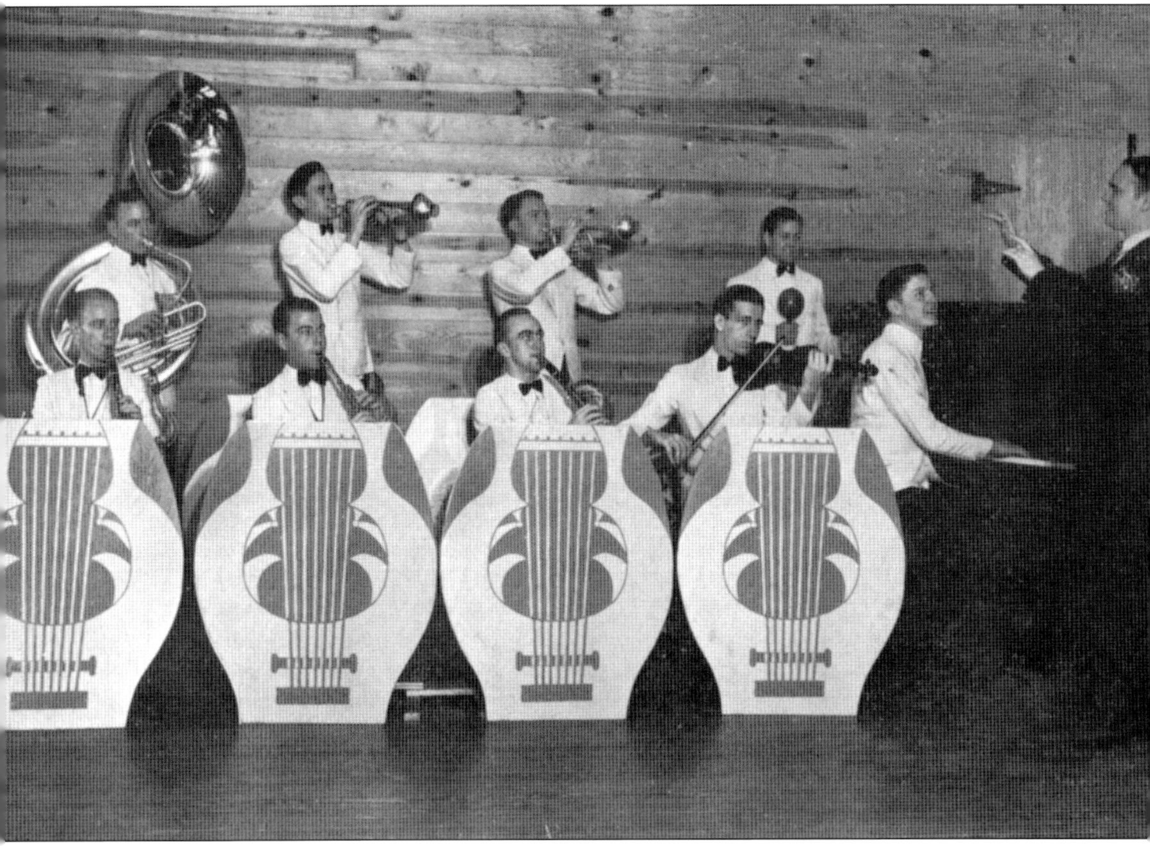

Several young instructors provided a wider worldview for their students during the 1930s. These men included several foreign language teachers, including Charles E. Hayden, who traveled to Europe each summer and gave a cosmopolitan flavor to the campus. Hayden, also a musician, conducted a student campus dance band, the Varsitonians. He guided summer tours for a Dallas travel agency and arranged for five Varsitonians to play for third class passengers on one voyage of the great French ocean liner *Normandie*. Two of those young musicians are pictured here: Walt Whitlow, first row, third from left, who played clarinet; and Sidney Smith, top row, third from left, who played trumpet. The five men, who also included Harold Gilbert, Herbert Lawrence, and Harold Hunsaker, visited Paris. Not knowing the French language, they could not read the latest news. They only realized when returning home on the *Normandie*, which was filled with passengers fleeing an expected war, that their adventure had occurred during the early days of the 1938 Munich Crisis when Nazi leader Adolf Hitler first threatened to go to war.

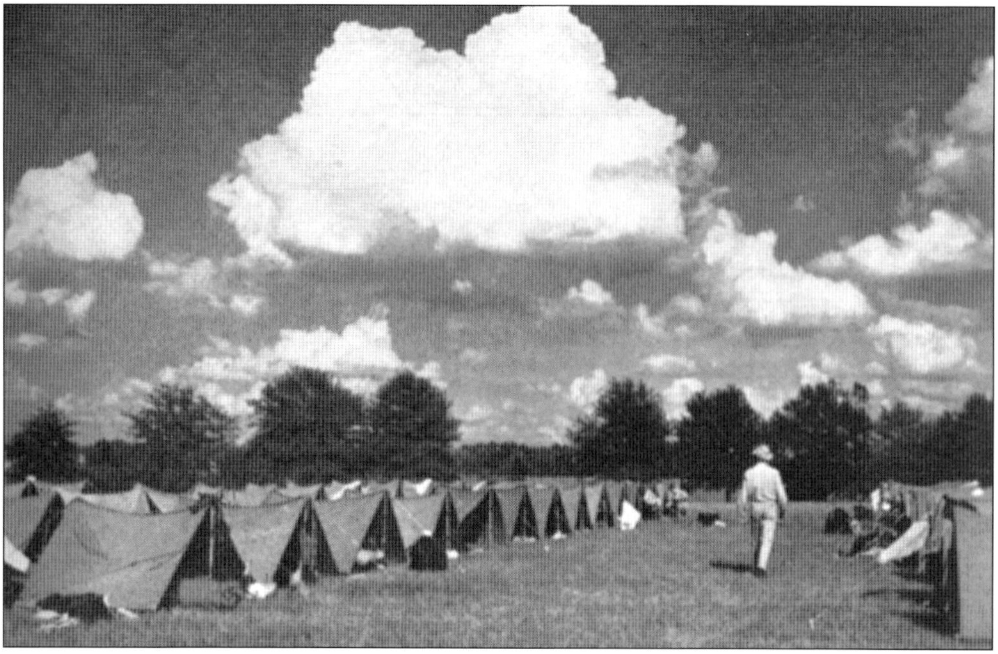

Magnolia A&M students trained twice a week as citizen soldiers of Arkansas National Guard companies at the armory on campus. Companies D (pictured) and B of the 153rd Infantry led by agriculture instructor Capt. Ves Godley were mobilized for one year's service in January 1941, a year before the United States entered World War II, and sent to prepare the defenses of Alaska. Just before the A&M student-soldiers were scheduled to return home, Japanese forces attacked the US fleet at Pearl Harbor. As a result, the former students remained in service for five years, one year longer than the war itself, until Japan surrendered in September 1945.

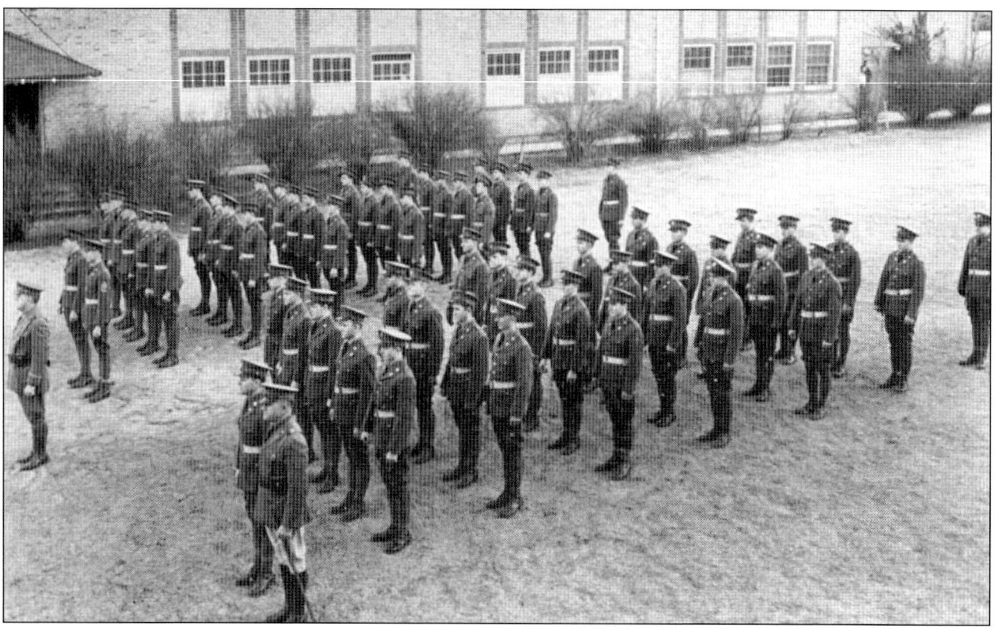

Col. Charles S. Wilkins became president of Magnolia A&M College on November 1, 1945. He had just returned from France after five years in the US Army. Although he earned a doctorate in agricultural economics from Texas A&M University, he preferred the title of colonel. Before he resigned in 1950, Wilkins assisted the board of trustees in deciding to turn A&M into a four-year, baccalaureate degree–granting institution.

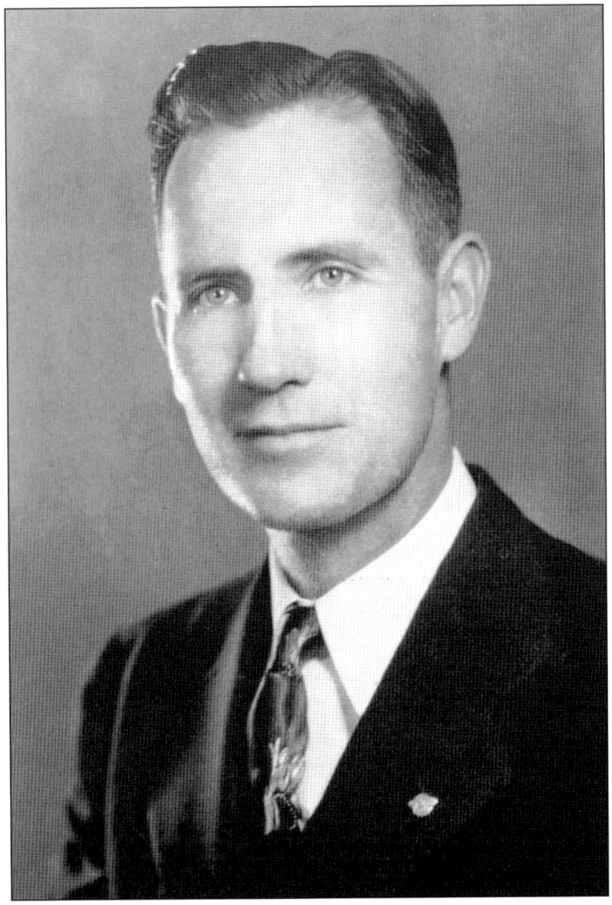

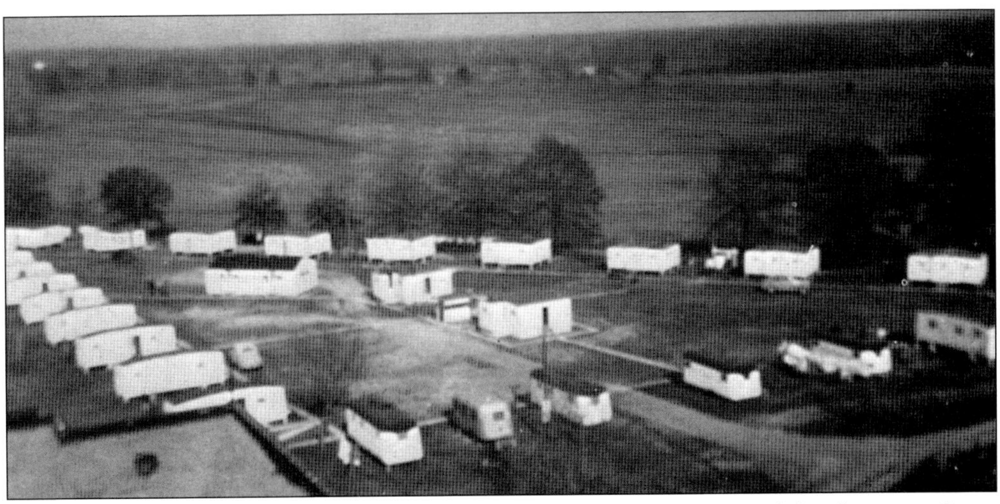

On the northern edge of campus, "Wilkinsville" housed veterans and families in military surplus trailers. The trailers were small, without running water or toilets. A common faucet, shower house, and bathroom served all the residents. Men and women who had endured the Great Depression and World War II put up with this latest hardship in order to earn a degree and the promise of a better life.

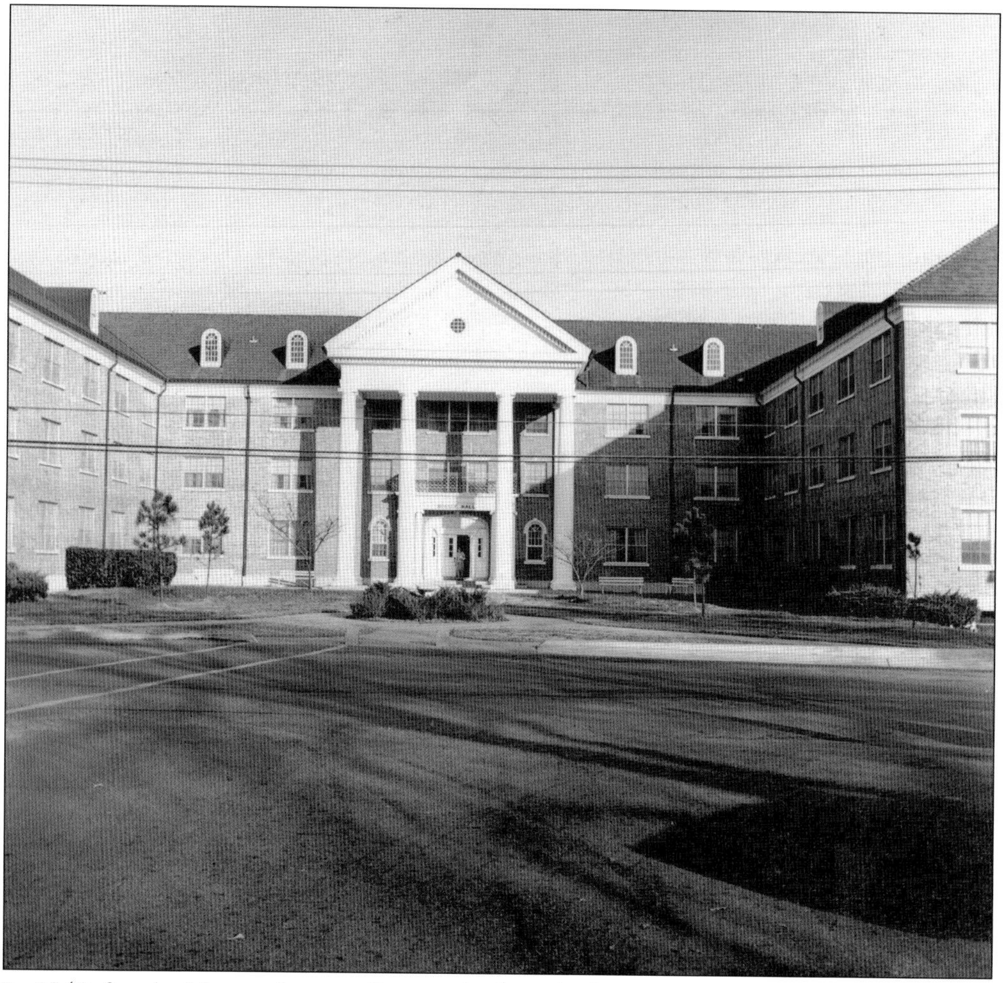

In 1949, faced with growing enrollment, the board of trustees accepted Colonel Wilkins's recommendation to issue bonds to build a new residence hall. There was discussion of two halls, exactly alike in appearance, at each end of the east-west road that passed in front of Old Main. Women would be housed in the hall on the east end, and men on the west. These residence halls would complement Overstreet Hall, using its English Georgian architectural design (sometimes referred to as Colonial Revival). Reminiscent of the classical Greek and Roman world, the buildings would have entrances framed by large columns topped with a triangular pediment. In the end, costs permitted only a women's hall. It opened in a snowstorm on Sunday, February 5, 1951, when all women students on campus moved their clothes and other possessions from older residence halls into the new one. In 1955, it was named for long-time dining director Caro Bussey.

Orval Childs headed the agriculture department from 1942 to 1976. Scores of young men would later say, "I never would have gone to college except for Mr. Childs and a job on the farm." Many of his students subsequently earned PhDs and became important agricultural researchers and university professors. Others became leaders in the agriculture industry, like Leland Tollett, CEO of Tyson Foods, the world's largest meat product company.

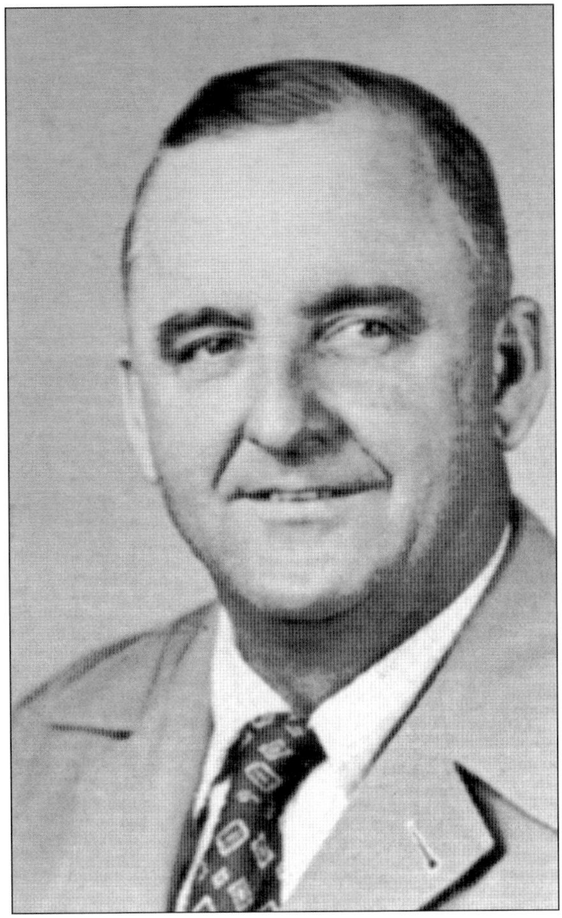

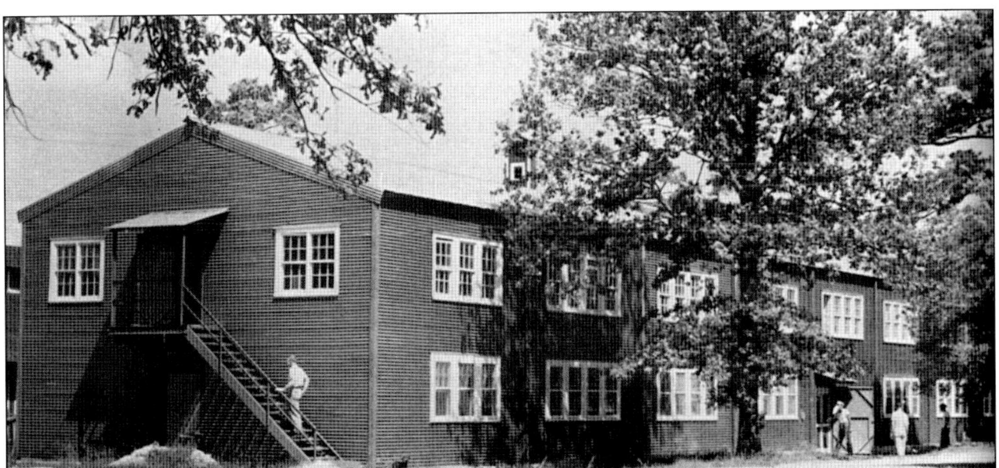

Among the surplus facilities that A&M acquired after World War II were two large, metal buildings for classrooms and housing. The Agriculture Building contained classrooms on the ground floor and residences upstairs for agriculture majors. It was located next to the barns on the northwest edge of campus. In the mid-1960s, after interior remodeling and exterior bricking, the building was renamed Childs Hall.

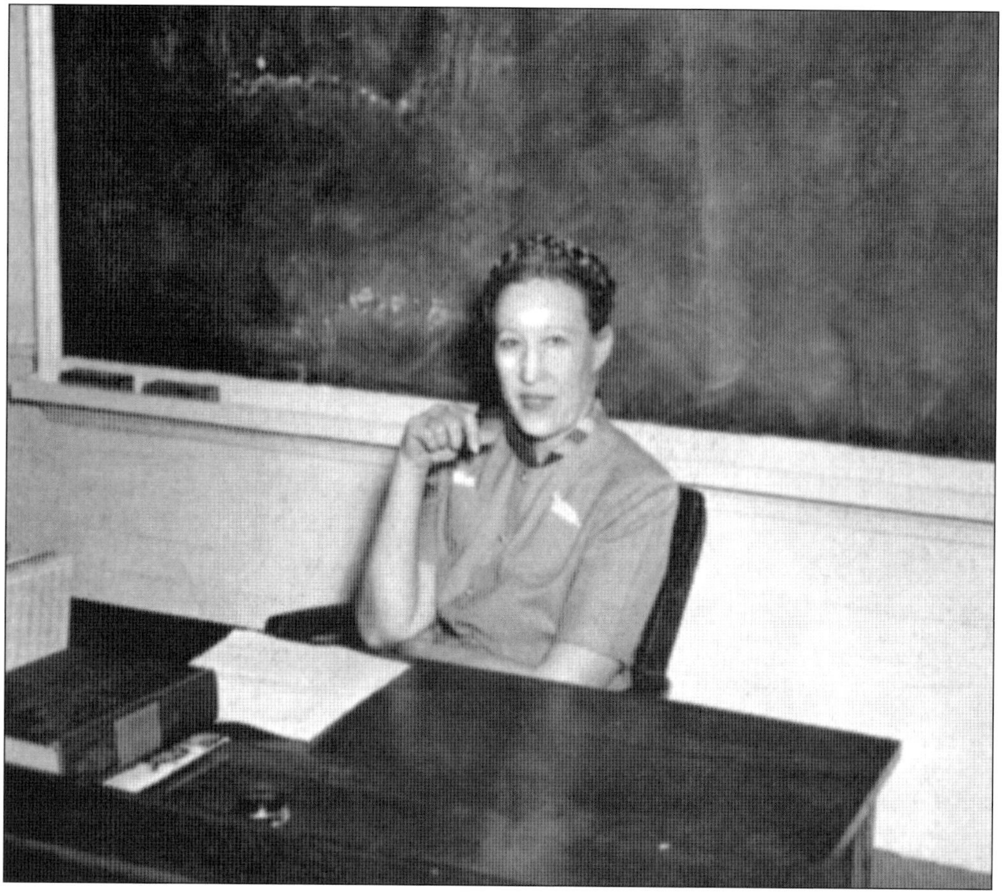

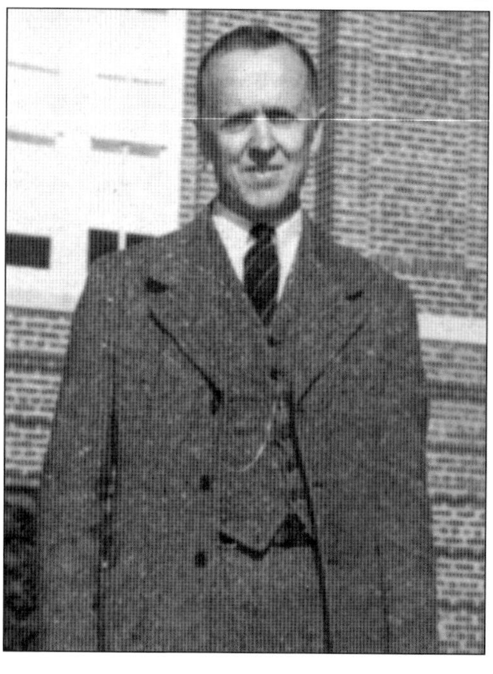

Inez Couch taught English from 1925 to 1963. When teaching British literature, she delighted students with risqué stories of English kings' misdeeds. But she also demanded high performance. Dr. Carl Benson, class of 1935, and later an Auburn University professor of English, said she was the best teacher he ever had. "Inez never got it into her head that one was a good student," he said. "One always had to prove it."

Among the new faculty after World War II, the most distinguished scholar was Dr. Samuel Denny Smith. He had earned a PhD from the University of North Carolina and was the author of the first full-length study of the first African Americans who served in the US Congress, *The Negro in Congress, 1870–1901* (1940). He, too, would settle for nothing less than the best effort from his students.

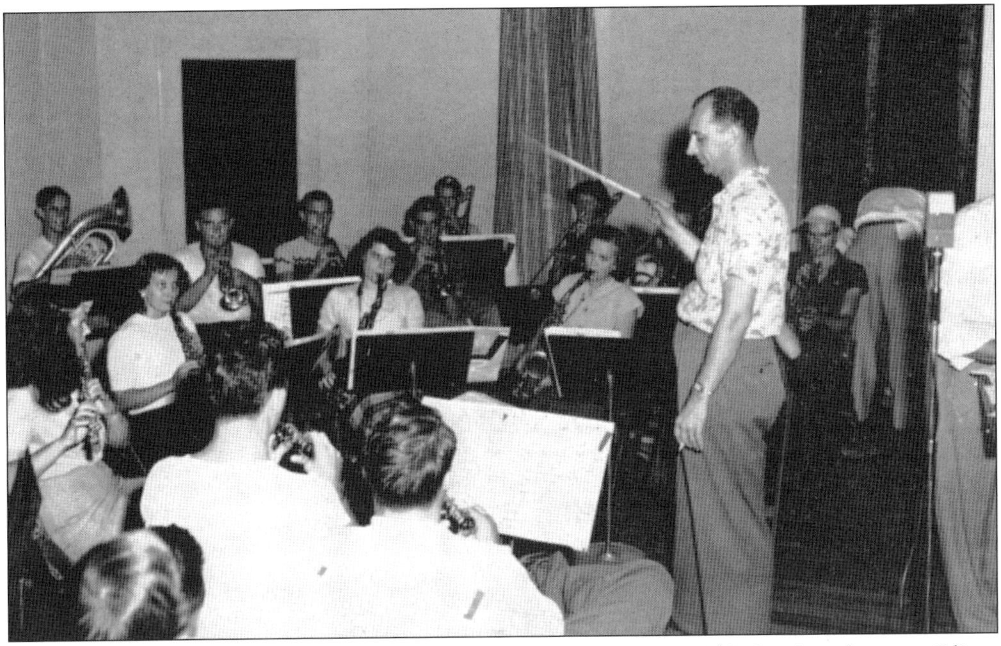

Richard Oliver became music professor and band director in 1948. During the war, Oliver had played in the US Navy fleet band at Pearl Harbor in Hawaii. Upon returning home, he completed a master's degree at the University of Oklahoma before moving to Magnolia A&M. He was chair of the music department and band director for two decades.

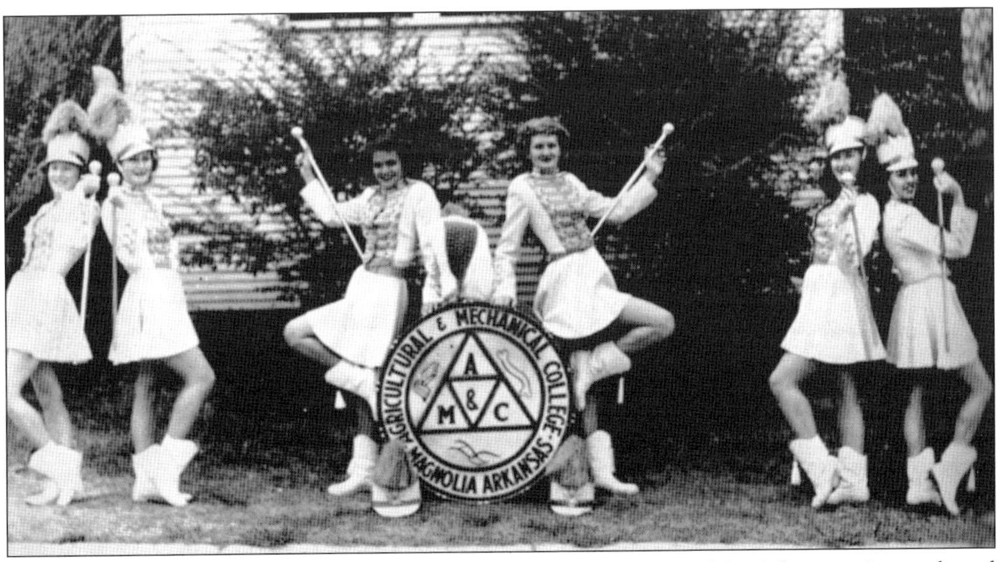

Magnolia A&M's music program was among the most respected in Arkansas. It produced some of the region's best horn men, including Jerry Horne, Bill and Jack Hardin, and Charles Colquitt. The marching band had excellent halftime shows at Mulerider football games. The band's majorettes in 1949–1950 were, from left to right, Elizabeth Hudson, Naomi Little, Elsie Elder, Jo Anne McAdams, Nell Urrey Mulligan, and Billye Dale Johnson.

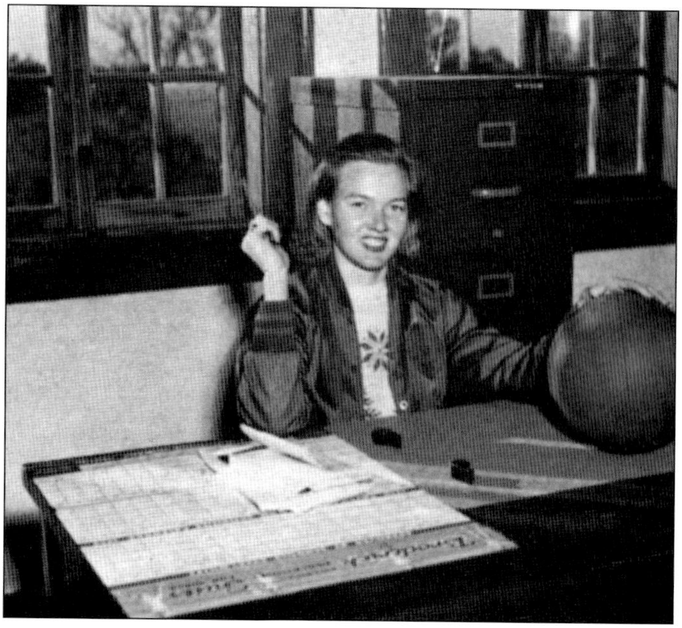

Coach Kathryn Smith (later Dr. Brown) came to A&M in 1946 as a 19-year-old physical education teacher, having graduated early from high school and college. She remained at A&M College and its successor institutions for 50 years, the longest service in school history. Among her accomplishments was renewing women's basketball. Named the A&M Kats, the team played only independent teams; there was no conference in Arkansas for women's college sports.

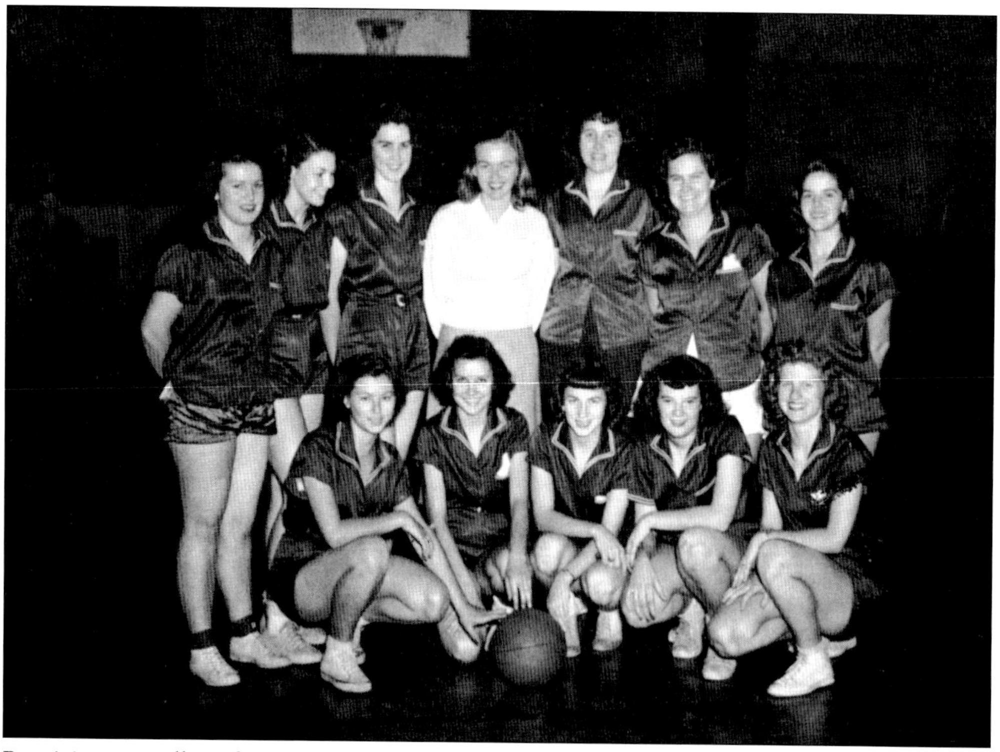

Receiving no college funding, Kathryn Smith-Brown raised travel donations from Magnolia businessmen. The 1949 team won the Amateur Athletic Union tournament's state championship. From left to right are (first row) Lucille Holley, Jean Moore, Pat Alexander, Pat Dodson, and Norma McMahen; (second row) Ann Mauney, Gene Lee, Mary Kat Simpson, Kathryn Smith-Brown, Evelyn Fee, Mickey Roling, and Rita Waller. College president Dolph Camp ended women's basketball during the 1950s, saying it was "unladylike."

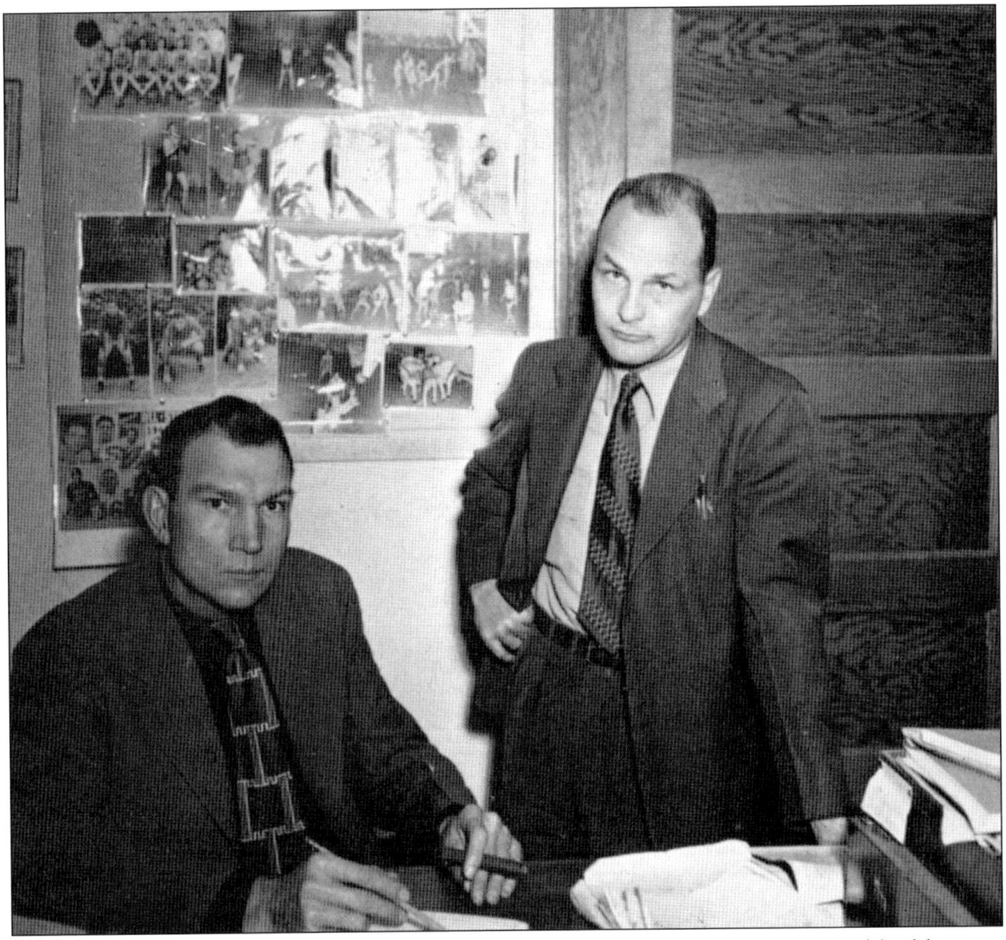

A&M's coaches after the war shared a name, Smith. To avoid confusion, they told athletes to use their given names, Coach Elmer, left, with perennial cigar in hand, and Coach Auburn, right. They also shared a football legacy, both having played for famed Hendrix College coach Ivan Groves. Coach Auburn was more approachable than Coach Elmer, who coached as he had played fullback, ruthlessly. Groves once said of him: "He could make yardage through a concrete wall." In a memoir, Coach Elmer wrote that fear was the best motivator. Players either hated him and dropped out of his program, or they endured his tough regime and admired him. He was also notable for loyalty and support from former players. Both Smiths coached football and basketball together until Coach Elmer left in 1955 to become an assistant coach at Texas A&M University. Their football and basketball teams during the 1940s usually ranked high in the standings and had outstanding players, including Prentice "Duddy" Waller in basketball, and in football, Charles "Charlie" McClendon, later a famed Louisiana State University coach.

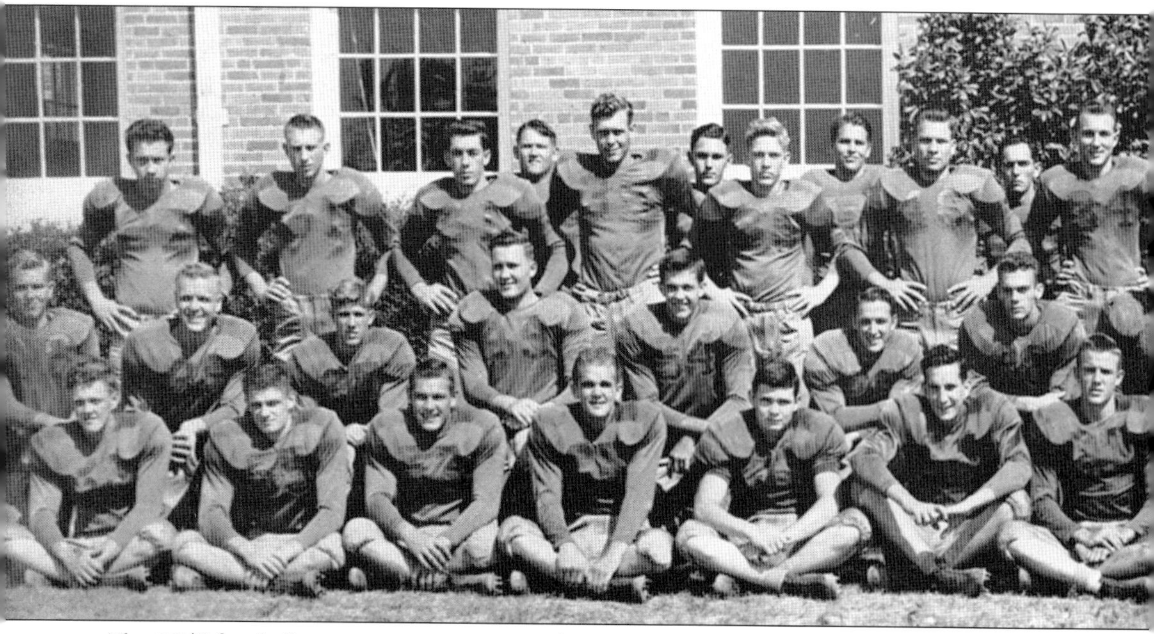

The 1948 football team was a great team, losing only to Arkansas Tech College. From left to right are (first row) James Ball, Rex Woodruff, Jack Wells, Ben Burton, Hoyt Watson, Harold Brinson, Mike McLean, James Etheridge, Weldon Rasberry, Lynn Burton, Delwin Ross, Jabo Womack, Joe Little, Sammy Furo, and Donald Crews; (second row) Walton Pettus, John Pierce, Kenneth Harris, J.E. Hooten, Jack Scott, Eugene Blendon, Ecil Birchfield, Carl Keese,

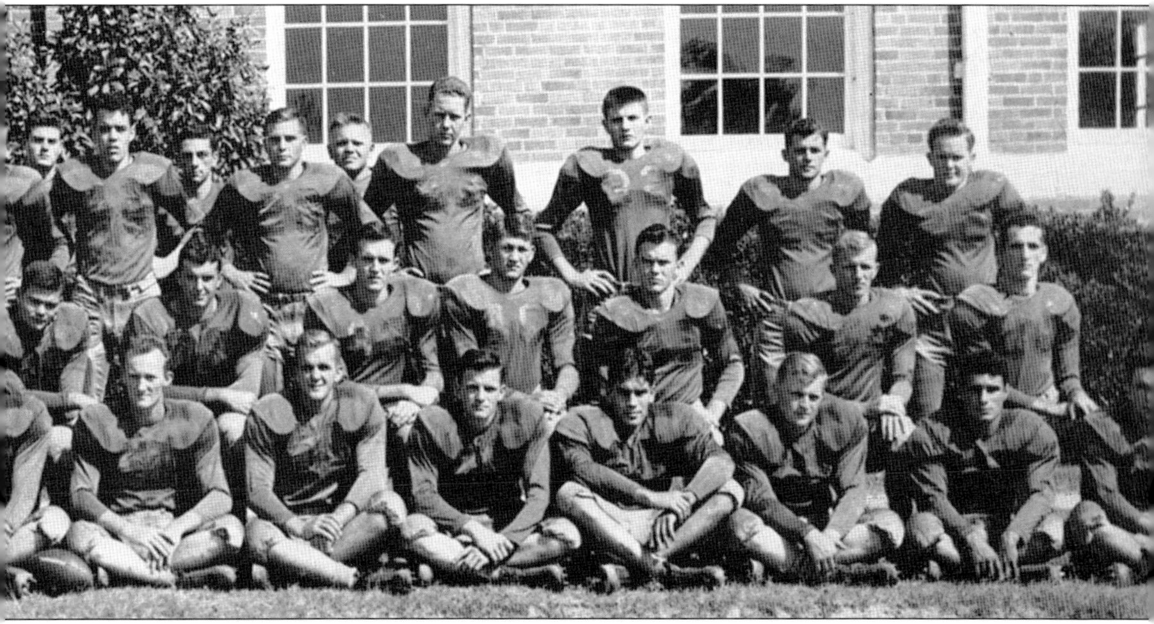

Vance Roberts, W.C. Owen, L.P. Elliot, Allen McClure, Doyle Wallace, Billy Gregory, and Charles Lanphere; (third row) Bill Burns, Roy Ledbetter, John Jones, Raymond Burchfield, Bill Roberts, Billy Joe McCann, Herman West, Joe Rooker, Clark Stancil, Wayne Taylor, Roderick Pinkett, Bob Keck, James Hope, and Russell McAllister; (fourth row) Bob Phillips, Harold Sunderman, Newell Puttman, Bill Perry, Buddy Horner, Pat Carrithers, and Harold Hime.

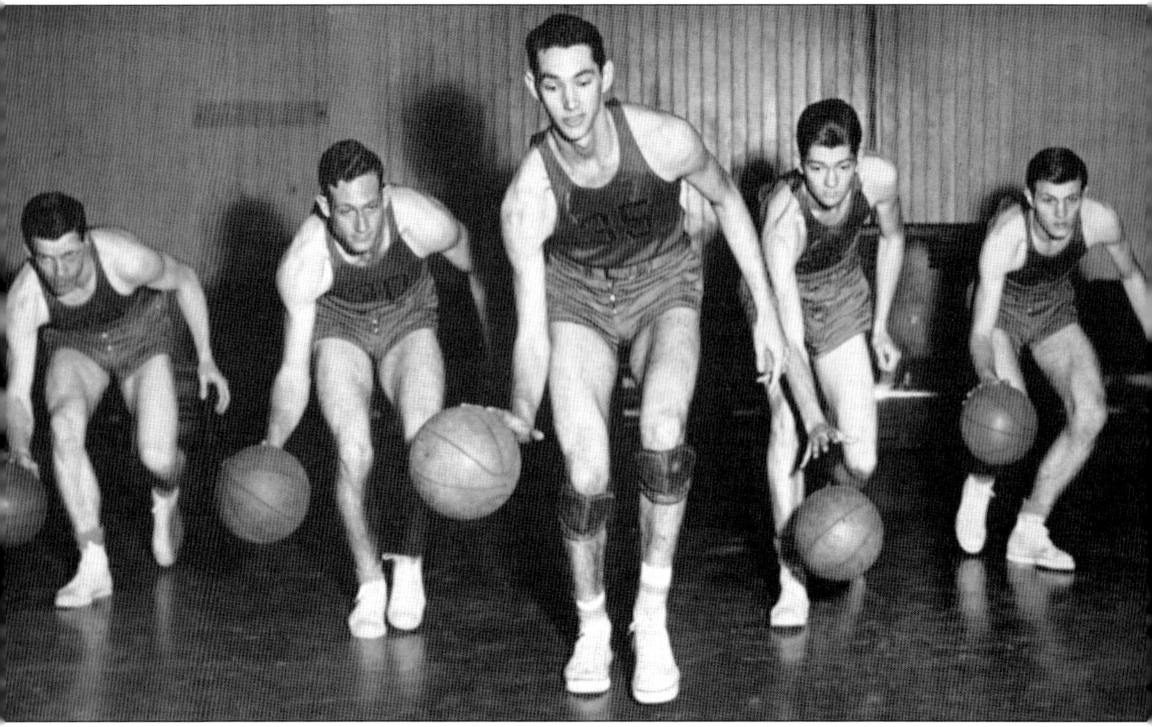

The 1948–1949 basketball teams had remarkable players. From left to right are Delwin Ross, guard; Prentice "Duddy" Waller, forward; Roger Layne, center; Bobby Talley, forward; and Bob Keck, guard. Waller was the leading scorer in 1949 when the team had 20 wins and 9 losses. He went on to fame as a player and later coach at the University of Arkansas. Ross was the only player on first teams in football and basketball. He returned to coach various sports, especially swimming, at his alma mater. Layne went on to play for the great Kentucky coach Adolph Rupp. There, he gained more fame for once declining to play than for playing. During a Southeast Conference (SEC) tournament game, he gave up a spot on the team so that a fellow player would have a chance to post an SEC record. Sportswriter Walter Stewart praised Layne for his gallantry and "spirit of unselfishness."

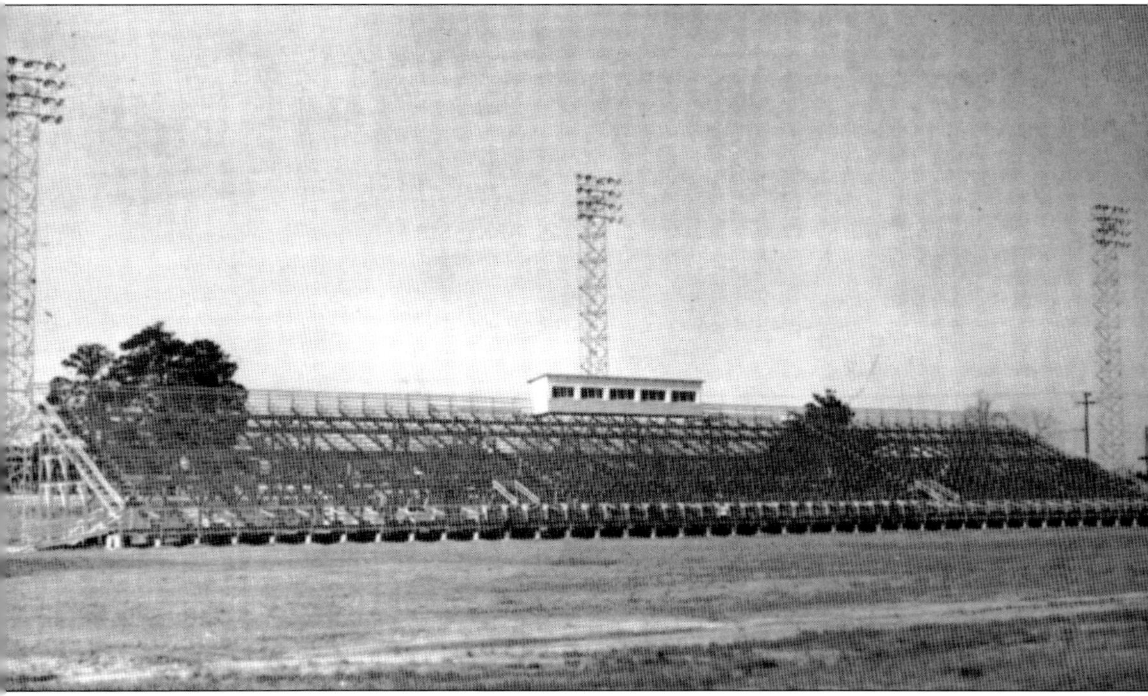

Until 1949, A&M football teams played at Columbia Stadium, a New Deal project of 1935 built so that both A&M and Magnolia High School teams could have more attractive home facilities than the open fields previously used. It was located at the corner of Stadium Drive and Olive Street, on the west side of Magnolia, halfway between the town square and the college. In 1949–1950, Mulerider Stadium, later renamed Wilkins Stadium, was constructed on the northeast edge of campus. It had steel bleachers seating 4,000 rather than the few hundred wooden seats of the older field. The new stadium had dressing rooms for both home and visiting teams, a facility also missing at Columbia Stadium. When a rain-soaked summer in 1950 delayed completion, Colonel Wilkins enlisted volunteers from Magnolia's citizens and earth-moving equipment and welding operators from local oil companies to handle an accelerated work schedule so that opening day would not have to be postponed.

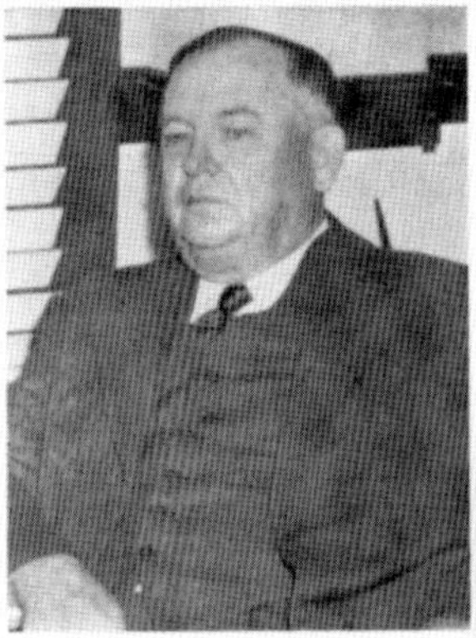

LUTHER LOWE
Garland

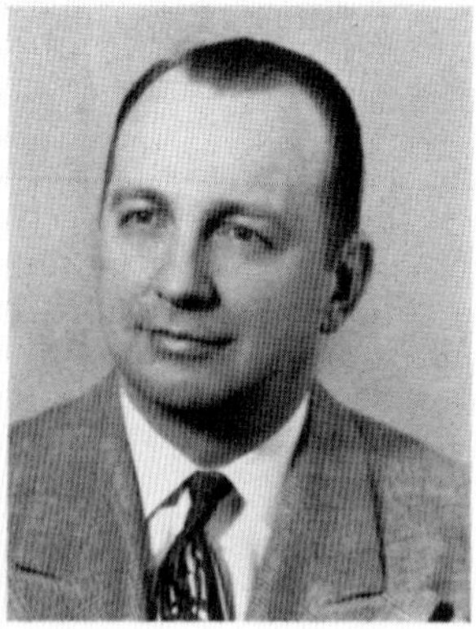

JOHN H. WILSON
Magnolia

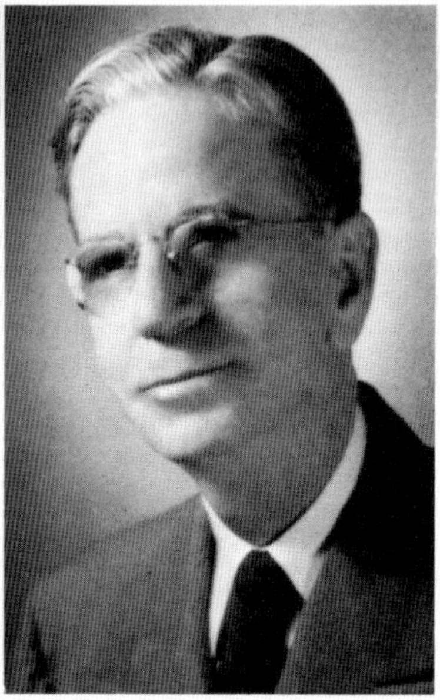

D. O. TALBOT
Chairman, Stamps

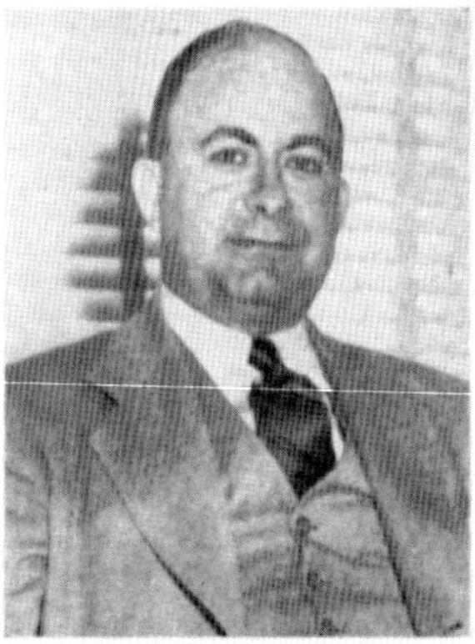

NED STEWART
Texarkana

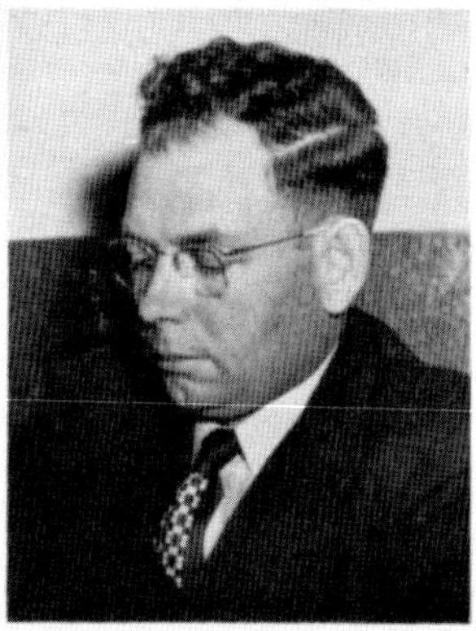

CLYDE THOMAS
Gillham

Through the years, as the other 1909 Arkansas agricultural schools sought four-year college status, A&M leaders repeatedly declined to do so. Their thinking was that students would benefit more from a strong, well-financed junior college than a struggling, poorly financed senior college. The schools at Jonesboro and Monticello changed status in 1933 and 1939, respectively. Arkansas Tech College in Russellville moved to four-year status in 1947–1948. A&M alumni called for their school to take the same step. Colonel Wilkins and the A&M board of trustees feared that as the state's only remaining junior college, their school would suffer in future competition for legislative funding. They decided on November 24, 1949, to elevate the school to the four-year rank. The state legislature acquiesced to this assertion of board power, based on Act 100 of 1909 and Amendment 33 of the Arkansas constitution, and merely acted to rename the school Southern State College in 1951.

Three

SOUTHERN STATE COLLEGE

Over the course of two decades, presidents Dr. Dolph Camp and Dr. Imon E. Bruce built Southern State College into an excellent regional state college. Dr. Camp became president in 1950, and within a few years, gained accreditation for the school from the North Central Association of Colleges and Secondary Schools.

Camp hired numerous faculty with PhDs from major universities, many attracted perhaps by an unusual offer of on-campus houses and apartments at nominal cost. SSC's faculty developed degree programs in a wide variety of fields.

Dr. Bruce, beginning in 1959, accelerated a building program begun by Dr. Camp that transformed the appearance of the campus, adding 15 new buildings by 1975. Construction necessitated the destruction of some older TDAS buildings. Enrollment grew to 2,700 in 1969, but declined in the early 1970s with the end of the Vietnam War.

The turbulence on many college campuses during the 1960s and early 1970s barely touched SSC. However, like college students everywhere in this era, SSC students pressed for relaxation of the most restrictive features of *in loco parentis*, the traditional practice of colleges supervising students' personal behavior in place of parents, which included curfew hours for female students and dress codes for all students.

Among the most important academic changes during Dr. Bruce's tenure were a nursing program and master's degrees in several fields of teacher education. Dr. Bruce also initiated the beginning of an endowment and scholarship program. SSC also used the federal government's Title Three program for higher education to pay for faculty to return to graduate school. The percentage of SSC professors with doctoral degrees increased from 12 to 40 percent.

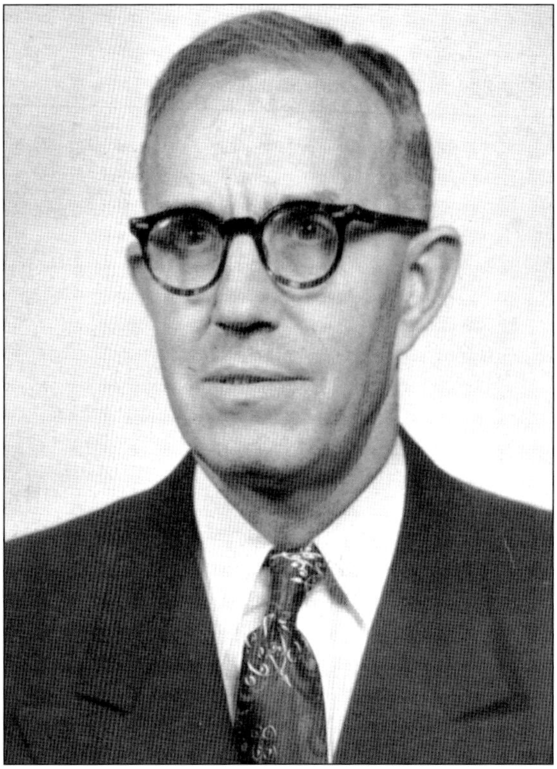

Dr. Dolph Camp became president of the new four-year-college in 1950, six months before it received its new name, Southern State College, in early 1951. A 1920 alumnus of the school, he subsequently earned an EdD in educational psychology from Syracuse University, served as president of the National Association of Guidance Supervisors, and created a guidance program for Arkansas public schools.

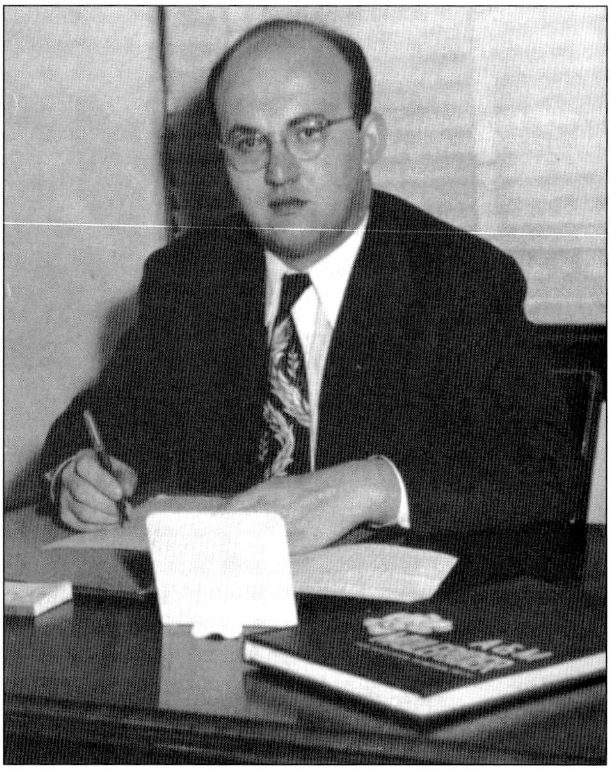

Robert J. Kibbee, a University of Chicago doctoral candidate, became senior college director in 1951. When SSC's initial bid for accreditation failed in 1953, he was made academic dean, led a new application effort, and gained approval of the North Central Association in 1955. As City University of New York's chancellor in 1974, Dr. Kibbee returned to SSC to deliver the May graduation address.

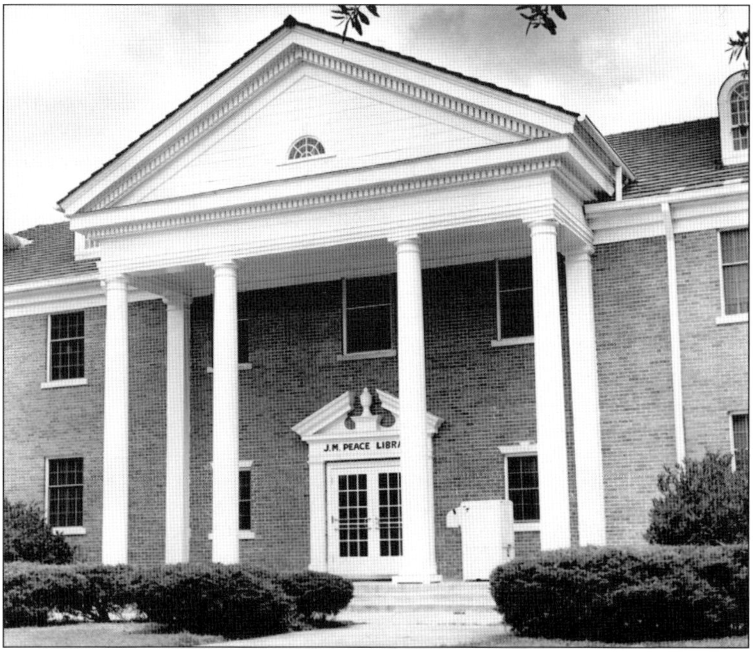

Becoming a four-year college required a new library. In 1953, a large, two-story library of Georgian architectural style, like Overstreet and Bussey Halls, was completed. Named for the school's first librarian, James M. Peace (1914–1949), it was located just north of the Greek Theater and was designed to hold 60,000 volumes.

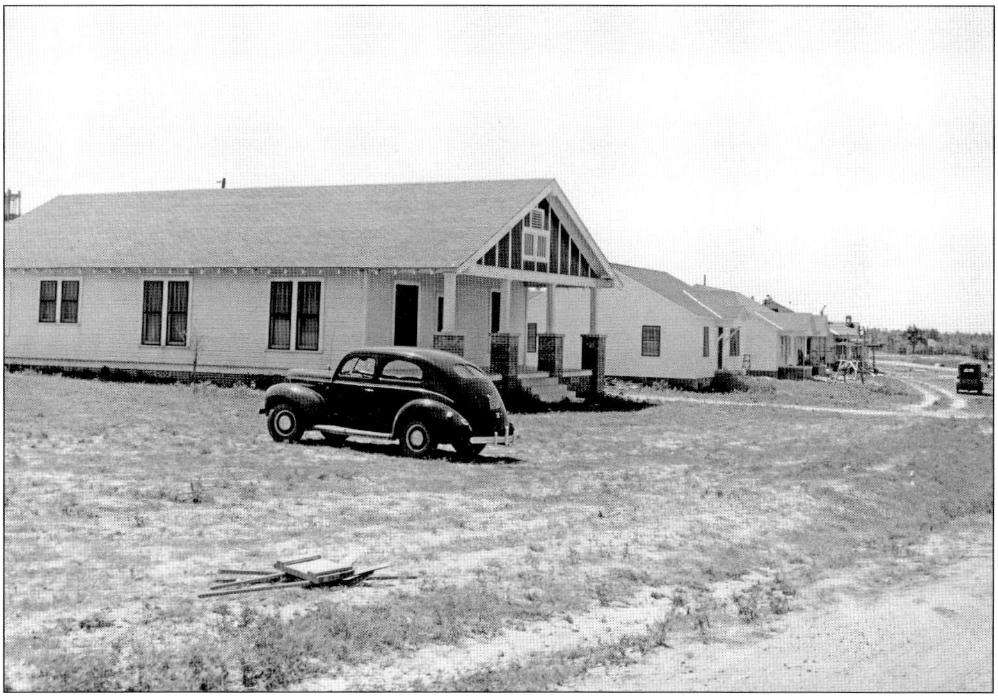

As a four-year college, SSC needed faculty with doctoral degrees. Competition among colleges and universities for faculty with PhDs was fierce during the early 1950s. Seeking an edge, SSC built increasing numbers of low-cost housing units on the campus's east side to add to those already on the west side. Eventually, SSC had housing for approximately 40 faculty members.

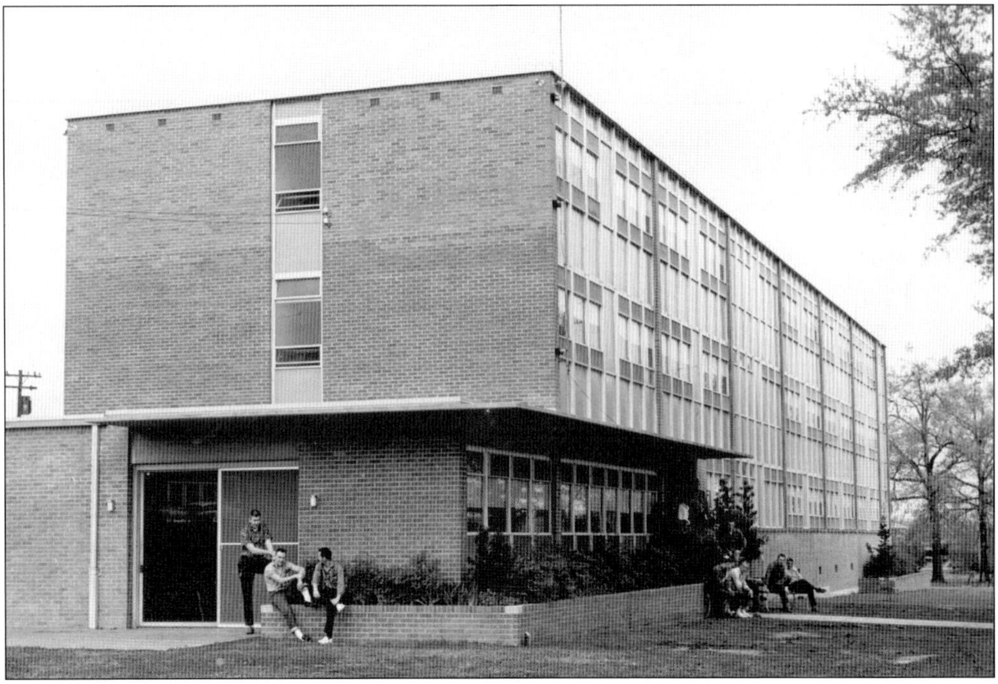

Increased enrollment prompted a new, large residence hall for men in 1955. Building a twin of Bussey Hall was rejected as too costly. The result was a three-story, modernistic structure that broke architectural continuity with Overstreet, Peace, and Bussey Halls. The building was named for the long-serving academic dean of Magnolia A&M College, Earle E. Graham.

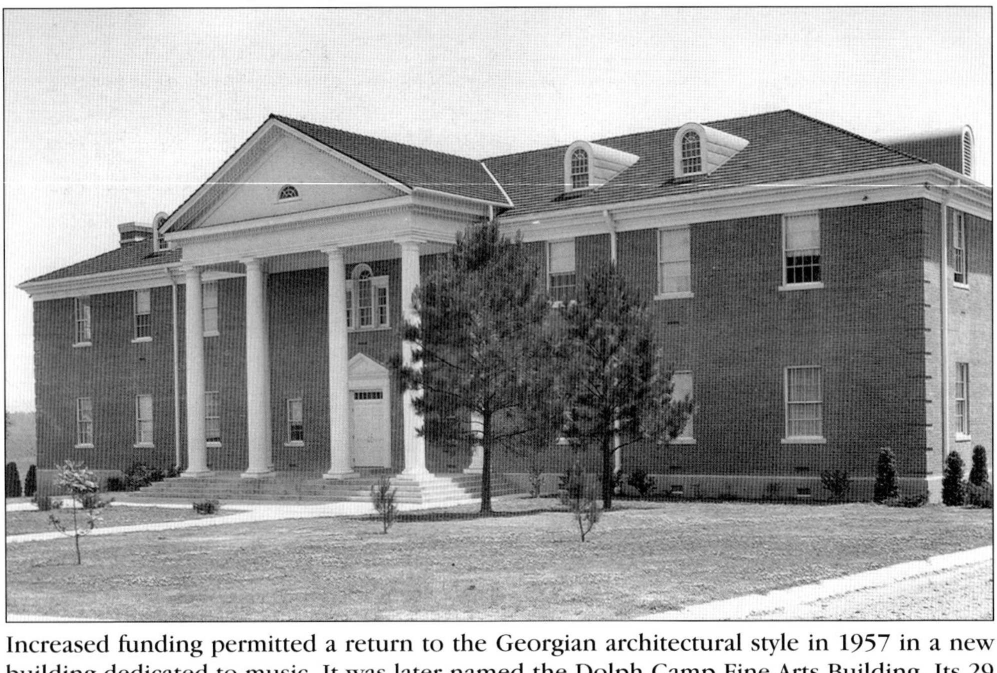

Increased funding permitted a return to the Georgian architectural style in 1957 in a new building dedicated to music. It was later named the Dolph Camp Fine Arts Building. Its 29 rooms provided offices, classrooms, a band hall, student rehearsal carrels, and a performance auditorium containing a large pipe organ and a nine-foot concert grand piano.

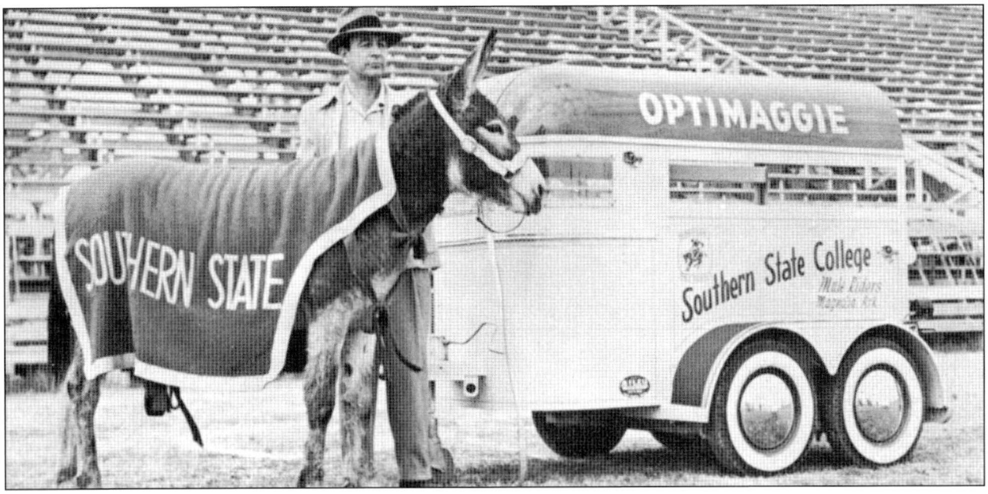

In 1950, the Muleriders were in a slump. The year turned around on October 14. At halftime that day, the Optimist Club of Magnolia presented a mascot to the school, Optimaggie, a Sicilian mule (donkey). Dr. Camp was eager to restore the tradition of the 1920s and early 1930s of a mule at games. Optimaggie attended all subsequent football games, even those on the road. The Muleriders did not lose again in 1950. During four seasons, from 1950 to 1953, the Muleriders racked up 17 straight wins in the Arkansas Intercollegiate Conference and won back-to-back AIC championships in 1951 and 1952. In 1953, when the team finally lost to College of the Ozarks, superstitious fans pointed to Optimaggie's absence at that game. Optimaggie sired an offspring named Adolphus, imitating the SSC president's name, Dolph. At games, cheerleaders managed the animals and prompted them to bray as though cheering the Muleriders.

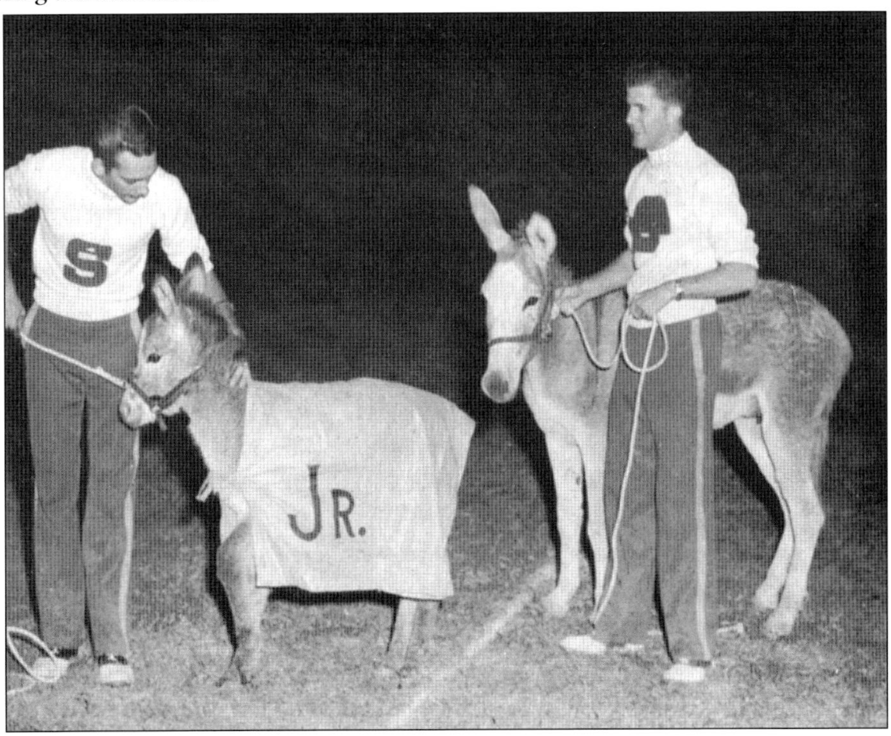

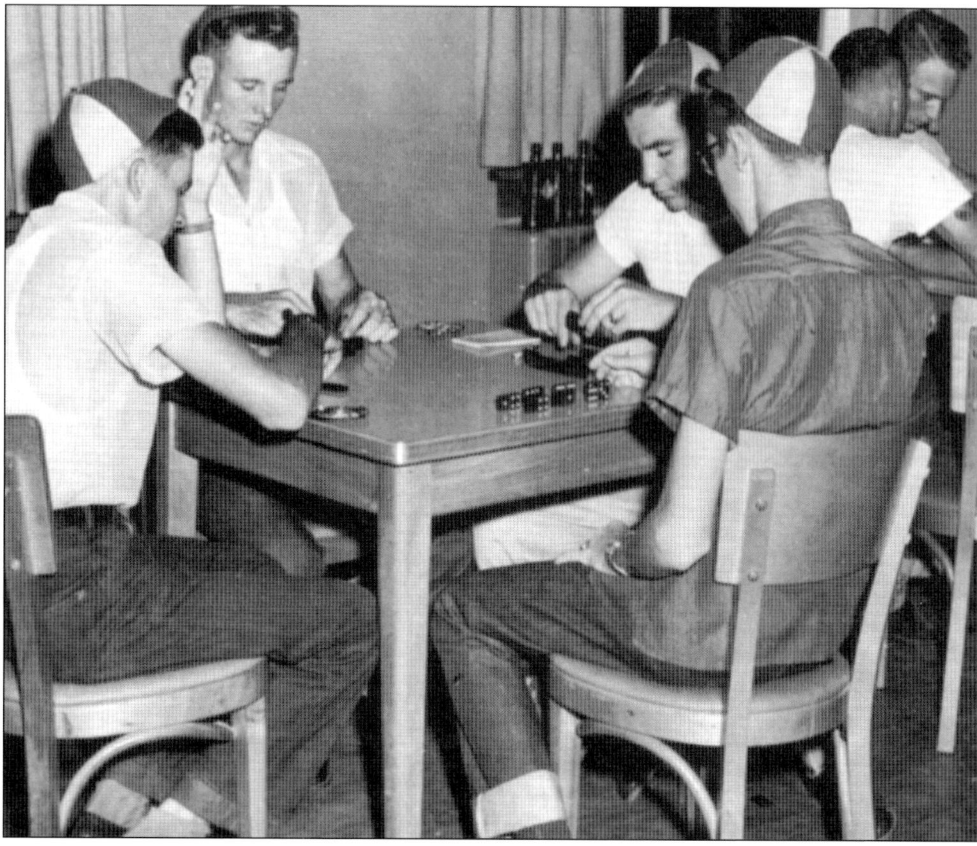

Freshman initiation sometimes wrongly turned into bullying. However, for most entering students, initiation was a lighthearted affair and involved little more than wearing the required blue and gold beanies for a few weeks, a practice begun in 1952. Upperclassmen could also stop a freshman student and demand recitation of the school's loyalty song or a fact about the institution's history.

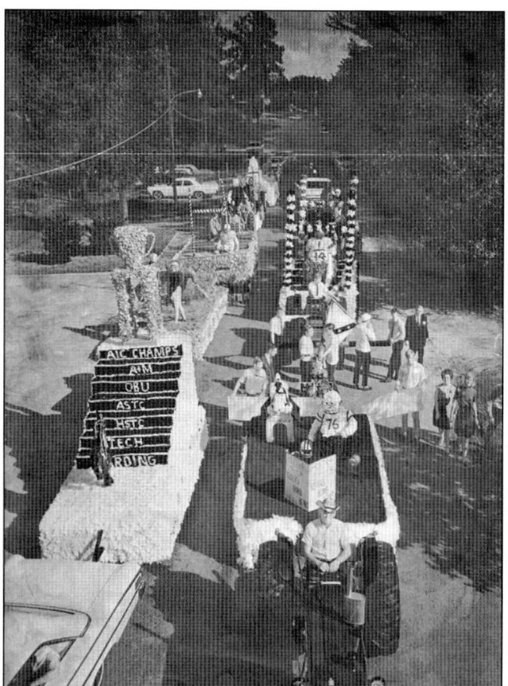

The biggest event held each fall at SSC was Homecoming. Selecting a Homecoming Court, holding pep rallies, and building floats consumed a week. Elaborately decorated floats featured slogans such as "Wreck Tech." Arkansas Tech College at Russellville was a principal football opponent. The floats paraded to the Magnolia town square, where hundreds of citizens cheered and waved.

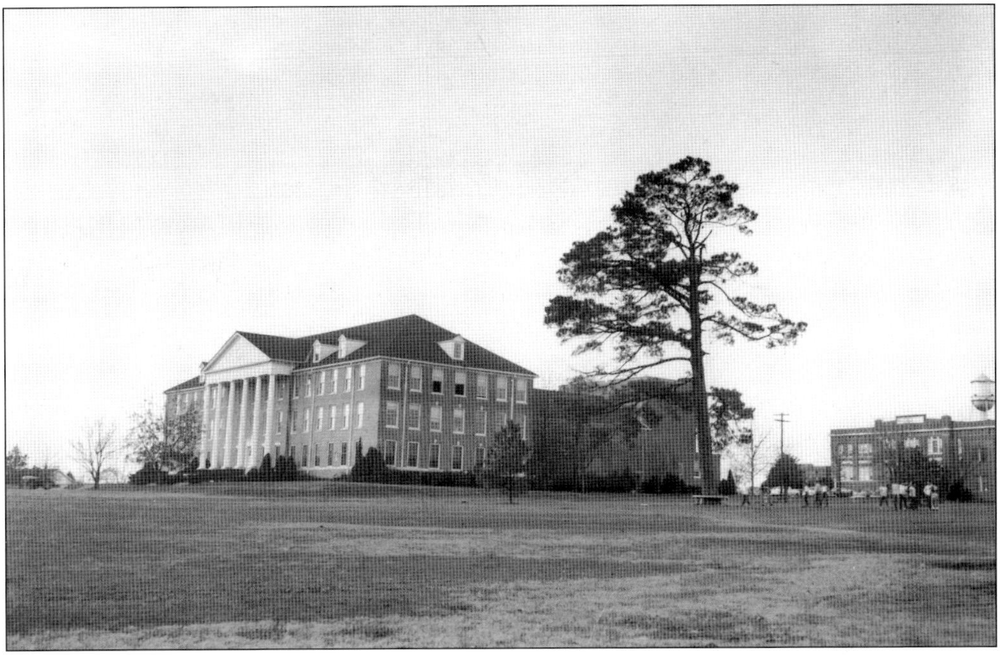

On February 21, 1956, a special school assembly in Overstreet Auditorium was held for the fallen Lone Pine Tree, pushed over by a strong storm. It had provided a trysting place for students since before World War I. Students and faculty gave speeches and read poems to mourn the passing of a school tradition. For some 40 years, hundreds of courting couples had sat under the tree to pledge their love, sometimes to become engaged to be married, hoping that their commitment would last as long as the tree that had for so long seemed indestructible.

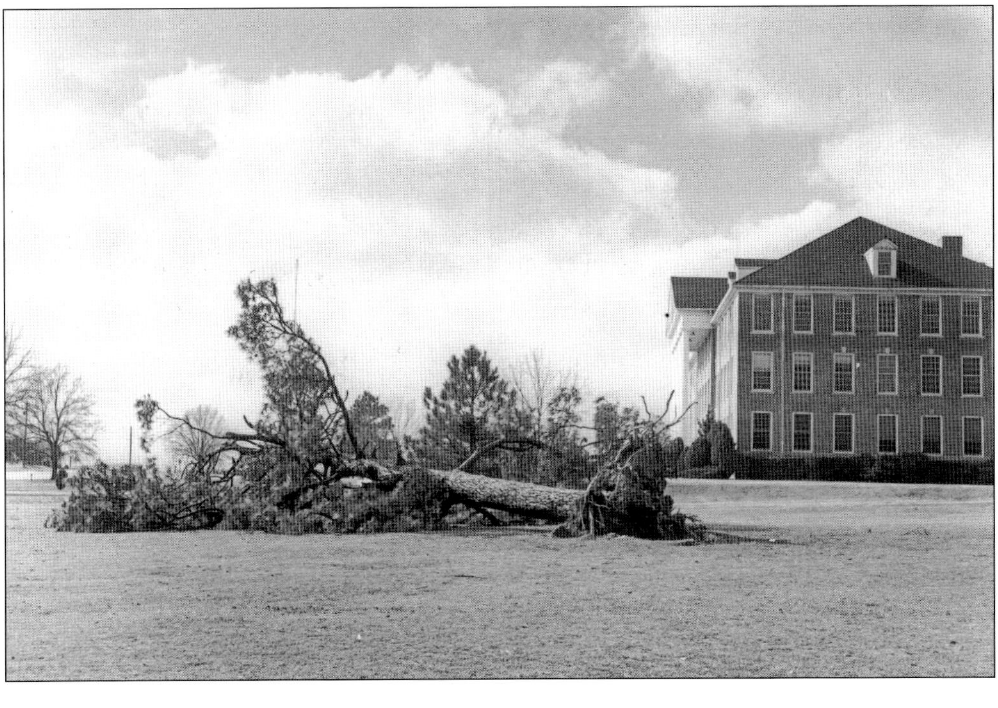

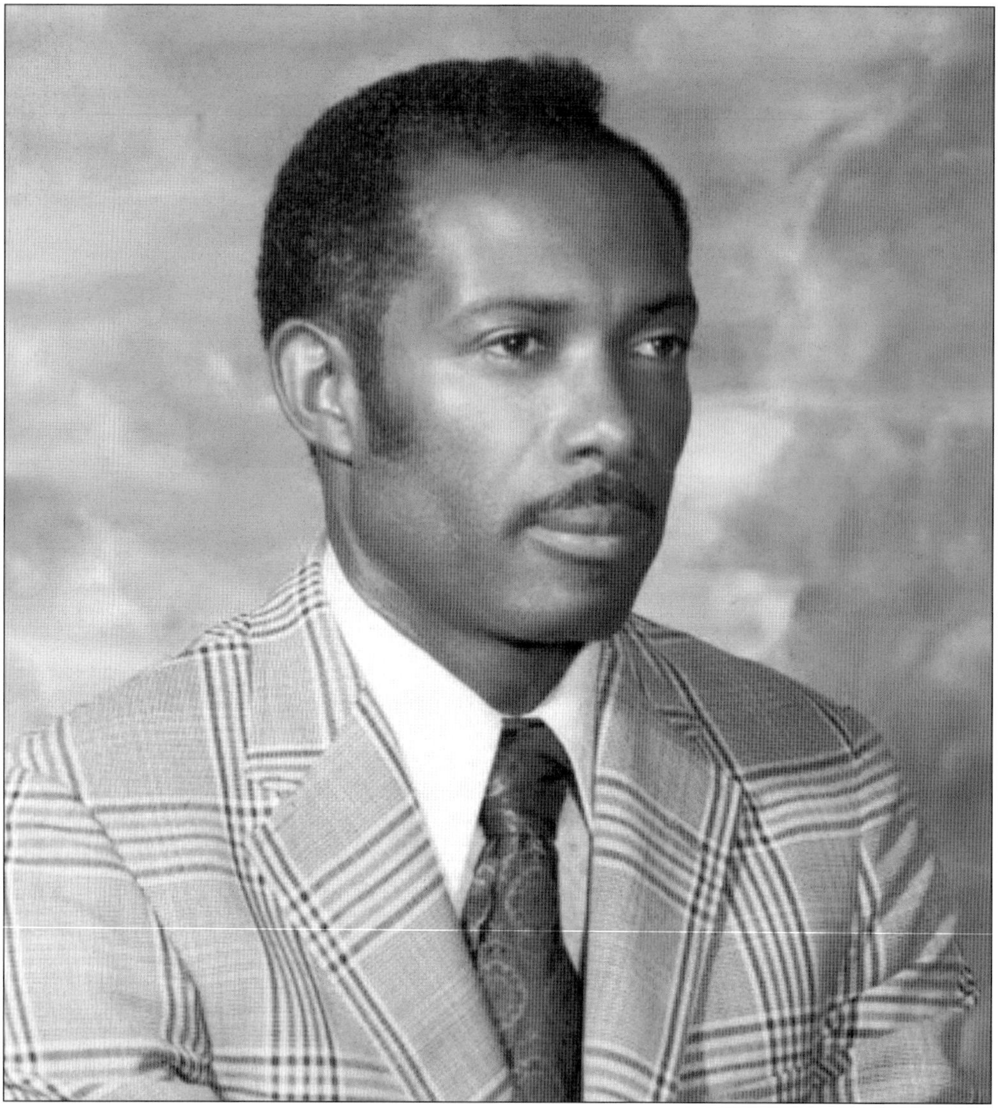

SSC was first integrated during fall semester 1955 with the admission of Wilmar B. Moss. His entry was a token, like the enrollment that year of a handful of black undergraduates at other public colleges in Arkansas. This action followed an advisory opinion of the Arkansas attorney general that the US Supreme Court's decisions prohibited discrimination. Even so, Moss had to threaten to ask for help from the National Association for the Advancement of Colored People before SSC's board of trustees relented. Moss attended one semester and then transferred to the traditionally all-black Arkansas AM&N College in Pine Bluff. Later, he served as a schoolteacher and as superintendent of the Walker School District in Columbia County. Prior to Moss's enrollment, two black schoolteachers from Stephens, Arkansas, Kathleen Jordan and James Epps, attended a graduate education extension class from the University of Arkansas taught on the SSC campus during the 1955 summer session. No record exists of any other black enrollment at SSC before passage of the 1964 Civil Rights Act.

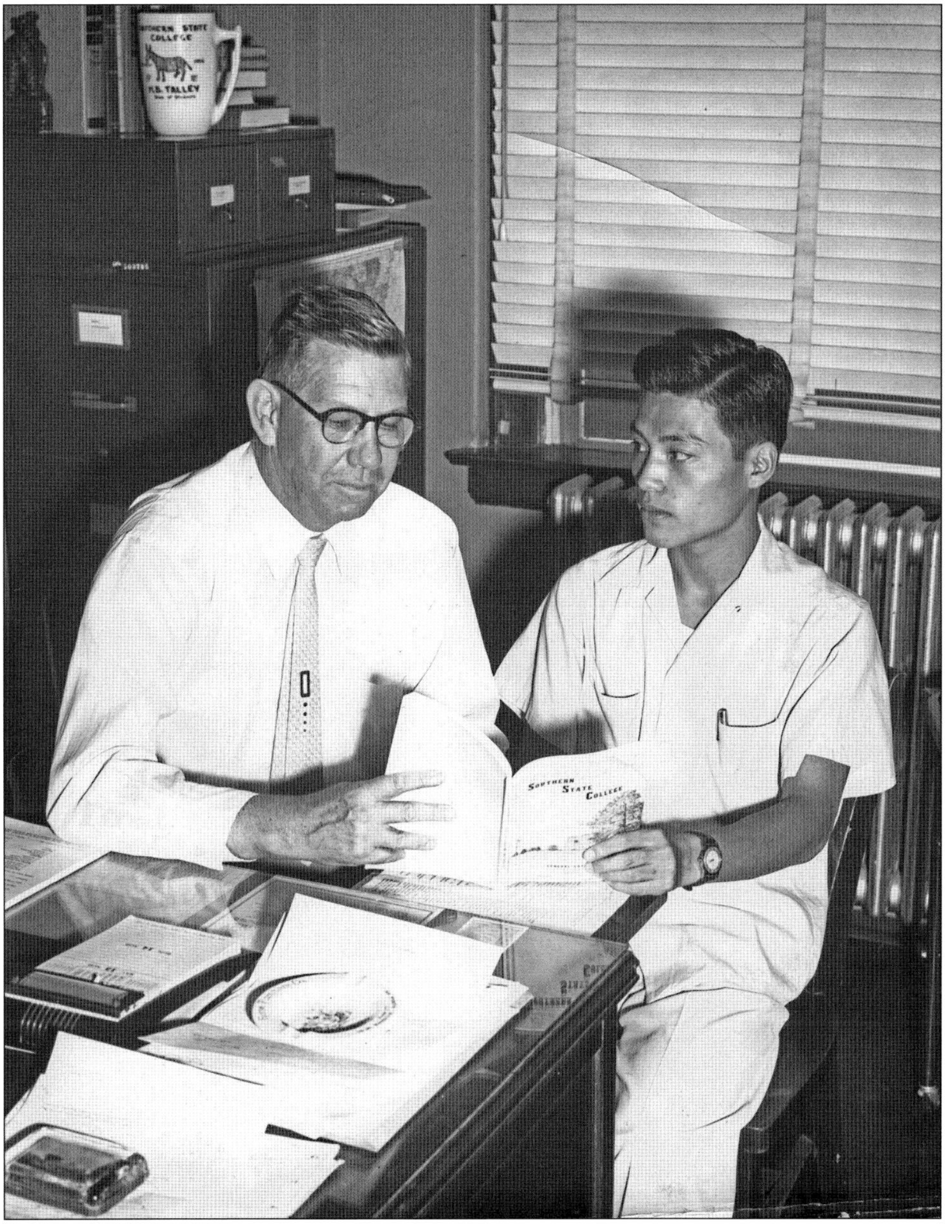

Dean of Students Milton Talley's door was always open to all students. He was especially supportive of SSC's international students, whom he advised. During the 1951 spring semester, Ben Kramer from the Netherlands was the college's first international student. The college had no study abroad program, but in 1953, Francis D. Loften Hampton, who graduated with a bachelor's degree in English, sailed for England carrying a Fulbright scholarship award to study library science at the University of London. Briefly, in the mid-1950s, SSC enrolled a small group of Hungarian freedom fighters who had survived the Soviet Union's invasion of their country in 1956. The first international student to graduate at SSC was Young-soo Kim (pictured) from Seoul, South Korea, in 1960, with a degree in industrial management. The largest number of international students at SSC during the late 1950s and 1960s were from Iran.

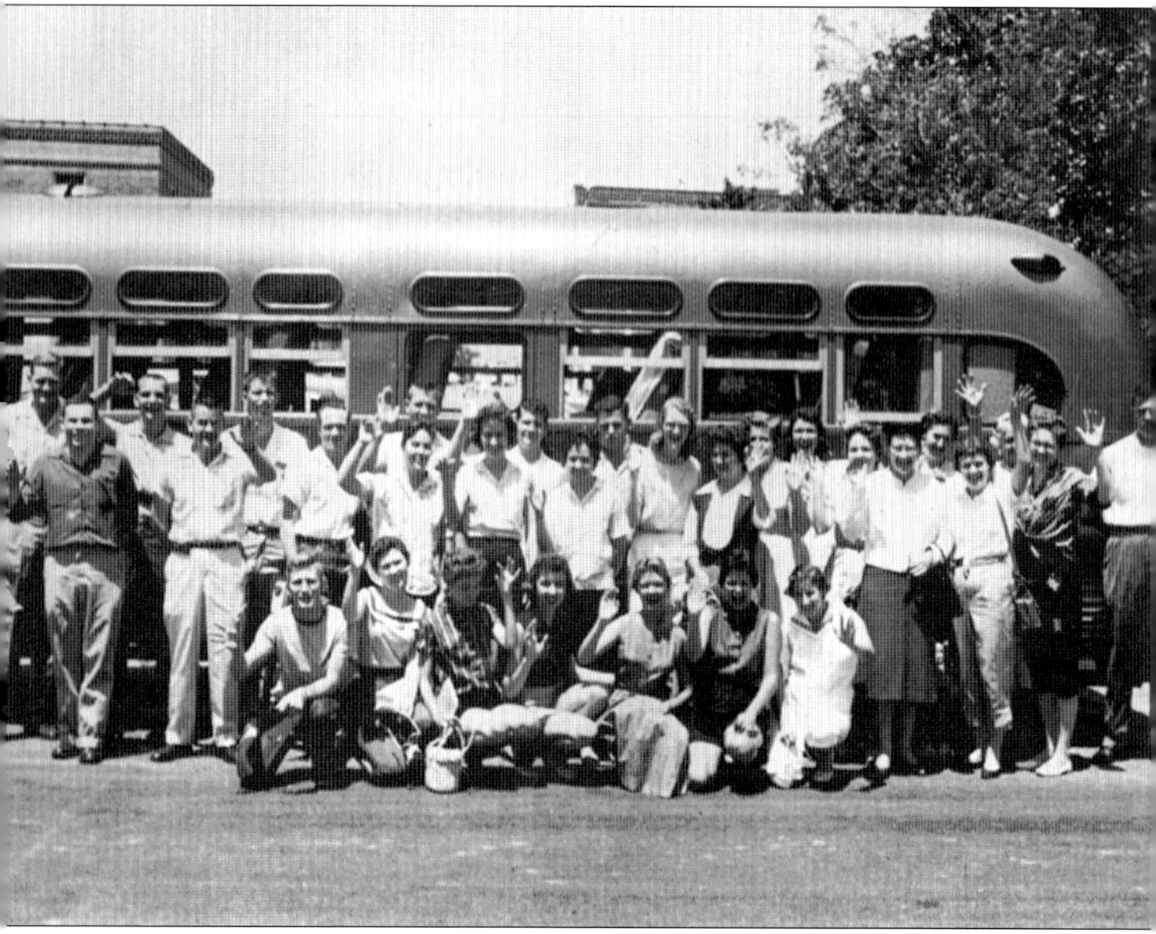

Southern State College first offered academic credit for study abroad in 1957 when sociology professor George Fay took a busload of students on a 38-day trip to Mexico. Students could earn six hours in history and sociology by taking notes and answering lengthy sets of questions about the 25 Mexican cities and innumerable historical and cultural sites that they visited. Essential to the venture's success was the bus driver, Earl Miller, in the early stage of his 50-year career at Southern State College and Southern Arkansas University, during which he took athletic teams and student groups all over the United States. In Mexico, Miller drove more than 5,000 miles across mountains, deserts, jungles, and busy city streets without incident. The group spent a week in Mexico City, arriving just in time to attend an afternoon bullfight. Students swam in the Pacific Ocean at Acapulco and stopped at Vera Cruz on Mexico's east coast on the way home. Earl Miller is in the back row at left. In front of him is George Fay.

Dr. Imon E. Bruce became SSC president in 1959. He was a 1933 alumnus of Magnolia A&M College, earned an EdD from Indiana University, and supervised teacher education at Arkansas State Teacher's College. Later, he served as superintendent of schools in the Hot Springs, Arkansas, district. Dr. Bruce established academic scholarships, essentially built a new campus, and managed the relatively smooth integration of SSC after 1964.

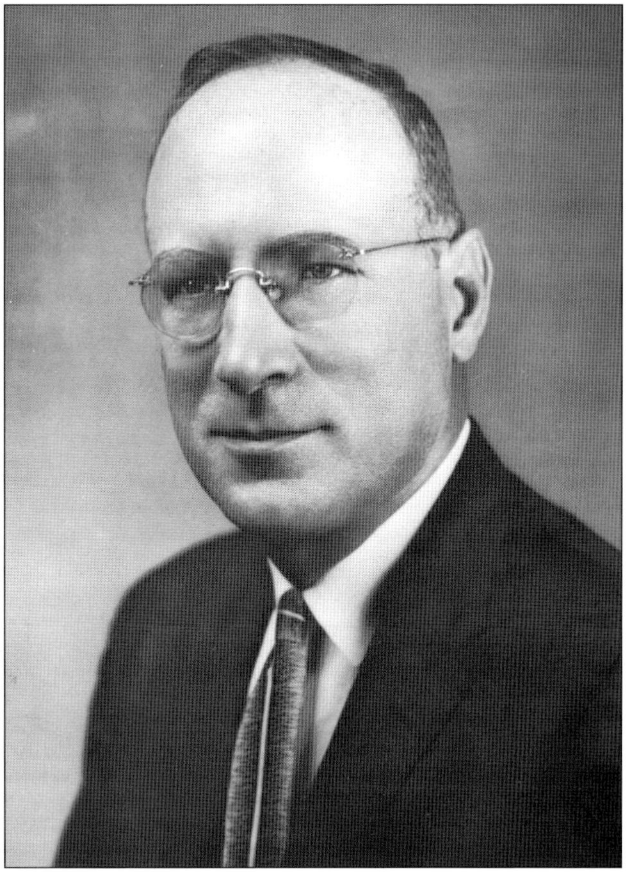

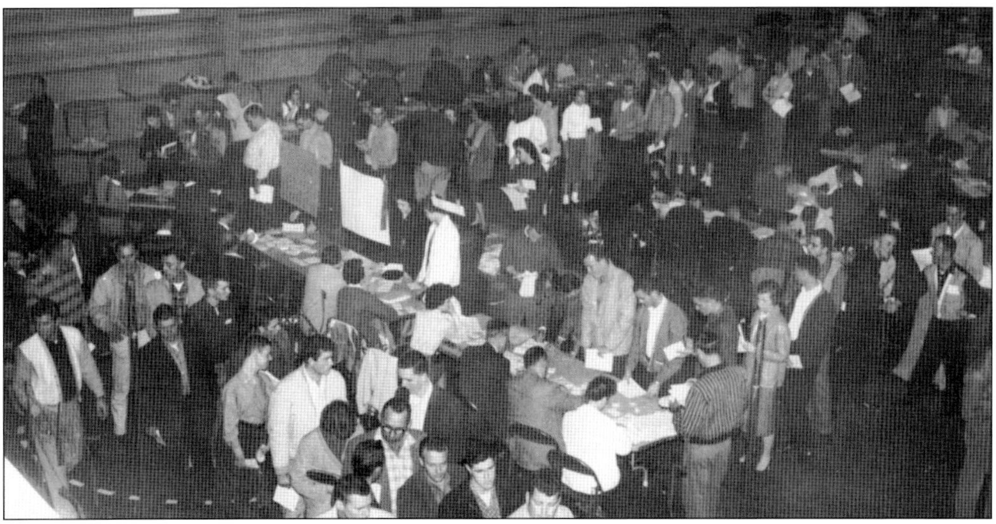

By the mid-1960s, registration for classes was crowded at all the nation's colleges as the baby boomers born after World War II enrolled in ever-larger numbers. Before the age of computers, registration was still conducted by hand, with faculty directly enrolling students in their classes, filling out a three-by-five-inch note card for each student. To accommodate these students, Dr. Bruce embarked on an extensive building program.

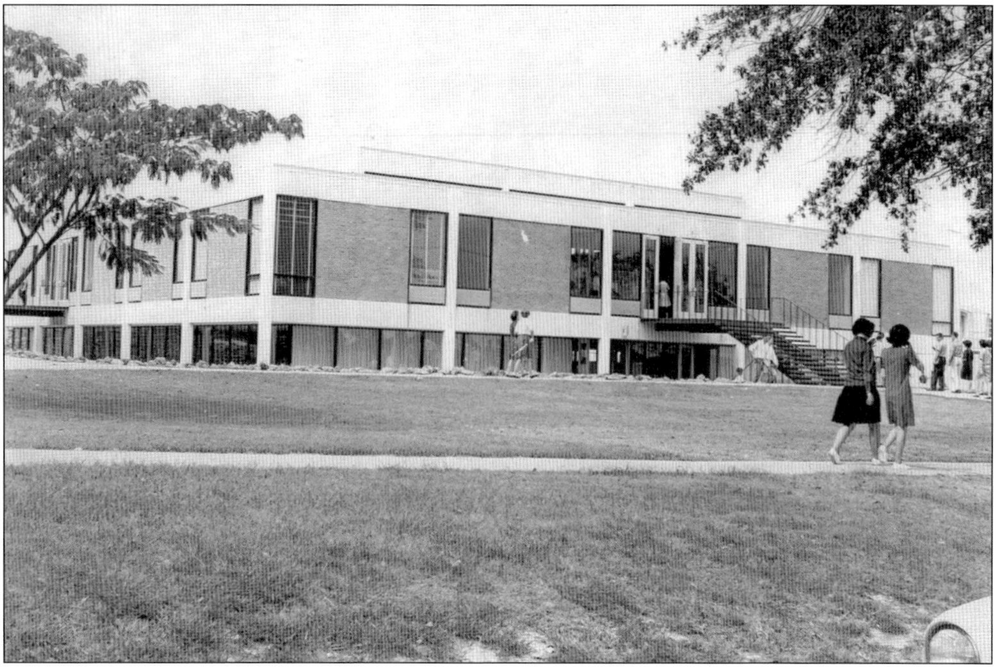

After a new student center was completed in 1963, the old student center, the 1913 dining hall, was torn down brick by brick. The new center, later named the Bruce Center, was the second building, after Graham Hall, to depart from the Georgian or Colonial architectural style first employed in Overstreet Hall. Bruce Center's first floor, sunken below ground level, housed a cafeteria. The upper floor contained a larger interior space for gatherings, including student dances, and a snack bar, post office, and bookstore, as well as offices for the dean of men and dean of women.

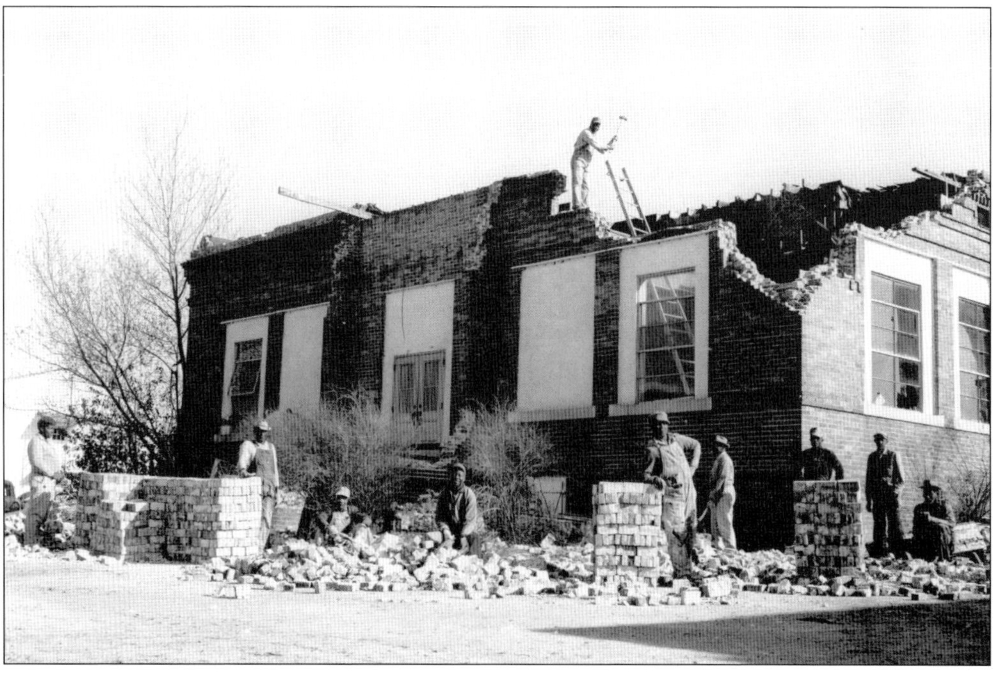

A new gymnasium in 1961–1962 was the first of many new buildings in the 1960s. It had the unusual feature of an Olympic-sized swimming pool. This permitted participation in AIC swim competition for the first time. The gym also had an arena that could seat crowds of 2,500, increasing by five-fold the number of fans who could cheer at Mulerider basketball games.

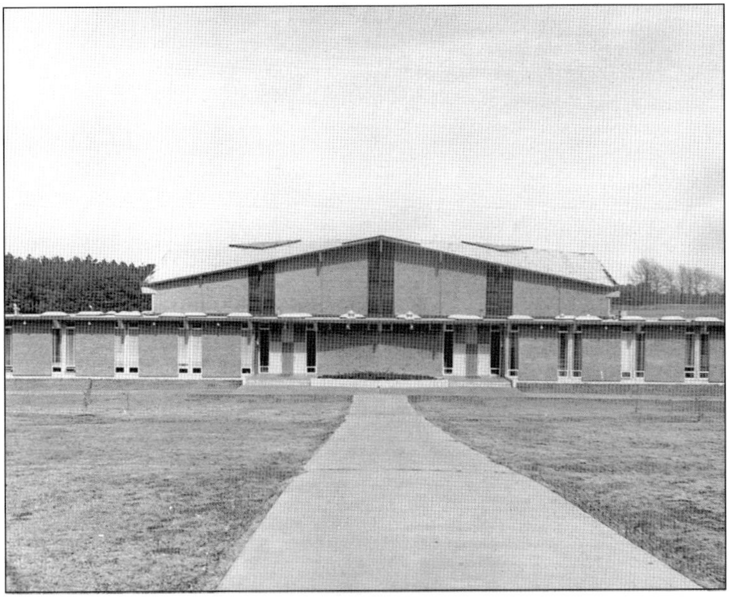

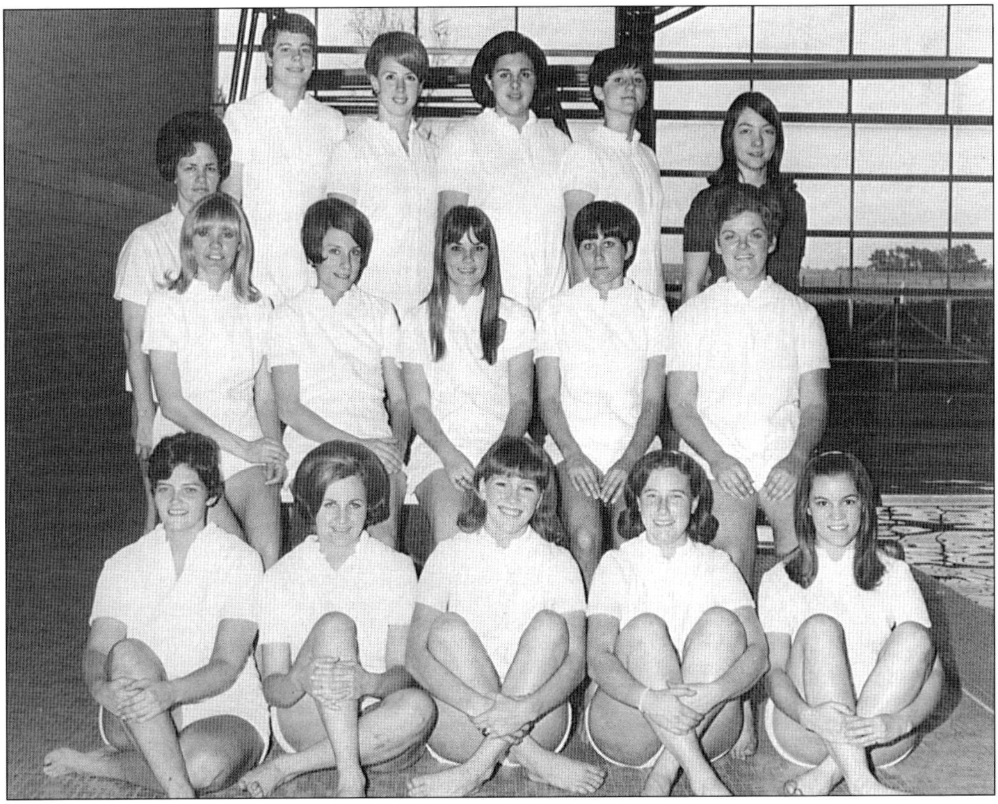

Women's swim teams were twice state champions in 1969 and 1970, led by the fast-paced swimming of Edith Frazer (back row, second from left). She was so fast that men's swim coach Dr. Delwin Ross also used her to beat male opponents. AIC authorities at first banned the practice. Coach Ross later used for four years Title IX's guarantee of gender equality as justification for including women on the men's team.

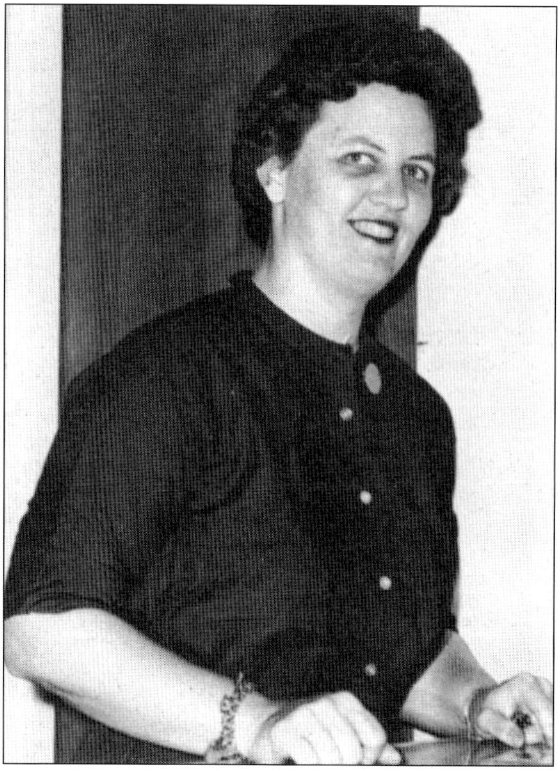

Pat Weaver, a 1954 SSC alumnus, earned a master's degree from the University of Arkansas and became director of SSC student activities in 1963. She also served as dean of women from 1967 to 1979, and afterwards as director of alumni affairs.

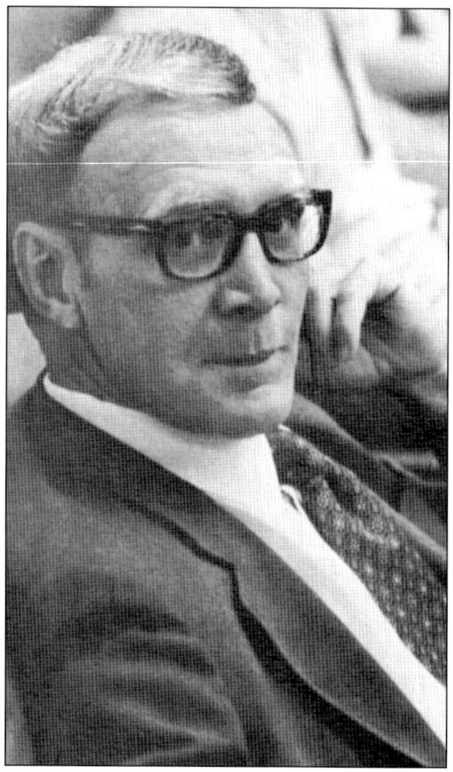

Dr. Donald Haefner replaced Milton Talley as dean of students in 1967. The Ohio native served the school and its students with much success during the next 30 years. He was largely responsible for keeping the school abreast of changes across the nation, as schools everywhere gave up the role of *in loco parentis* and began to treat students as adults rather than children.

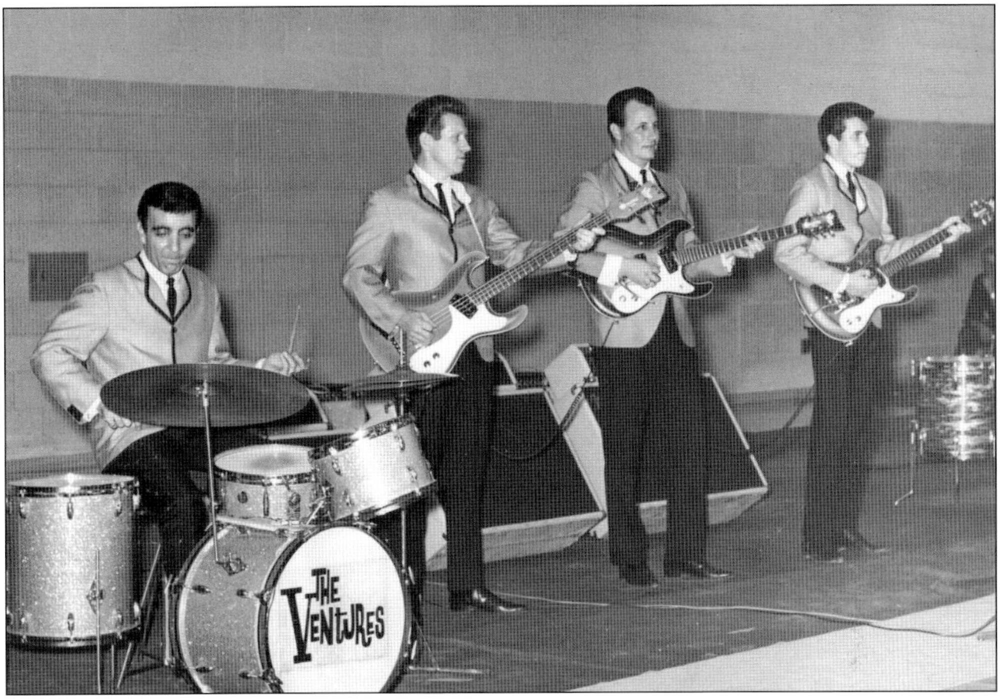

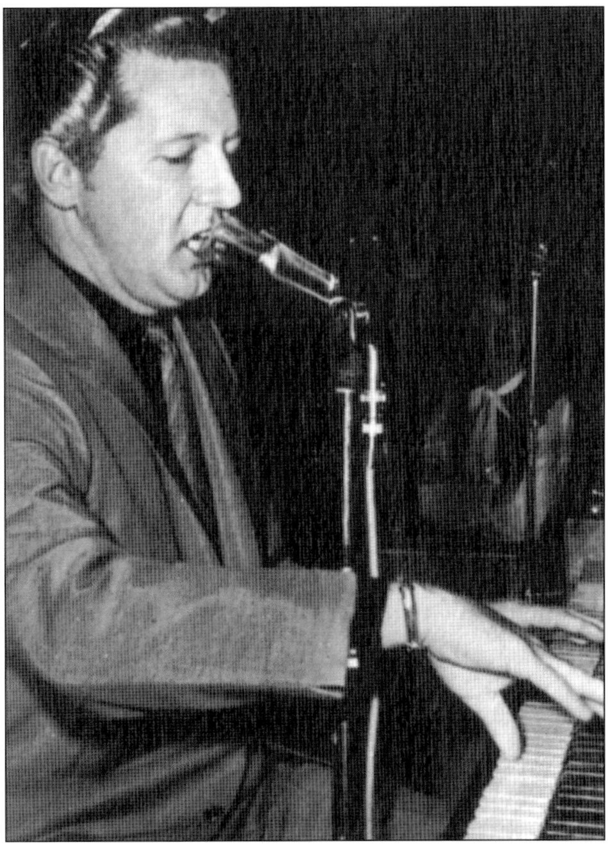

With the assistance of activities director Pat Weaver, several entrepreneurial presidents of the Student Government Association during the mid-1960s arranged rock concerts in the new SSC gymnasium. Most of the musicians toured in Dick Clark's Caravan of Stars. The number and variety of rockers who came to SSC was remarkable. The fall 1966 concert at SSC, for example, featured Gary Lewis & the Playboys, Sam the Sham & the Pharaohs, The Yardbirds, and the Distant Cousins. At other times, the performers included Paul Revere & the Raiders, Billy Joe Royal, Steve Alaimo, the Knickerbockers, the Viceroys, Linda Scott, the Ventures (pictured above), the Four Seasons, B.J. Thomas, Johnny Tillotson, Johnny Rivers, Bobby Goldsboro, the Kingsmen, and the Lettermen. On one occasion, even Jerry Lee Lewis (right), past his prime but still famous, pounded the piano keys at SSC.

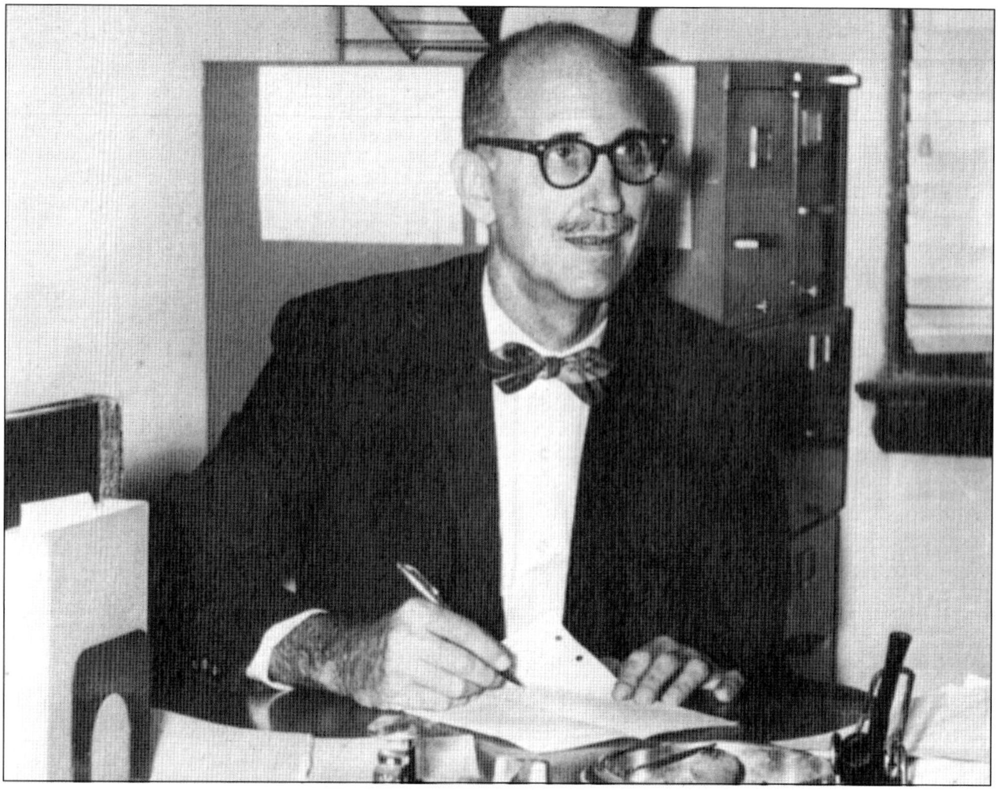

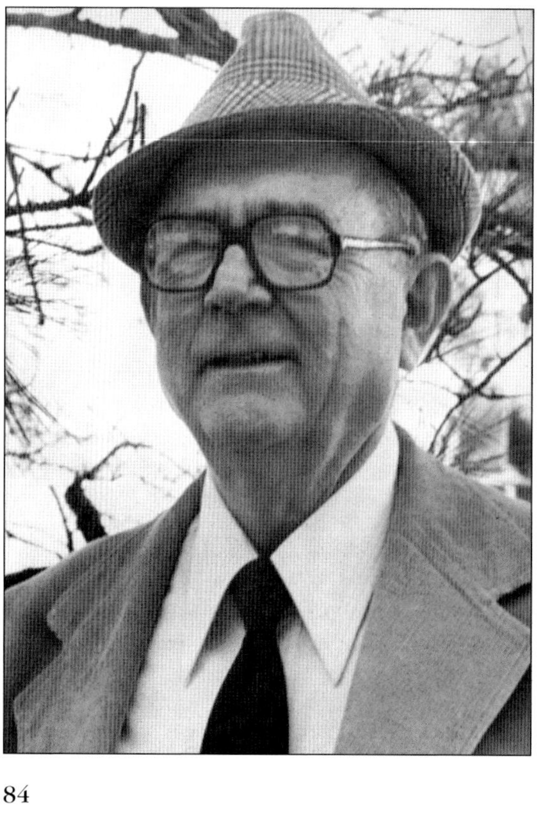

During the SSC years, two teachers were honored with the title of distinguished professor: Dr. George Sixbey (above) and Dr. Robert Walz (left) were masters of the classroom. The power of their personalities drew students into their courses' subjects. A Yale University PhD, Sixbey was noted for emotional poetry readings and discussions of beloved books. Walz, a University of Texas PhD, never gave a formal lecture. Constantly in motion, he talked informally and experimented with the various media of his time—records, movies, and film slides, some made from his own trips to historical sites in the United States—to bring history alive in his classroom.

A small number of black students entered SSC after passage of the Civil Rights Act of 1964. Among them was Virginia Marks, daughter of a Magnolia funeral home director. She earned a bachelor's degree in 1968, and later a master's degree. She returned to her alma mater 20 years later as Virginia Marks Todd to serve on the board of trustees, including a term as its president.

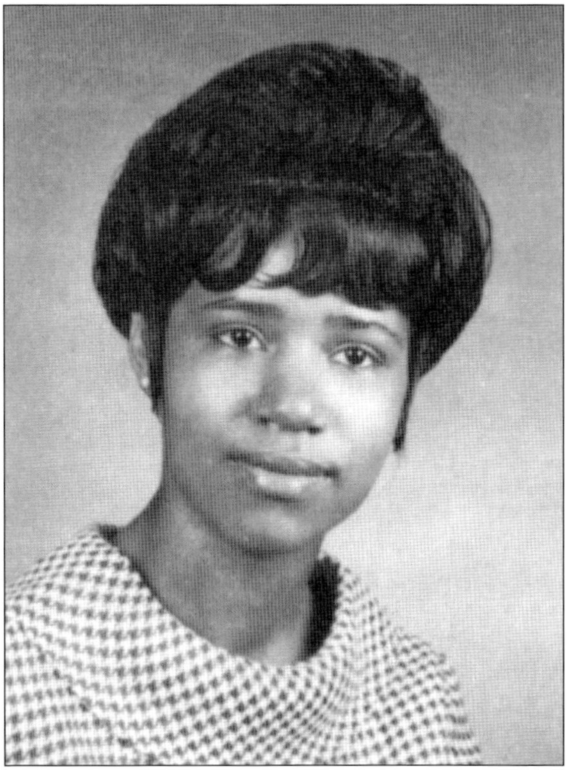

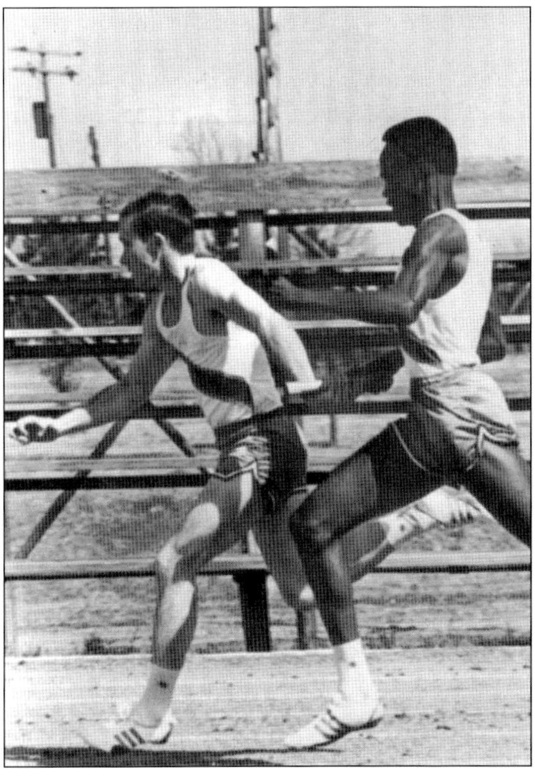

In 1965, more black students, including Archie Walker, came to integrate SSC. Dan Veach and Walker were fierce competitors on the track but otherwise friends living in the same residence hall. Veach, from Philadelphia, Pennsylvania, and other trackmen, went with Walker one night into the 66-Kitchen Café, an all-night diner popular with students. Almost inadvertently, they integrated this eatery for the first time, as Magnolia slowly adjusted to change.

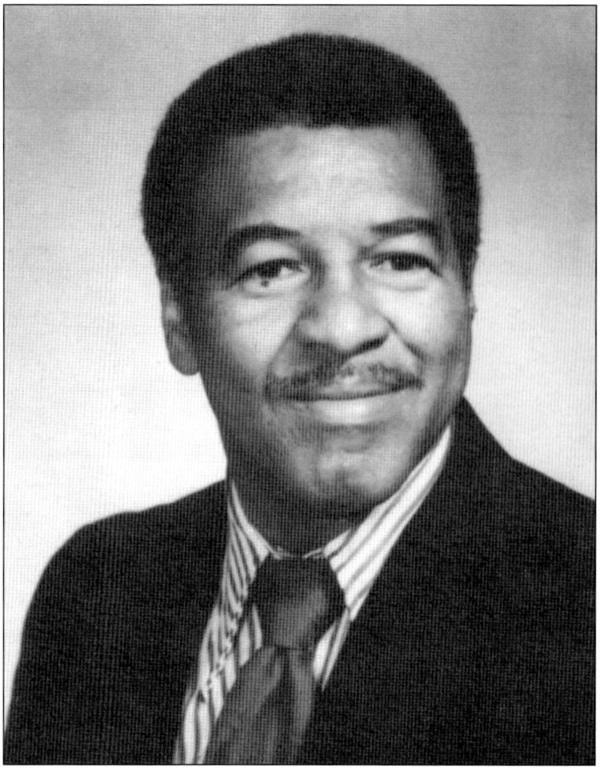

The integration of SSC's faculty and staff occurred more slowly than the student body. Alvin Brannon (pictured) was hired as a counselor in 1970 and worked closely with the student affairs office and with black student organizations. Marie Brown was employed in the nursing department beginning in 1971, first in the lab and later as a nursing instructor. Irene Brannon became an assistant librarian in 1974.

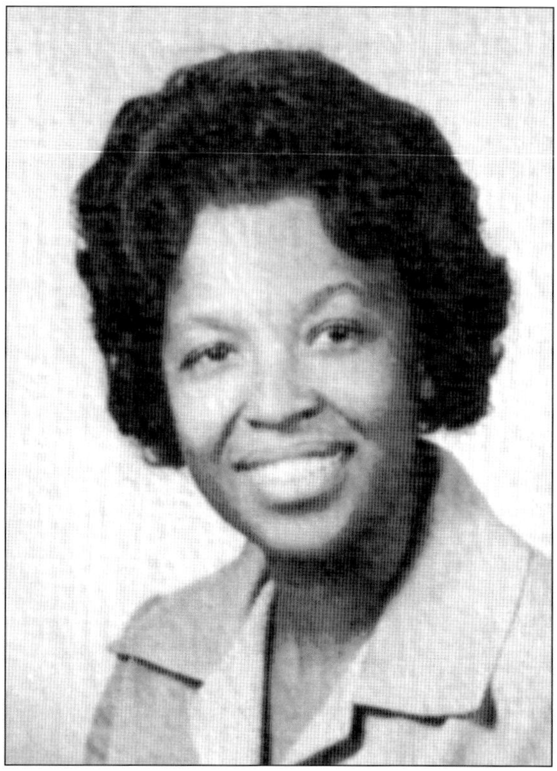

The first full-time black faculty member in the classroom was Kathleen Jordan, an instructor of English, in the fall 1974 semester. While teaching at SSC, Jordan earned a doctoral degree from the University of Nebraska and married a second time. A generation of students knew her as Dr. Kathleen Jordan Mallory, a much beloved teacher at the institution for more than 30 years.

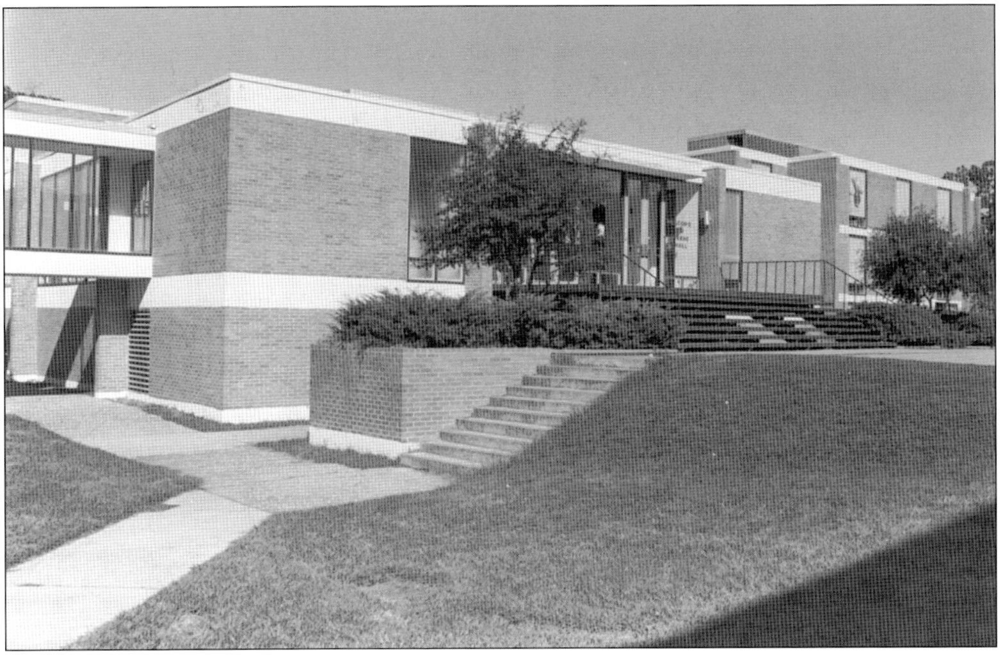

To meet Dr. Bruce's urgent need to house the baby boomers, work began on a twin residence hall, Greene Hall (below), even before construction of Talbot Hall (above) was completed. By 1964, a third residence hall, Talley Hall, matching Talbot and Greene Halls, had been completed. Together with the older Graham Hall, these buildings sat in a triangle of land on the north edge of campus, where "Wilkinsville" had once stood. Greene Hall was named to honor Lake Greene, physical plant director from 1943 to 1963. Talley Hall was named for Milton B. Talley, dean of students from 1953 to 1967. Talbot Hall was named to honor D.O. Talbot, member of the board of trustees from 1938 to 1975.

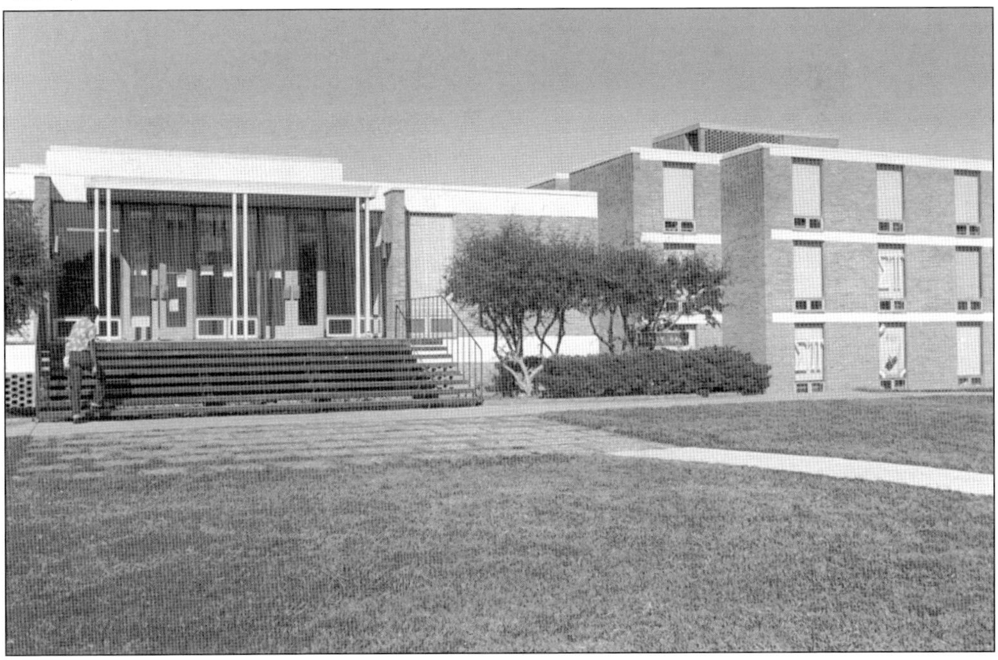

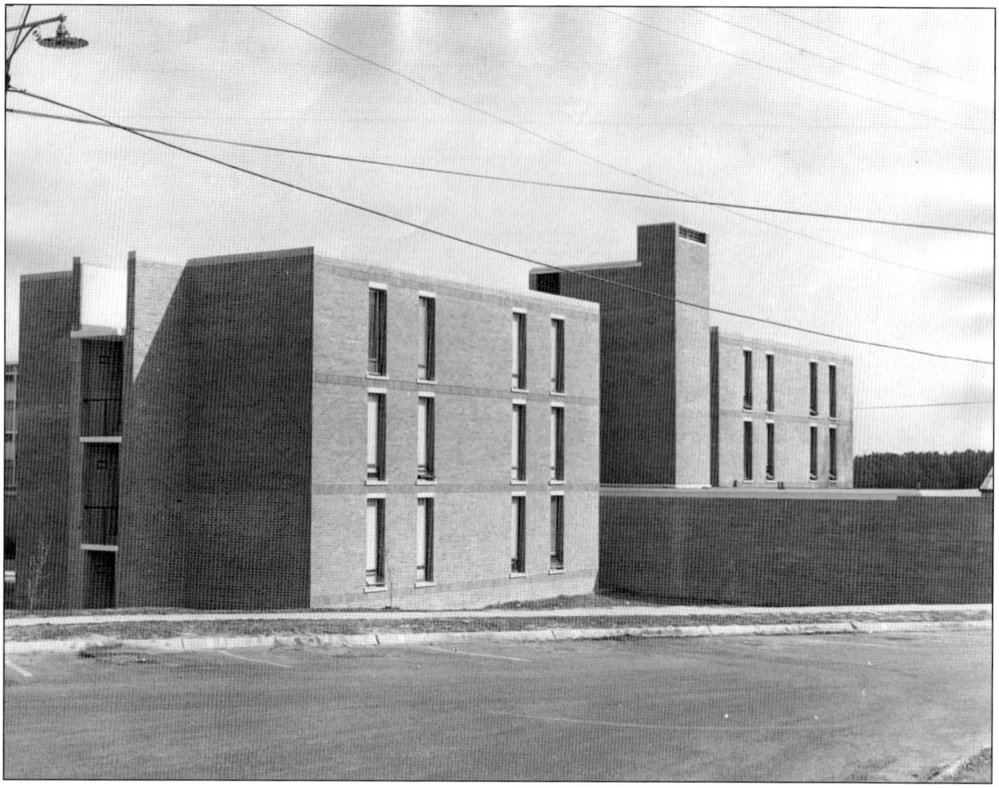

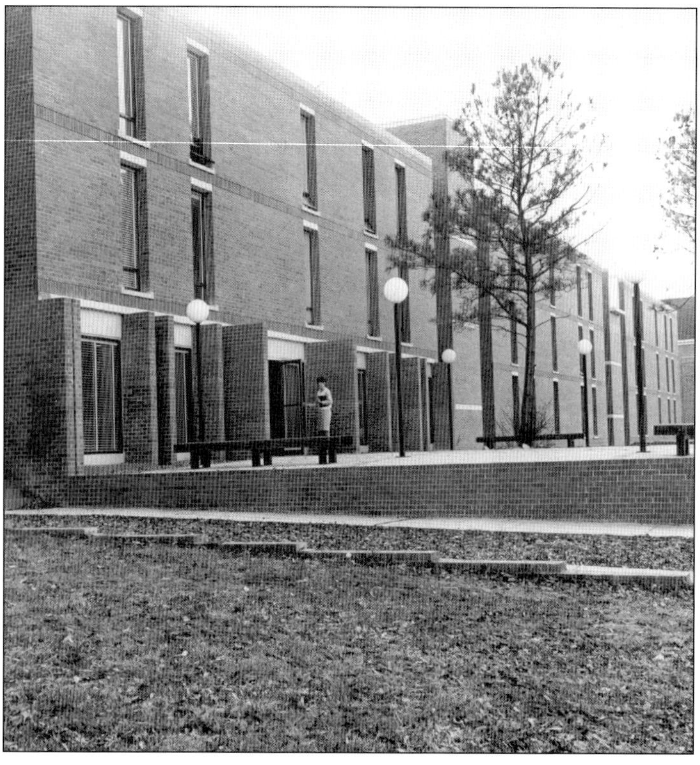

In 1965, a fifth new men's residence hall, Graham Hall Annex (above), was attached to the south end of Graham Hall, and a new women's hall, Harrod Hall (left), was constructed east of Overstreet Hall. Graham Hall Annex extended the honor paid to former academic dean Earle E. Graham. Harrod Hall was named to honor Margie Harrod, dean of women from 1954 to 1967. These two buildings completed Dr. Bruce's planned expansion of housing for students on campus. By 1968, all residence halls were full as total student enrollment peaked at 2,755.

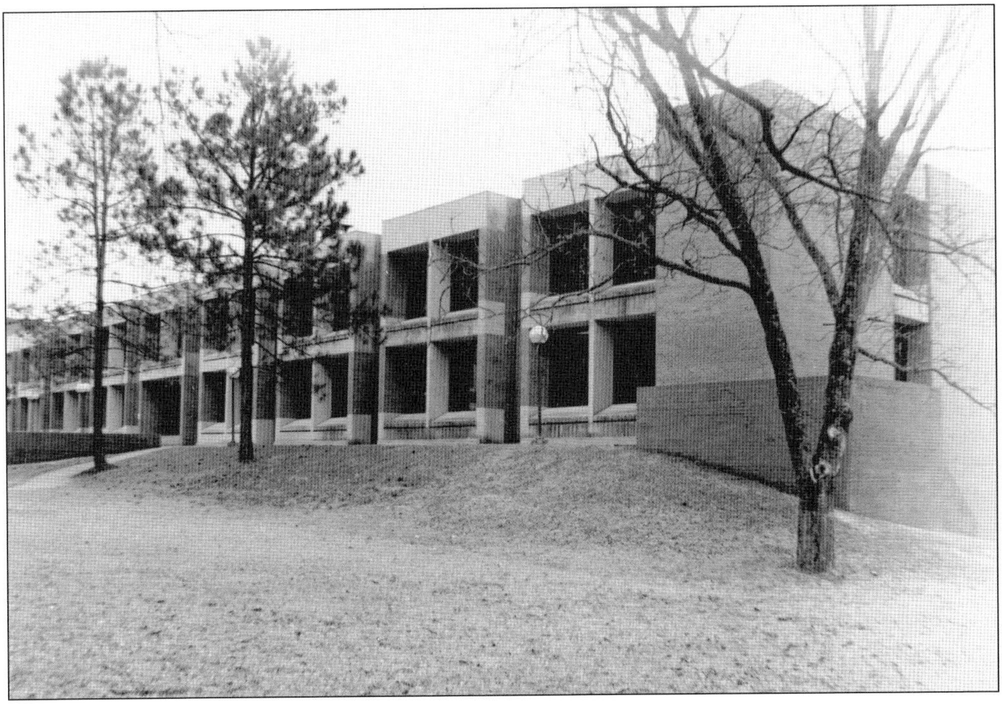

New classroom space was added in 1970 with the completion of Wilson Hall (above), named to honor Magnolia A&M College alumnus Dr. John H. Wilson, who served as a college trustee from 1945 to 1976. Science and mathematics offices and classrooms occupied the first and second floors. Also on the first floor was SSC's first mainframe computer from IBM, which Professor Ivan Brown, director of data processing, proudly shows Dr. Bruce at right. The school's main computer would ever after be named "Ivan" in honor of Brown. Wilson Hall's third floor housed offices and classrooms for English and foreign languages.

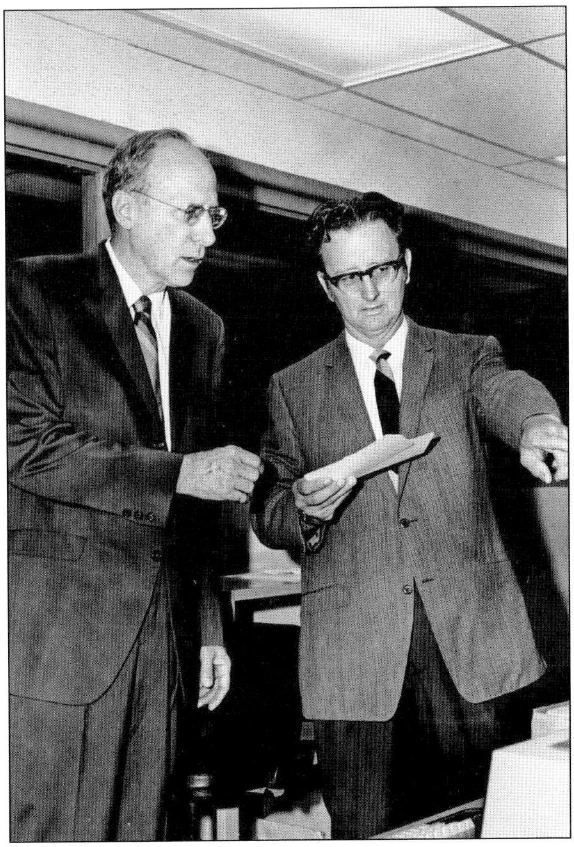

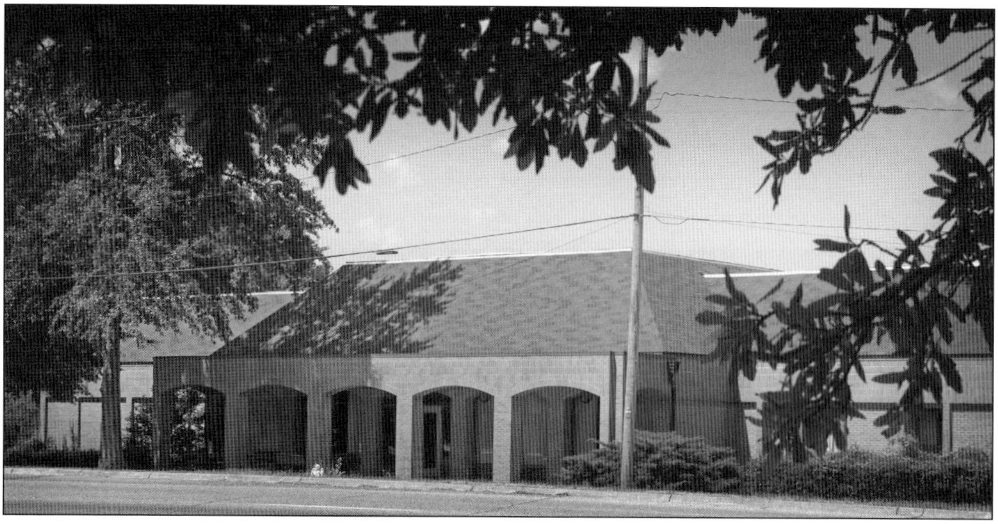

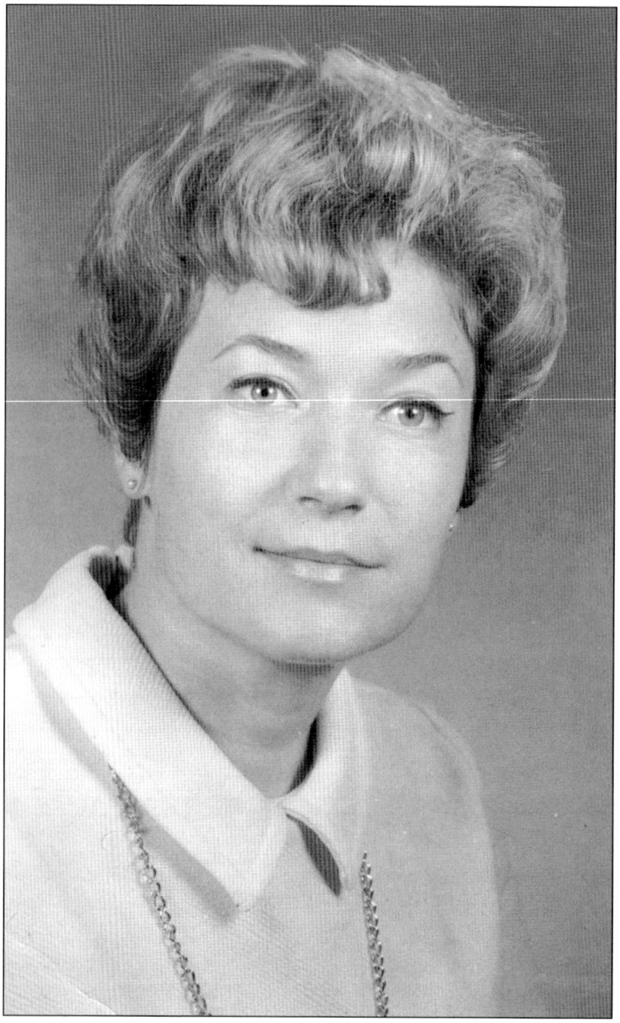

In 1972, Wharton Nursing Building, a new home for the nursing department, was completed on the west side of campus across Highway 371, where faculty houses had once stood. It was funded from Clara Barton's generous gift and Dr. Bruce's typical financial wizardry. At Barton's request, the building was named to honor her family's deceased physician, Dr. Joseph B. Wharton, founder of Warner-Brown Hospital in El Dorado, Arkansas. The nursing program began in 1968 with the arrival on campus of Pat Williams (left), former assistant director of the school of nursing at Methodist Hospital in Lubbock, Texas. Despite long commutes for both faculty and students to area hospitals in south Arkansas, the program flourished.

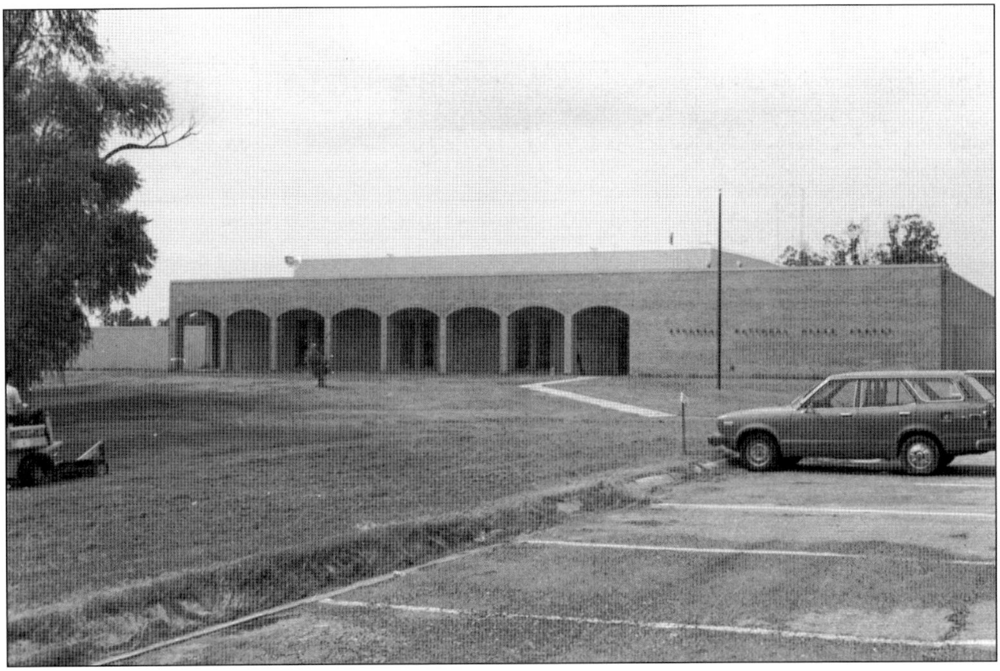

In 1976, SSC's ROTC program moved from the old 1926 armory to a newly constructed Arkansas National Guard Armory on the southwest edge of campus. ROTC began at SSC in 1972, at a time when many colleges were abandoning military training due to antiwar sentiment. Within a year, SSC had a higher rate of student participation than any other college in the state. A number of SSC's ROTC students became career military officers. Larry Banks, battalion commander in 1973–1974, was among the first African Americans in the United States to lead an integrated ROTC unit. With the end of the Cold War, the army discontinued SSC's ROTC unit, as well as other units at small colleges in Arkansas.

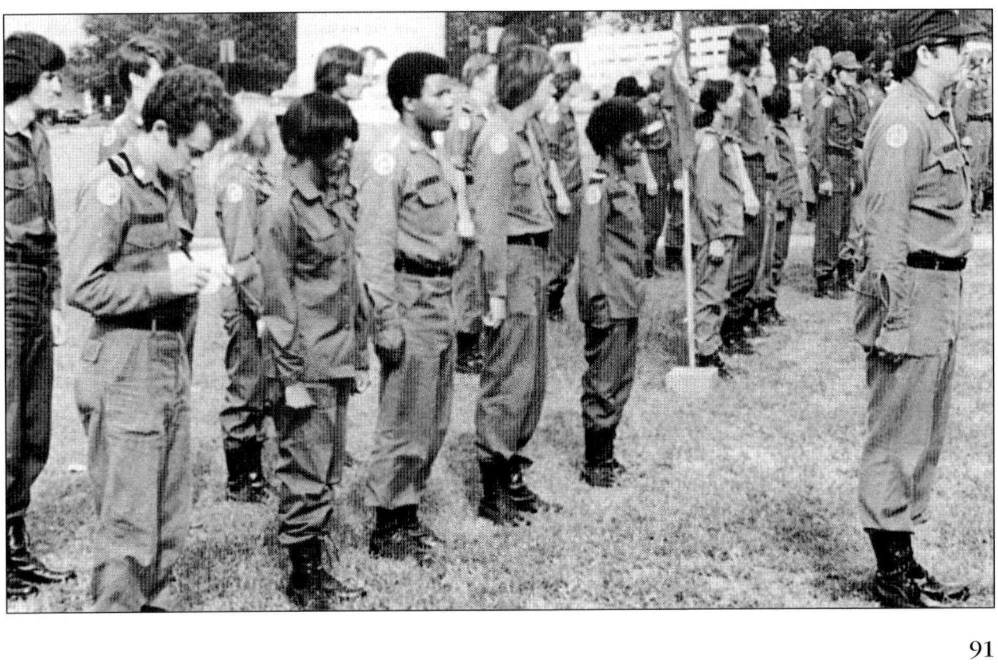

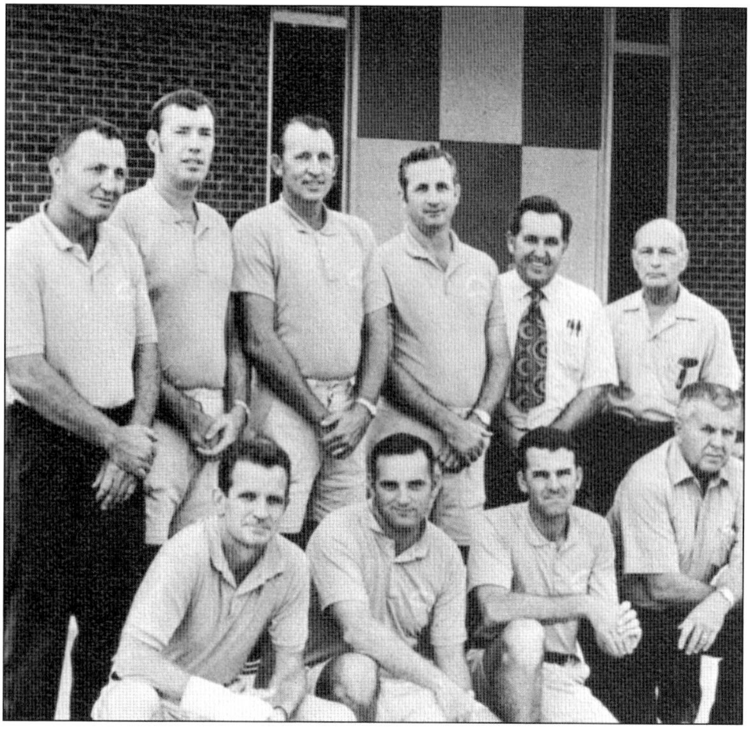

Coaches of men's sports in this 1973 photograph are, from left to right, (first row) Delwin Ross, Sonny Whittington, Eldon Hawley, and George Henry; (second row) Rip Powell, Monroe Ingram, Calvin Neal, W.T. Watson, Richard Carter, and director of athletics Auburn Smith. SSC's sports program was often the best in the AIC. SSC won the AIC all-sports trophy for the best combined record of its teams five times between 1968 and 1974.

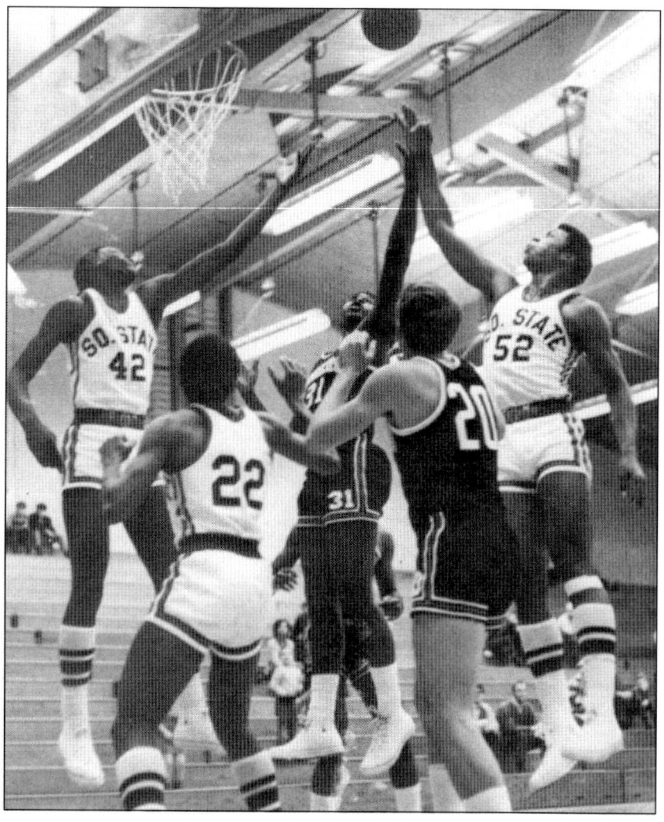

The most successful men's coach was W.T. Watson. His basketball program had only three losing season in 17 years. The greatest player was six-foot-five center Bill Barnes, SSC's first black basketball player, on the right in this photograph taken during the 1969–1970 season. Barnes's immense popularity helped smooth the local community's response to SSC's integration.

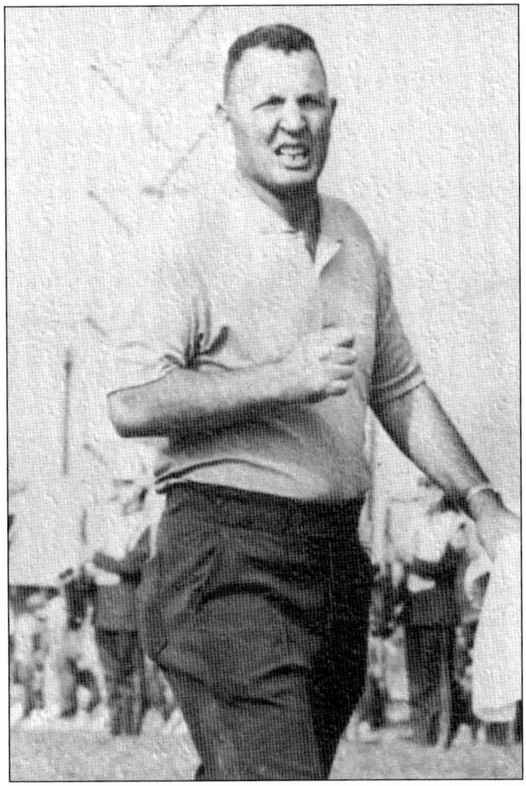

Coach Raymond "Rip" Powell was a fierce competitor on the field; elsewhere, he was a modest man with a big heart. From 1971 to 1974, with assistants Calvin Neal and James "Sonny" Whittington, Powell compiled the best football record in school history, ranking nationally several times. His best team, pictured below in the dark jerseys, won the AIC championship in 1972. Tommy Tuberville was an unremarkable player who persuaded Powell to let him watch film and listen to the coaches plan game strategy. Later, as a coach, Tuberville became one of the best NCAA Division I football coaches of his era at Auburn and other universities.

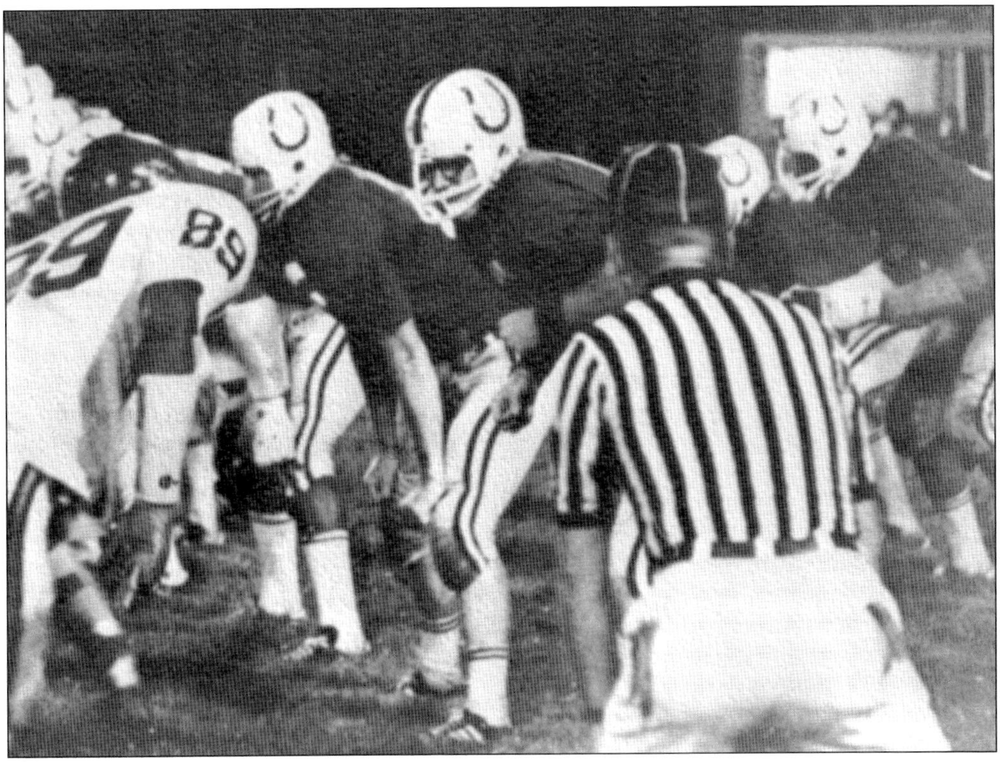

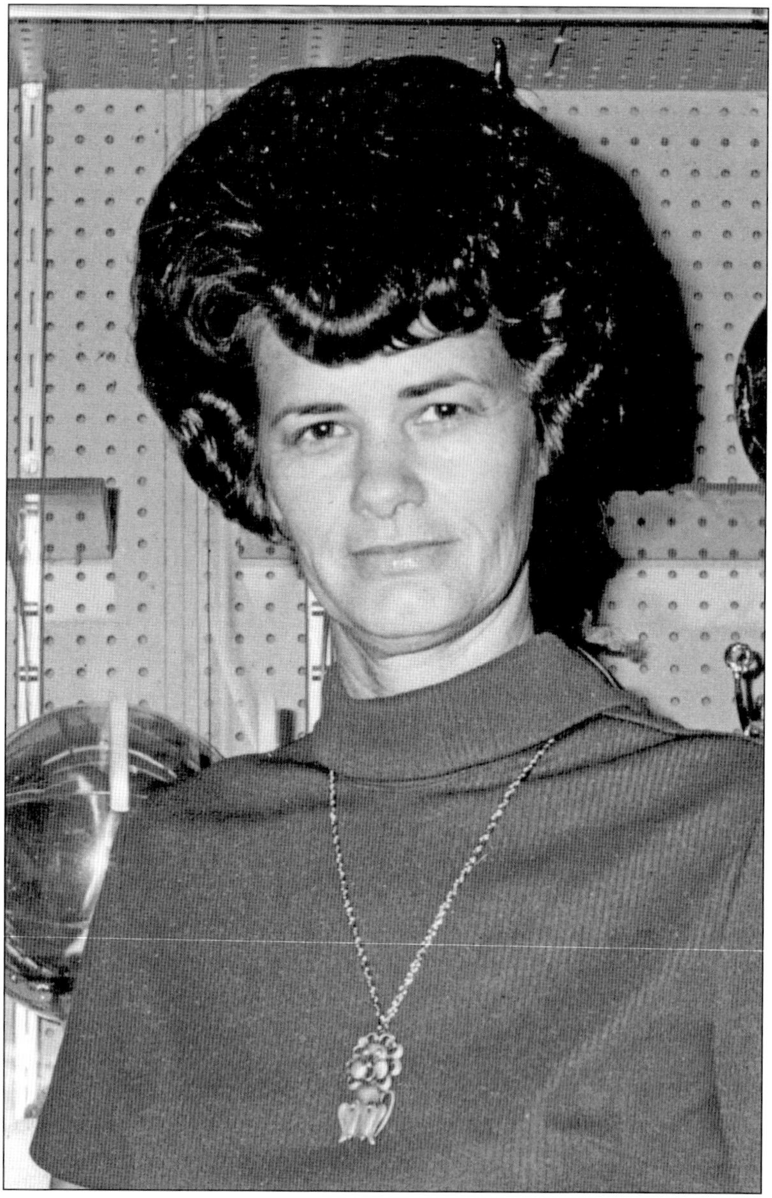

Coach Margaret Downing was a national leader in the rise of women's intercollegiate basketball. She was inducted into the National Association of Intercollegiate Athletics Hall of Fame in 1987. She twice served as manager of the US women's basketball teams in the Pan-American Games, and as president and treasurer of the US Olympic committee for women's basketball. She was head coach at Connecticut College for Women and at Central Connecticut State College before returning home to Arkansas to head Ouachita Baptist College's basketball program. In 1965, Downing came to SSC, where she coached swimming, volleyball, and basketball, leading teams to championships in each sport. Her basketball teams won eight championships over two decades, the second most titles in women's or men's sports in school history. Dr. Downing was also an outstanding teacher. She earned a doctoral degree at Texas Women's University and ended her career at SSC as dean of the school of education.

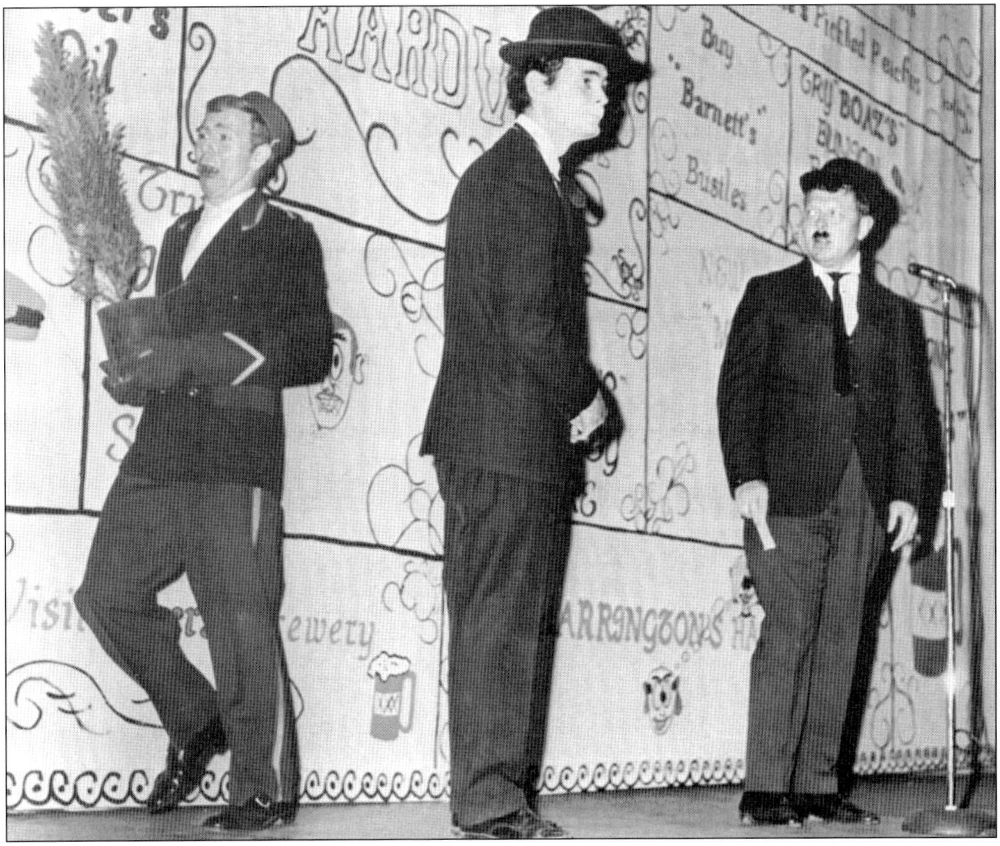

In addition to sports, SSC students in the 1960s and early 1970s participated in many other extracurricular activities. *Aardvark*, an annual production sponsored by the speech and theater department, showcased talents of a broad cross-section of students. Performers often included faculty, such as Jake Whitehead, pictured playing Oliver Hardy to Billy Barnett's Stan Laurel.

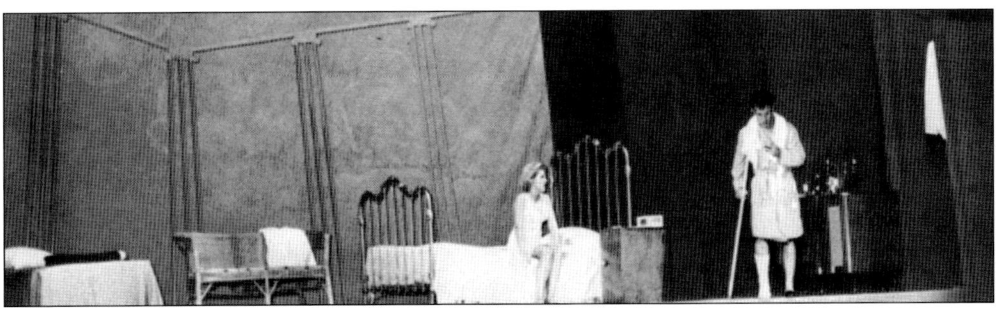

SSC theater productions became more sophisticated, and controversial, for Magnolia audiences after director Jerry Cortez arrived. In 1966, crowds so large that people were turned away came to see Tennessee Williams's *Cat on a Hot Tin Roof*. The administration required a disclaimer that the college did not condone the language or the play's theme. The story of Brick and Maggie's tortured marriage starred students Charles Burton and Linda Reynolds.

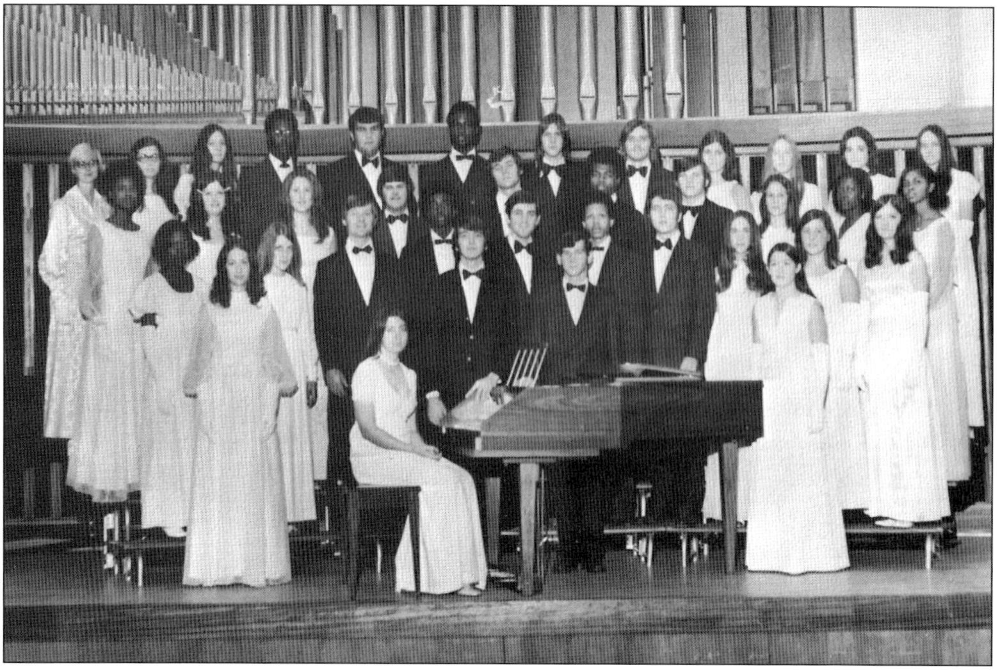

Among extracurricular activities available for SSC students, the choir (pictured here in 1973) was among the most important. Under the leadership of choir director Dr. Gene Kellsay, SSC's singers always performed to widespread acclaim on annual tours. The choir was part of SSC's strong music department. Under the leadership of Dr. Robert Campbell, the department gained accreditation from the National Music Association, a signal accomplishment for a small college music department.

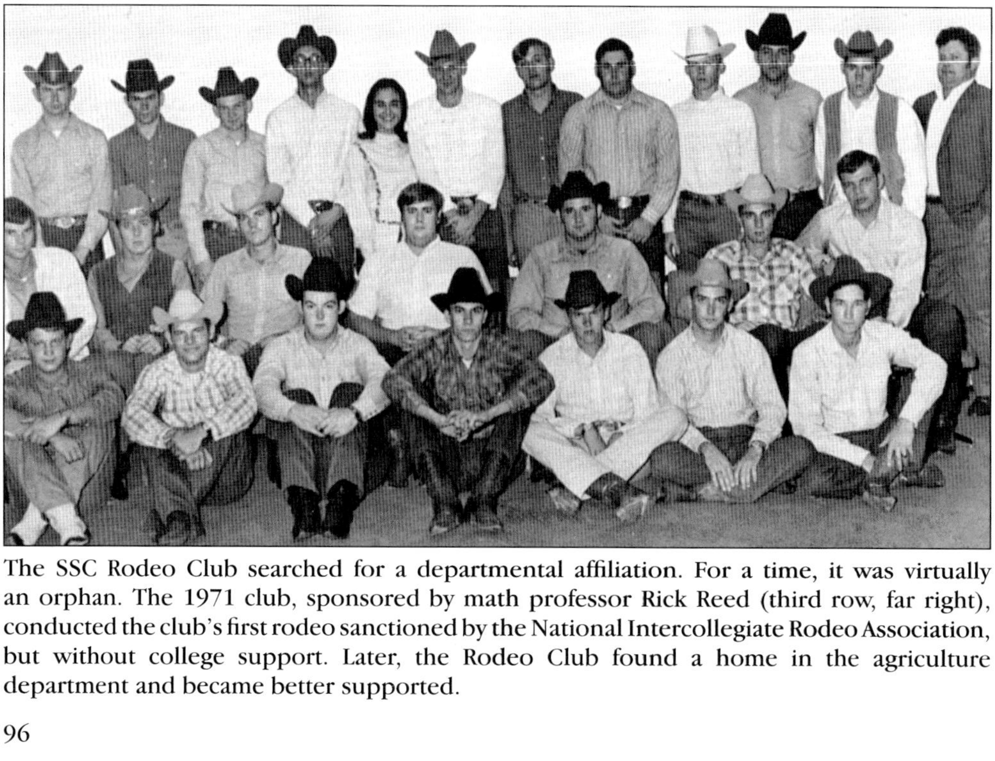

The SSC Rodeo Club searched for a departmental affiliation. For a time, it was virtually an orphan. The 1971 club, sponsored by math professor Rick Reed (third row, far right), conducted the club's first rodeo sanctioned by the National Intercollegiate Rodeo Association, but without college support. Later, the Rodeo Club found a home in the agriculture department and became better supported.

In the early 1970s, several notable personalities spoke at SSC. Among them was famed cultural anthropologist Dr. Margaret Mead, whose controversial reports on South Pacific and Southeast Asian traditional cultures' attitudes toward sex influenced the 1960s American sexual revolution. At SSC, she spoke in an environmental series titled "What Price Survival," following SSC's participation in the first Earth Day in 1970.

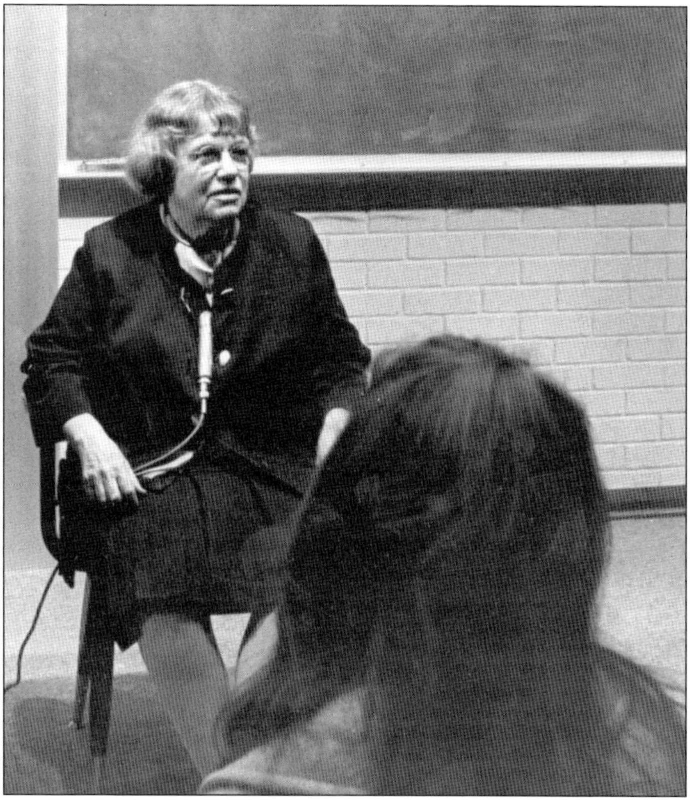

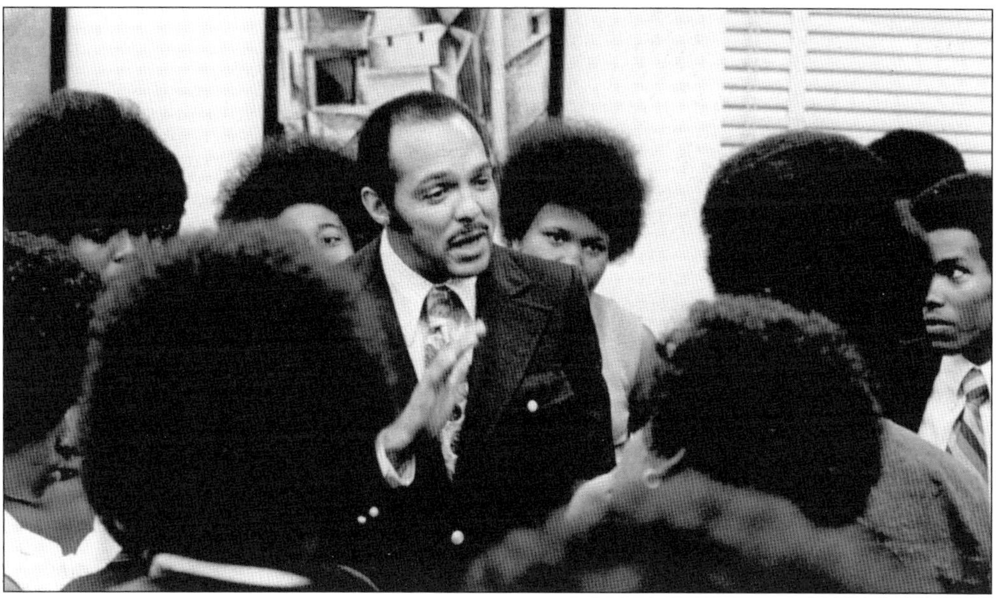

Famous black politicians and civil rights leaders also spoke, including Carl Stokes (pictured), first African American mayor of Cleveland, Ohio, and Julian Bond, a founder of the Student Nonviolent Coordinating Committee. Such speakers and programs provided SSC students opportunities to become more aware of and involved in the cultural and political currents that were changing America during this era.

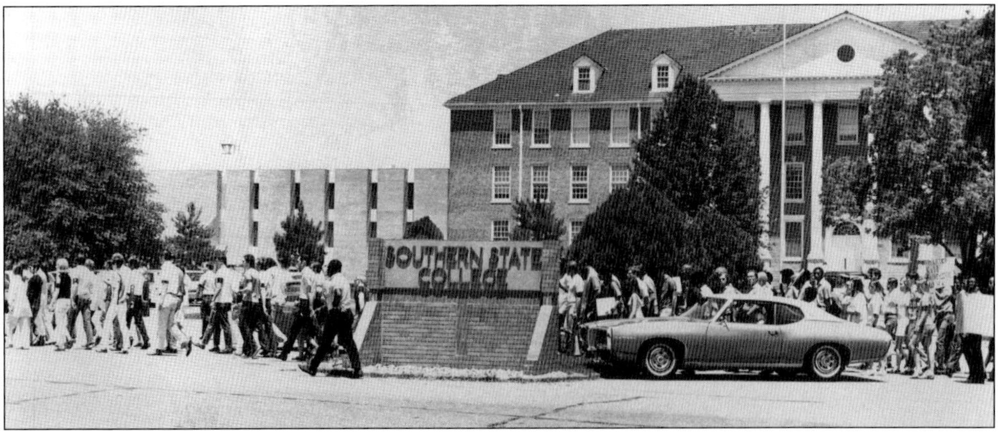

The protest movements that swept across the United States during the 1960s had faint echoes at SSC, but for the most part, the college and city of Magnolia watched the upheavals from afar. A single protest march at SSC occurred on May 12, 1970, to express sympathy for students killed at Kent State University a few days earlier.

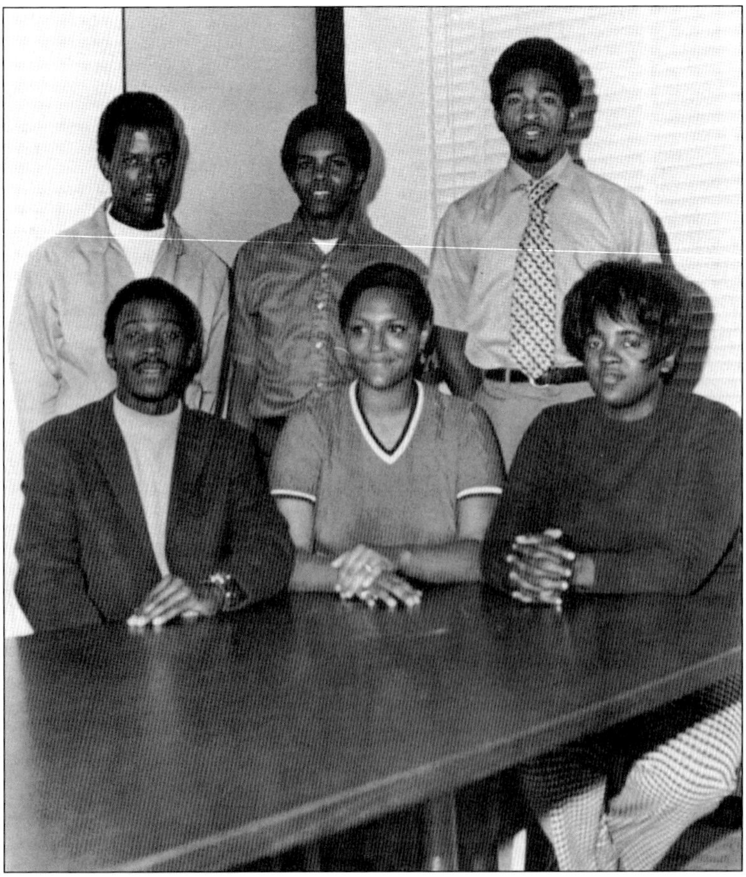

In 1969, SSC's administration banned a biracial student organization known as Students United for Rights and Equality, mistakenly thought too radical. Its successor was the Black Students Association. Its president for several years was Kandi Korbett, first row center, from Brooklyn, New York. Other officers in 1970–1971 included, from left to right, (first row) Tony Knight and Yvonne Riggins; (second row) Larry Roach, Thomas Williams, and Jerry Hayes.

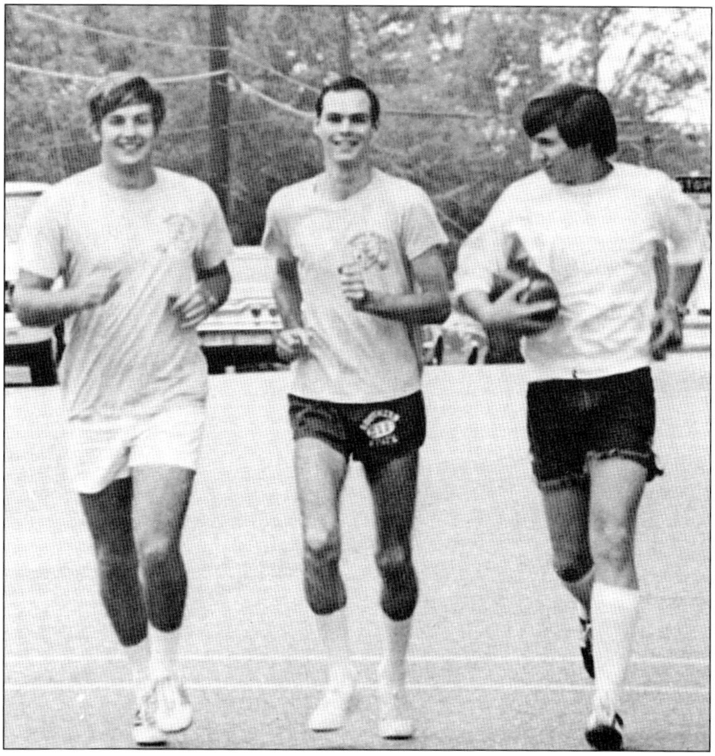

Established in May 1970, the Tauran Society was SSC's first fraternity. It folded in 1975 without acquiring national affiliation. Pictured here from left to right, Mike Waters, Alan Bailey, and James "Bubba" Wrentz are jogging the last relay of several Tauran teams that ran from Magnolia during a two-day trek to Conway to support the Muleriders playing against the Bears of the State College of Arkansas. Many social groups later affiliated with national organizations.

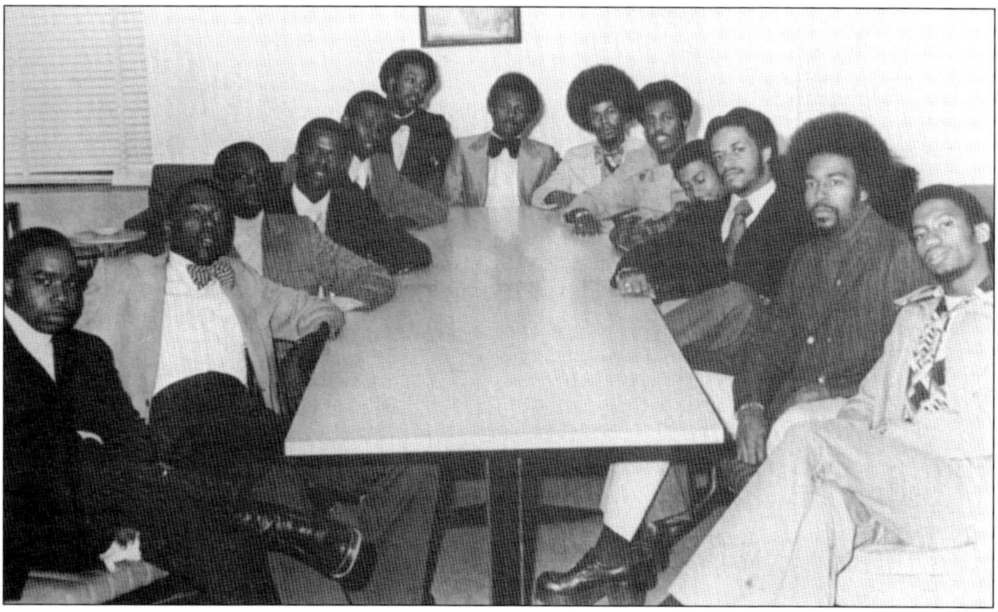

The first black fraternity, Omega Kappa Alpha, was organized in February 1973. Members pictured here include, from left to right, James Fort, Shady Patton, Vain Caldwell, Johnny Turner, Terry Calahan, Wilbur King, Tony Knight, Johnny Biddle, Kerry Hill, James Christopher, Larry Banks, James Phillips, Lawrence McKinney, and James Berry. The group affiliated nationally in 1974 with Omega Psi Phi. At about the same time, a black sorority joined Delta Sigma Theta.

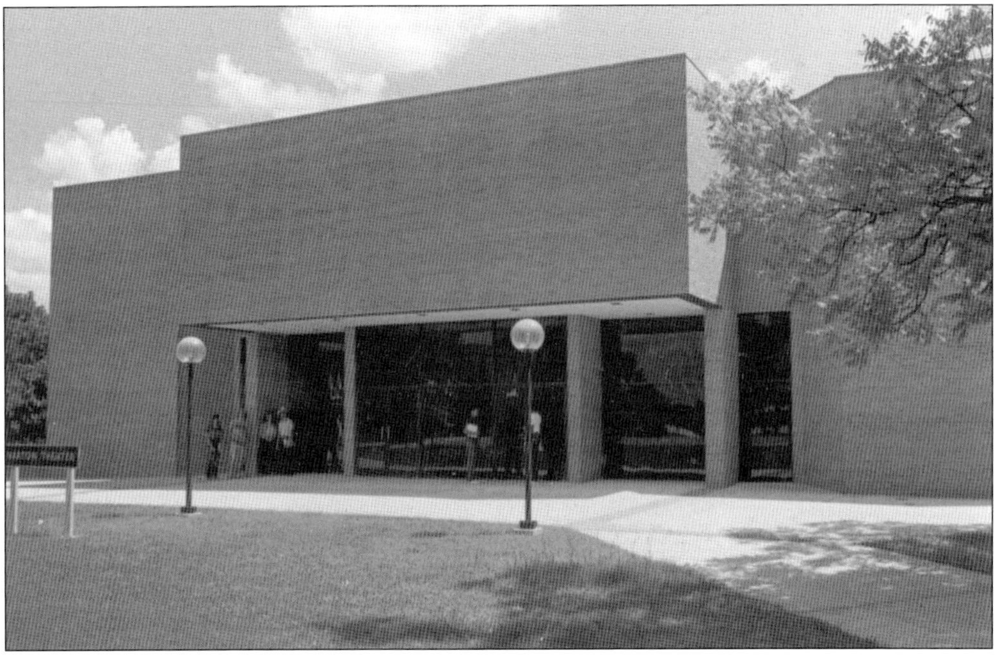

Dr. Bruce's building program continued into the 1970s. In 1974–1975, Harton Theater, a thoroughly modern 500-seat theater, replaced Overstreet Auditorium. It was named for Margaret Harton, professor of speech and director of theater from 1945 to 1975, who cut the ribbon at the dedication of the new building. Miss Harton (her preferred name) directed two generations of student actors in plays that had appeared on Broadway. Often in the 1940s and 1950s, she was forced to conform to local mores. On occasion, she allowed students to protest slyly. For example, in a scene from Noel Coward's *Blithe Spirit*, buttermilk was once used as a substitute for alcoholic cocktails. Magnolia was staunchly prohibitionist in sentiment and policy at the time. Miss Harton taught several student actors who were later successful in show business, including Harry Thomason, Hollywood producer and director of award-winning television series such as *Designing Women* and *The Blue and the Gray*.

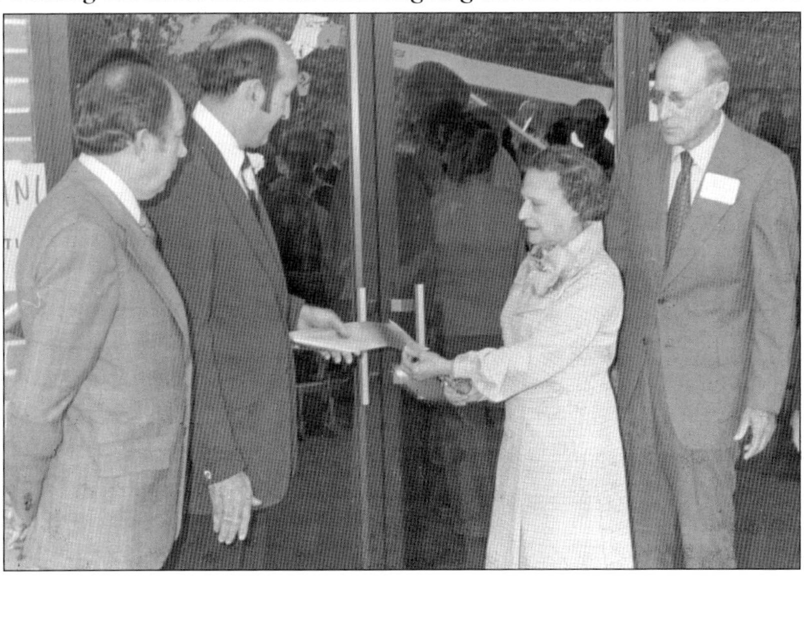

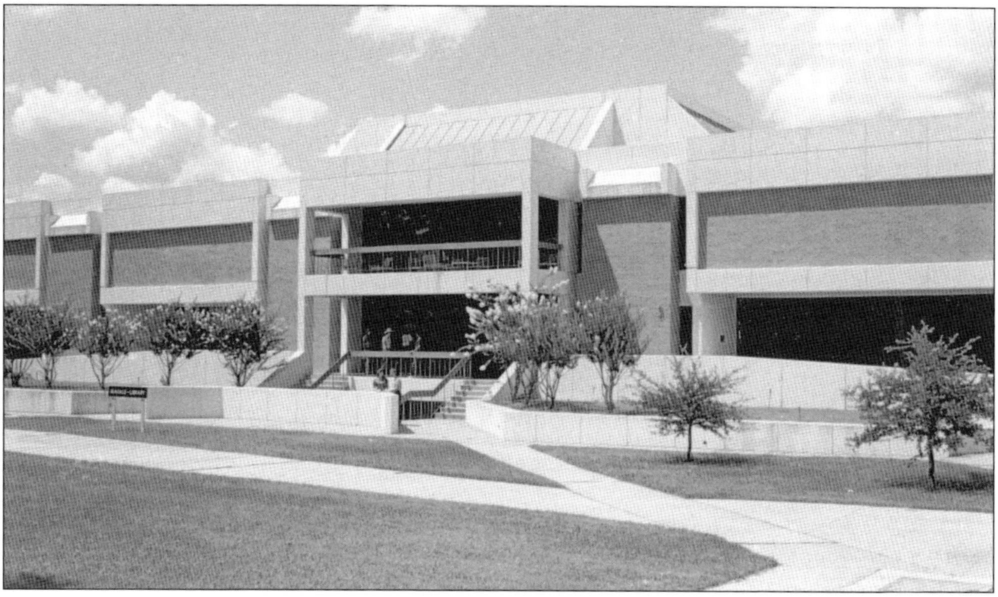

Construction of a new SSC library was completed in 1974 on the site of the 1913 dining hall and 1937 library. A three-story structure of modernistic style, it was named for John F. and Joanna G. Magale in recognition of the Magale Foundation's gift of $525,000 dedicated to the purchase of books.

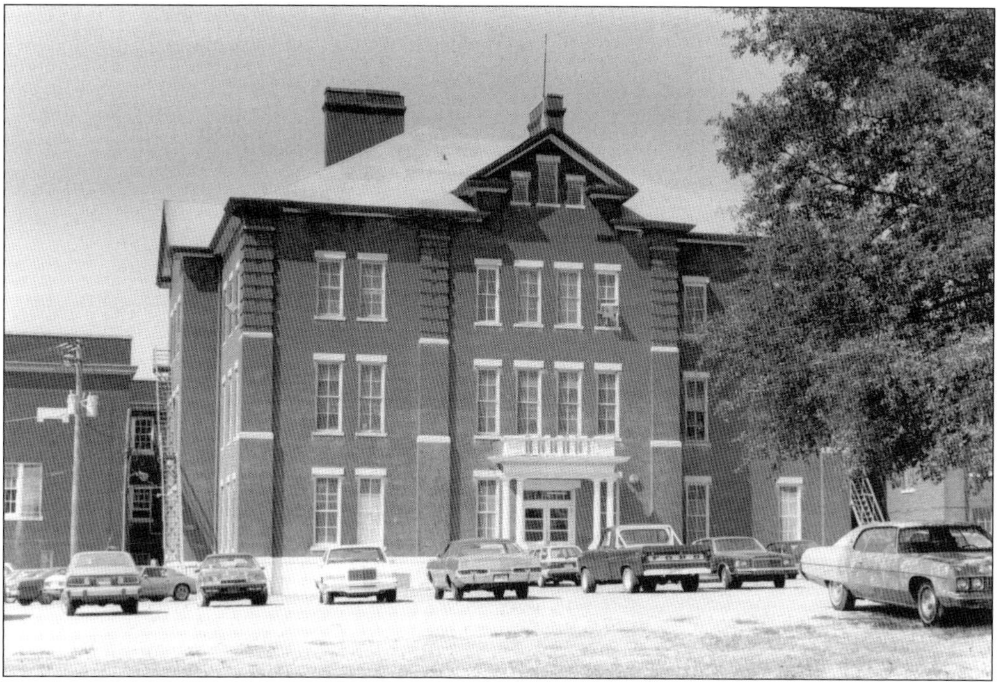

In 1975, the Arkansas legislature in Act 171 made SSC a three-campus system, with two-year community colleges in El Dorado and Camden. Without sufficient funding from the legislature for 10 years, the El Dorado branch had to use an old public school building; it subsequently became an independent institution. In 1975, the legislature, through Act 343, also authorized SSC to choose a new university name.

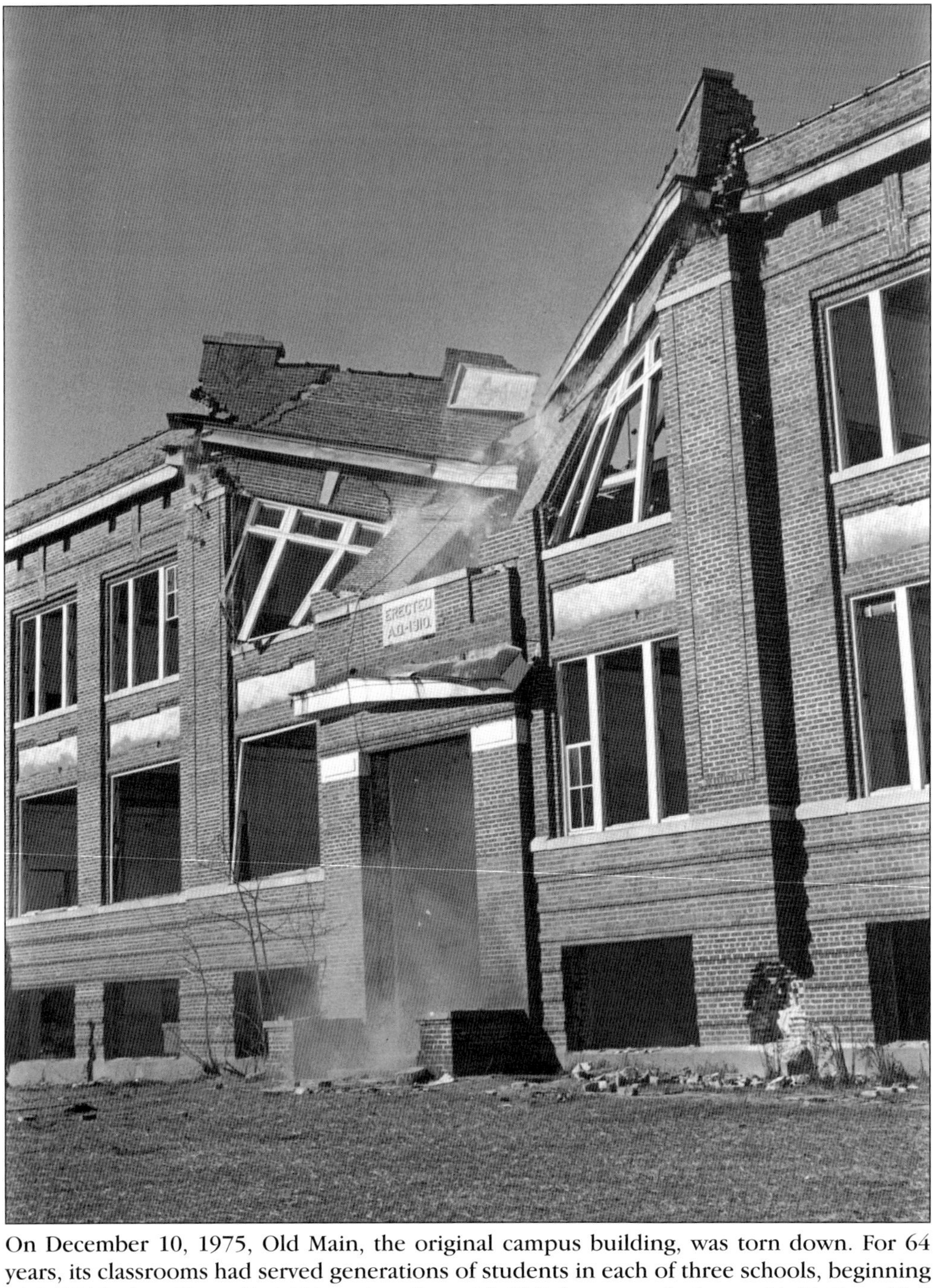

On December 10, 1975, Old Main, the original campus building, was torn down. For 64 years, its classrooms had served generations of students in each of three schools, beginning with TDAS, then Magnolia A&M, and ending with SSC. Its removal, along with McCrary Hall and Holt Hall, opened a wide mall between Magale Library and Harton Theater and gave the school a new appearance to match the forthcoming change to a new name, Southern Arkansas University. Many alumni wanted to save one or more of the older buildings to use as a museum and a reminder to students of the simple origins of the school. Such sentiment never galvanized into an organized effort to raise sufficient funds for the purpose.

Four

Southern Arkansas University

Dr. Harold T. Brinson became Southern Arkansas University's new president in 1976. National economic problems forced careful budgeting and efforts to increase privately funded endowments through a foundation. After a decline, enrollment reached 1960s levels again by the late 1980s. Dr. Steven G. Gamble, serving as president from 1992 to 2001, was also constrained by limited growth in budgets and enrollments along with other challenges, such as technological changes. He responded with strategic planning, building renovations, student retention initiatives, and new programs.

Dr. David F. Rankin's presidency from 2002 to 2015 was marked by enrollment and construction increases not seen since the 1960s. With bond issues and private gifts, Dr. Rankin managed construction of more than $100 million in new and remodeled buildings, including the Donald W. Reynolds Campus and Community Center, several residence halls, new buildings for the agriculture and science departments, upgrades to athletic facilities, a student activities building, and a new band hall. Especially noteworthy was a $2 million gift to build the Story Arena, home of the nationally competitive SAU rodeo team.

The single most important academic change during the Rankin years was the creation of the School of Graduate Studies, which led to a doubling of graduate enrollment to more than 1,000 students.

Growing enrollments and development of new academic programs continued with the appointment of Dr. Trey Berry as president in 2015. The size of the student body reached 4,771 in 2016. Three new residence halls were quickly built to keep pace with the growth. Particularly important among new academic majors was the creation of an engineering degree together with a $1 million gift for remodeling of the former National Guard armory into the Engineering Building.

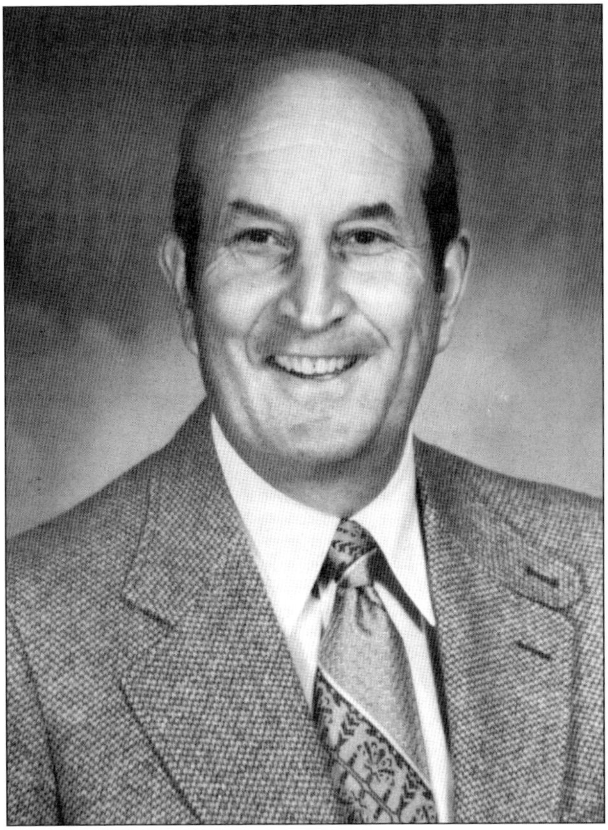

On July 9, 1976, the new president, Dr. Harold T. Brinson, formally announced the school's new name: Southern Arkansas University. An alumnus of Magnolia A&M College, Dr. Brinson later earned masters and doctoral degrees from the University of Texas. Prior to returning to his alma mater, he served as superintendent of Abilene, Texas, Independent School District. During several years of his presidency, SAU suffered from uncertain state finances. Brinson responded with successful private fundraising and established the SAU Foundation in 1980 to grow endowments. One of Brinson's first fundraising efforts placed a pink granite cube atop a brick pedestal as the focal point of newly constructed Overstreet Plaza. Inscribed on the cube were the dates and seals of the four schools that had occupied the grounds since 1909.

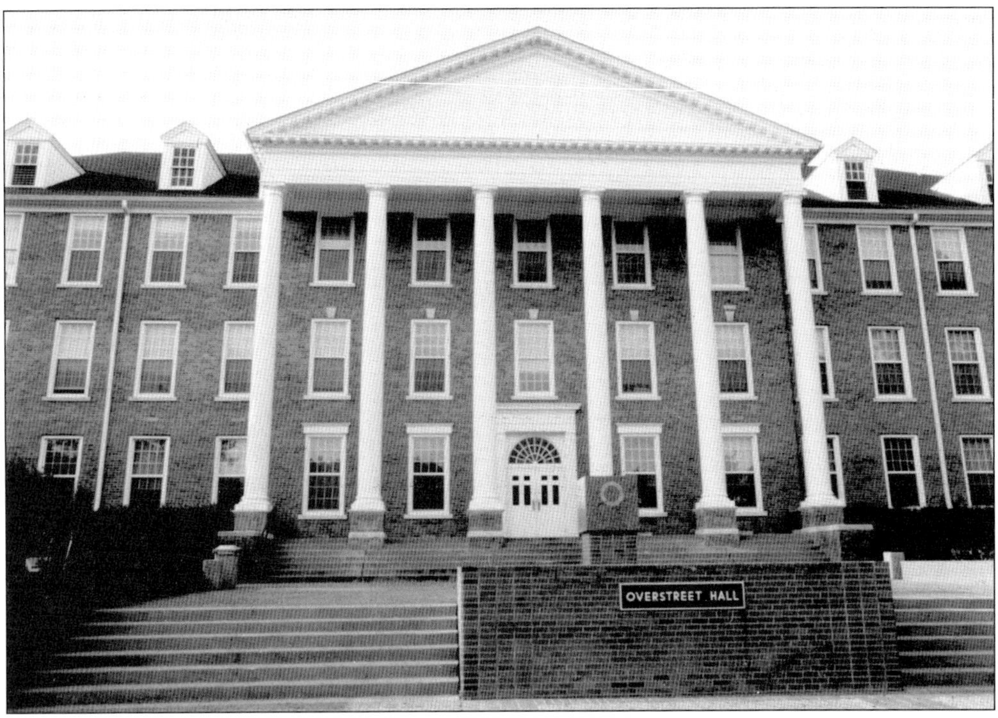

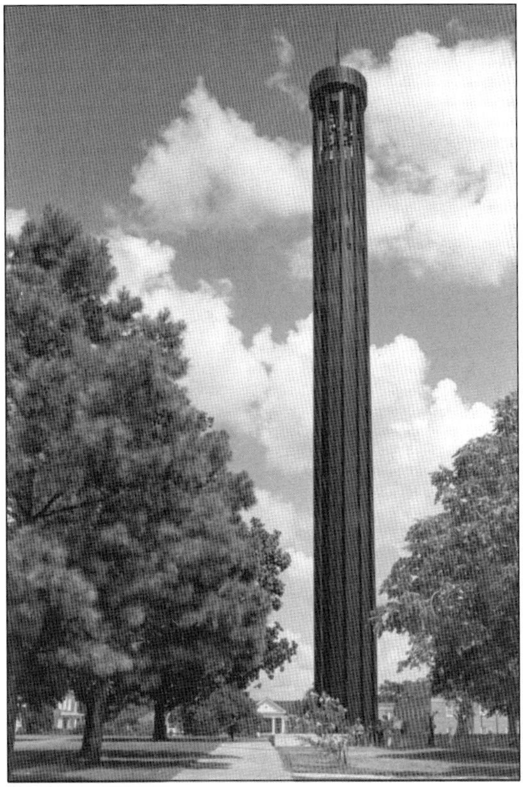

One of Dr. Brinson's early fundraising efforts placed a carillon from France atop the Bell Tower. In 1980, fourteen bells were ordered from Paccard Founderie de Clothes in the ancient French city of Annecy. After inspection by Brinson and his wife, Gene Lee Brinson, the bells were placed atop the tower. The Bell Tower, the last of Dr. Imon E. Bruce's construction projects, was an award-winning ornamental water tank that replaced an older, unsightly tank. A structure of oxidized weathering steel, the tower reaches 187 feet into the sky. SAU became the only college in Arkansas with genuine bell chimes. Visible at some distance from the school, the Bell Tower became one of SAU's enduring landmarks, as well as an often-used symbol of the school.

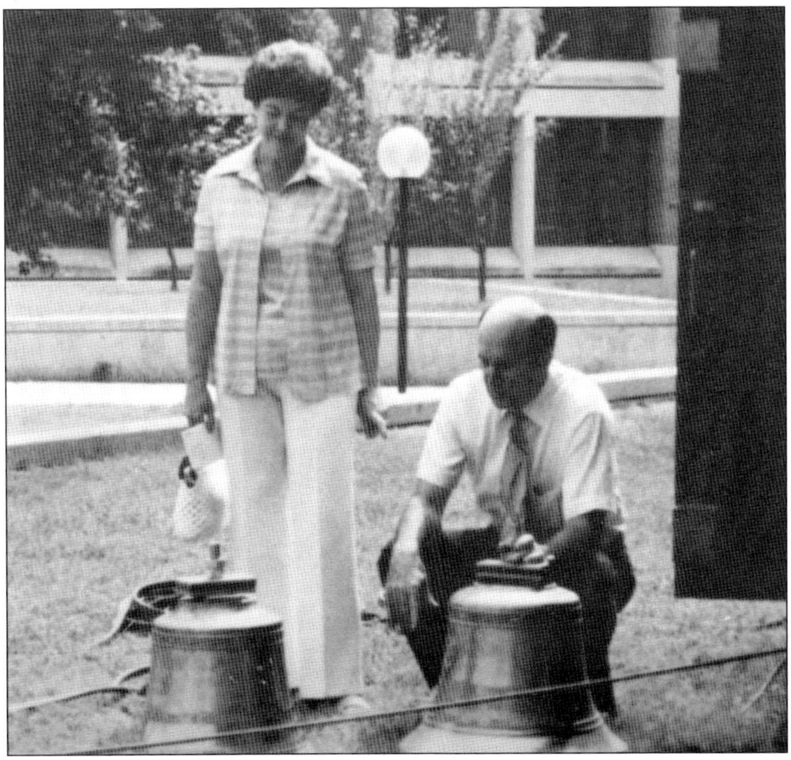

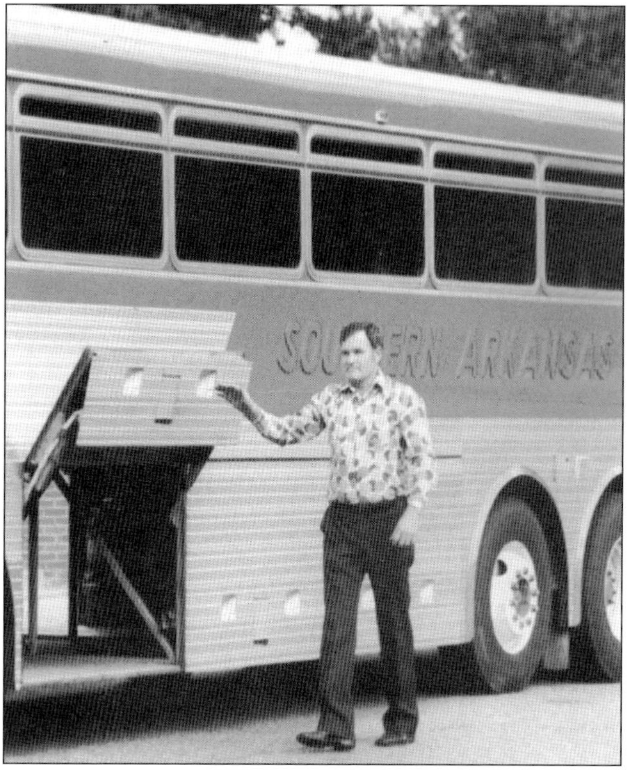

The individuals who were essential in SAU's day-to-day operations were the hard-working secretaries and other staff, especially those employed by the physical plant. No staff person was more widely known or better liked than Earl Miller (left), who drove the SSC and SAU buses, carrying students to athletic games and other events for almost a half century. The secretaries and staff pictured below in 1975–1976 are, from left to right, (seated, first row) Cassie Farrar, Wilma McWilliams, and Dorothy Knowles; (seated, second row) Dorothy Duncan, Glenda Gunnels, Kathy Stueart, and Johnnie Bray; (standing) Dianne Kimbell, Jimmie Watson, Curtistine Walz, Arvia Askew, Arlene Bacon, Wilma Williams, and Carolyn Wyrick.

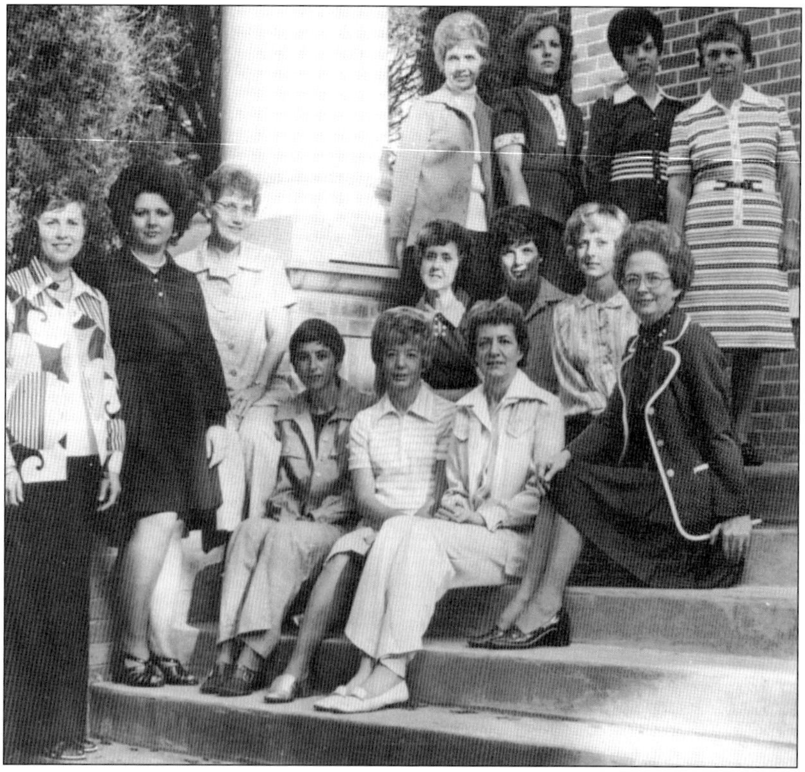

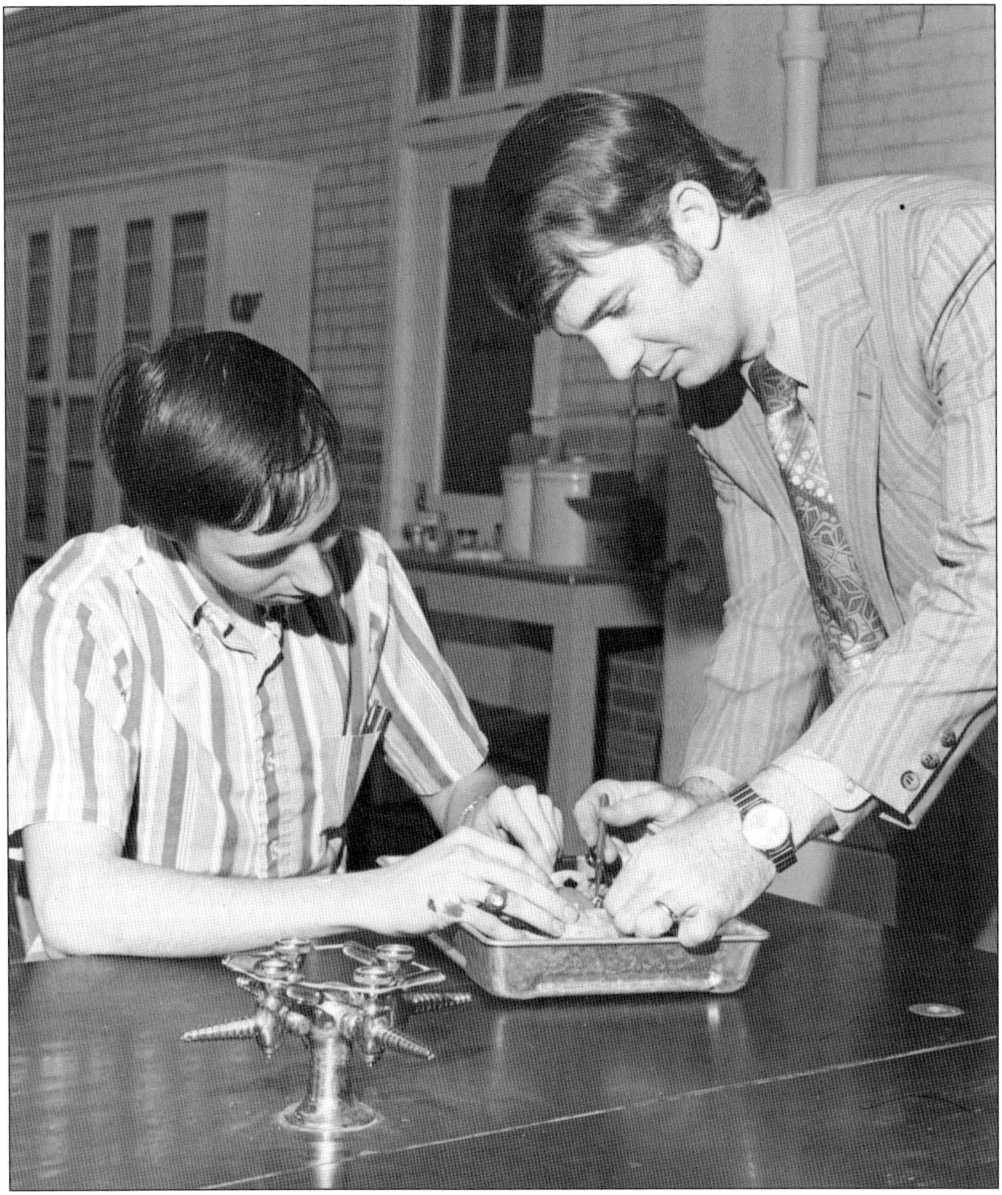

Dr. Henry Robison was the most distinguished scholar at SAU during the era of his service. After receiving his PhD in zoology from Oklahoma State University in 1971, he taught for 37 years at SSC and SAU, achieving the rank of distinguished professor while also holding the Dr. L.A. Logan chair in biology. Robison had both a national and international reputation in his field. During weekend trips, he documented fishes in the state's stream and lakes with the help of undergraduates. He discovered 14 previously unknown species. His first was in 1974, and the Smithsonian Institution named *Cambarellus robison* in his honor. The author of several books and more than a hundred articles, his best known works include *Fishes of Oklahoma*, *Fishes of Arkansas*, and *Only in Arkansas: A Study of the Endemic Plants and Animals of the State*, which describes those found nowhere outside the state of Arkansas. Robison served on the editorial board of *Copeia*, the premier journal of the American Society of Ichthyologists and Herpetologists.

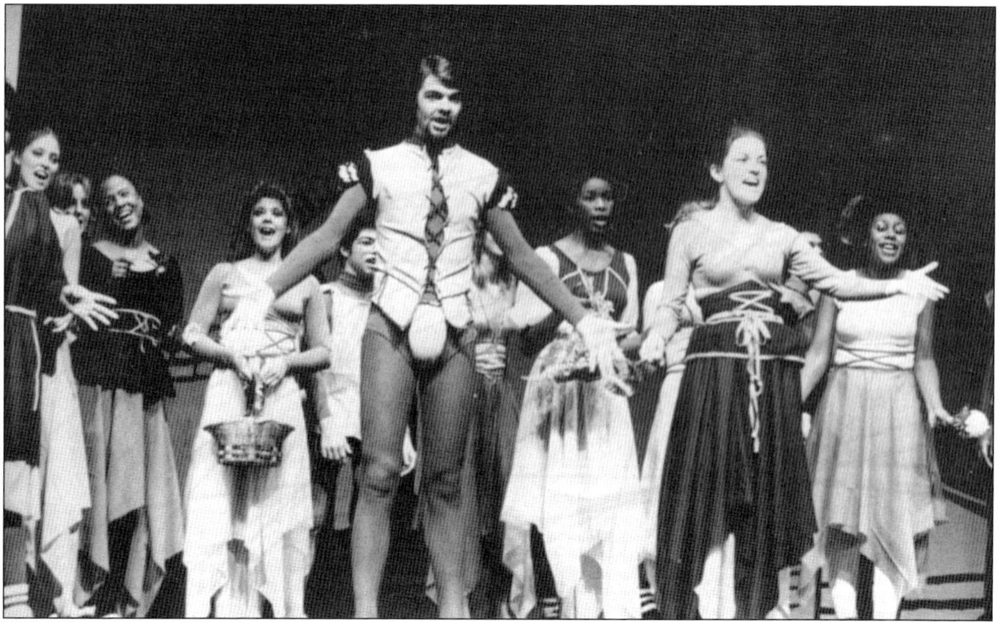

From 1971 to 1994, Professors Janelle Viertel, from the music department, and Jerry Cortez and Jake Whitehead, from the speech and theater department, produced an annual spring musical, including many Broadway hits. In 1980, *Kiss Me Kate* starred theater major Mitch Brian and English instructor Linda Ruston. Perhaps the most elaborate of all the musical plays performed at SAU was *1776,* which served as SAU's principal contribution to nationwide celebrations in the bicentennial year. For several years, Dr. Brinson used opening night of these productions to raise funds for the SAU Foundation. Another musical group at SAU was Encore, led by speech instructor Judy Vasser. Encore performed on occasion at SAU but primarily appeared at area public schools, where the performers entertained and helped inform students about SAU.

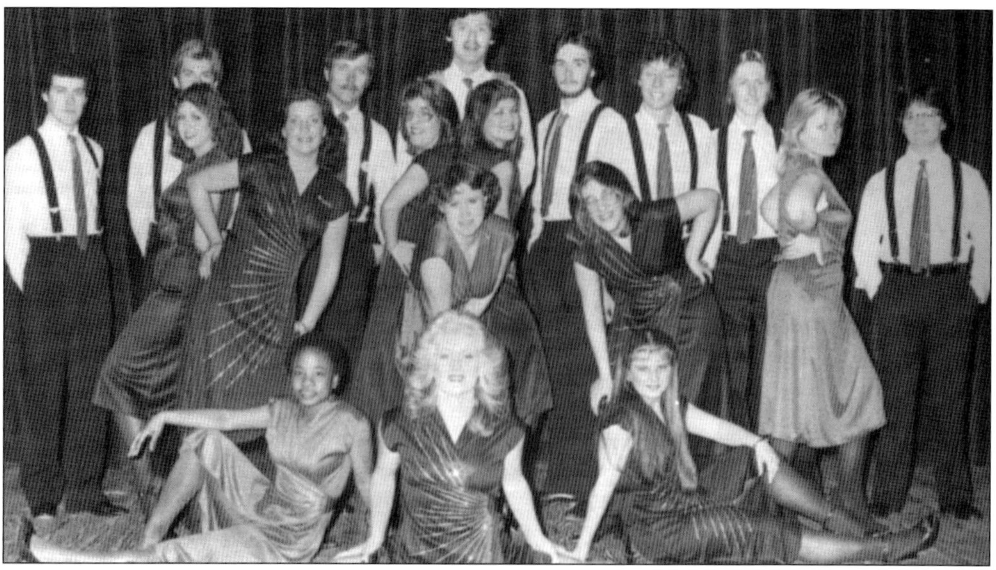

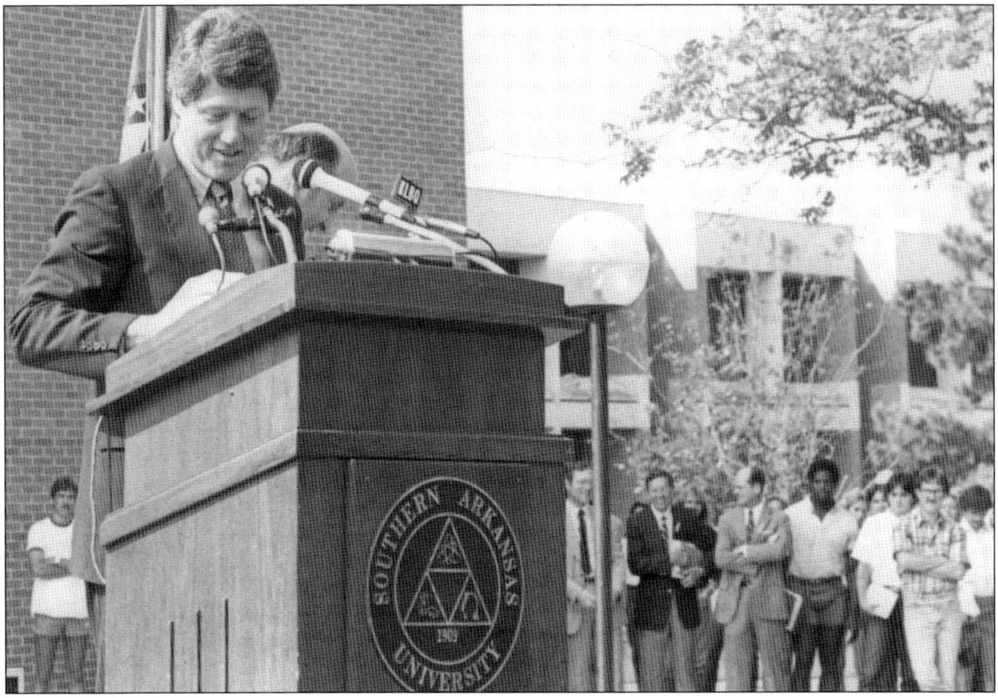

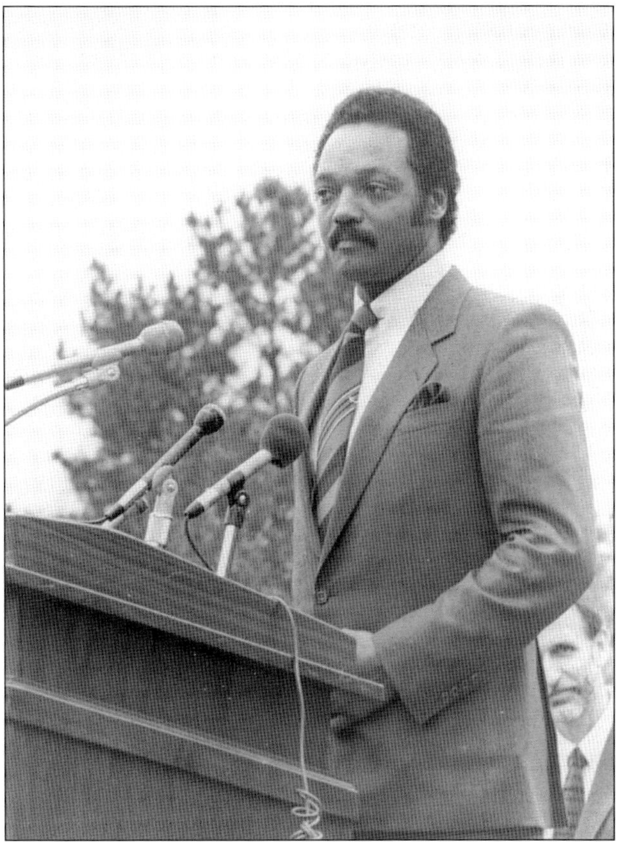

Arkansas governor Bill Clinton came to SAU in 1983 to promote his blue ribbon campaign for new taxes to reform education in the state. Many students and faculty stood on the mall between Harton Theater and Magale Library, wore a blue ribbon, and cheered for his pledge to increase funding for universities as well as for public schools. Clinton had first come to campus when campaigning in 1977 for the office of attorney general, and appeared at least twice more to deliver commencement addresses. Jesse Jackson campaigned in 1988 for the Democratic Party's nomination for president. Although losing the nomination to Michael Dukakis, Jackson continued to barnstorm for election of Democrats to office in 1988 and came to SAU to encourage students to register and vote. A huge crowd greeted him with enthusiasm.

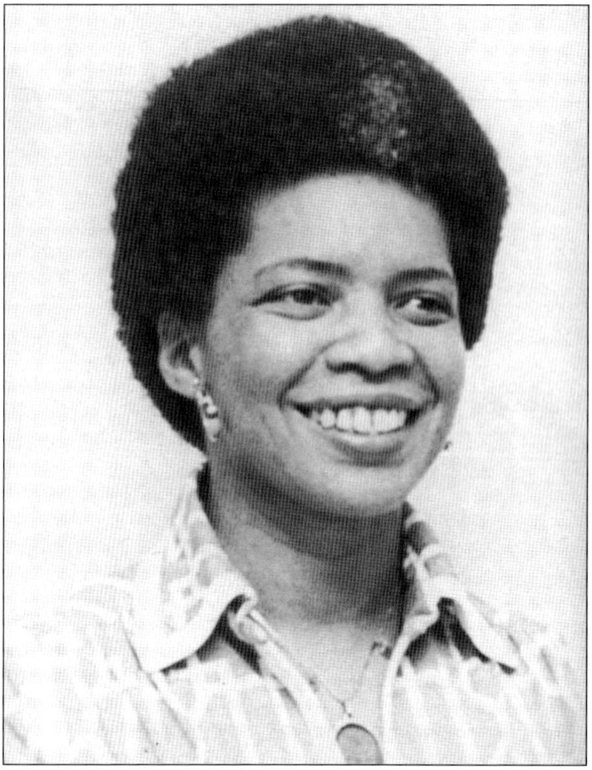

By the 1980s, black students seemed fully included in the school's life. Emmie Gamble, left, became the first black member of the board of trustees to serve full terms of office, beginning in 1977. Regina Collins was *The Bray's* first black editor in 1979. Georgina Johnson, below, the School of Business's outstanding marketing major, was also the first black Homecoming queen in 1981. Fred Coleman, elected in 1986, was the first black student body president. Other presidents and Homecoming queens soon followed. Black athletes continued to excel, including John Holmes, the first basketball player in school history named a first team NAIA All-American in 1989.

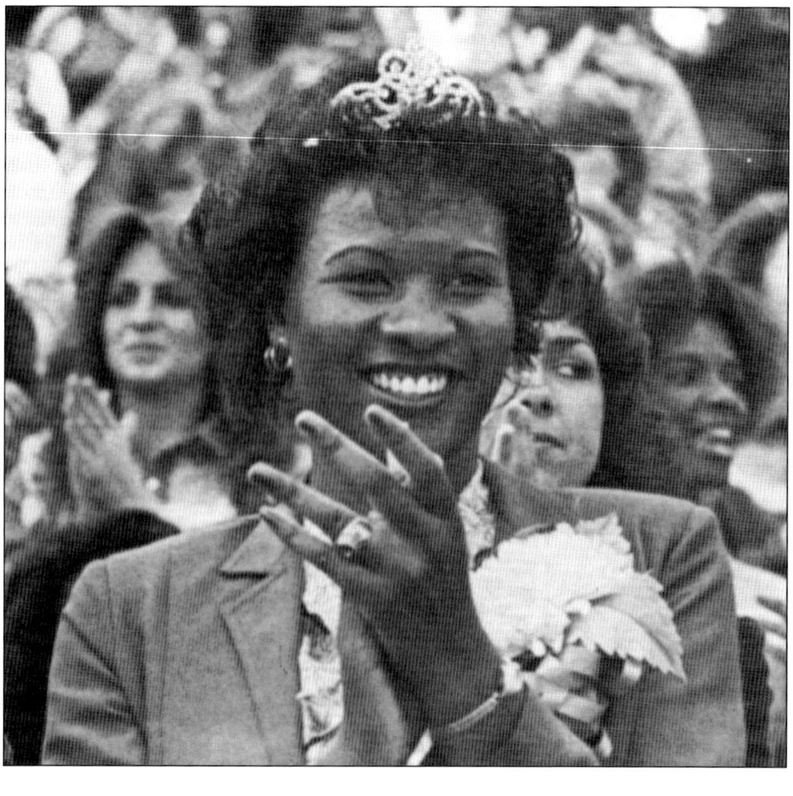

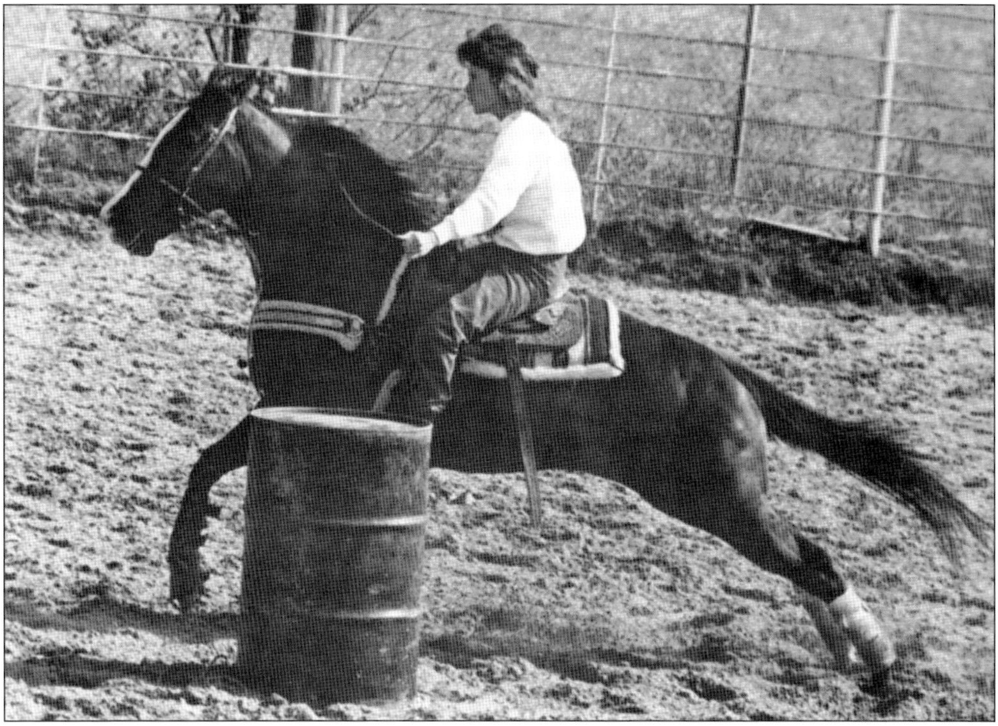

So-called minor sports had notable players and triumphs during SAU's initial decades. SAU's rodeo women gained national recognition, winning the national college rodeo championship at the finals in Bozeman, Montana, in 1986. Three SAU women—Nancy Rae, Sherry Lynn Rosser (above), and Cathy Dennis—successively won the individual title as National All-around Cowgirl during the 1980s. Men's tennis dominated Arkansas college teams in this era, due especially to Baylor Guy, first as a player and later coach, pictured below (back row, right) with the 1986–1987 championship team. Other outstanding players in these years included Peter, Pat, and Eric Sixbey, John Witter, Jeff White, Kurt Lehigh, Chris Blair, John Balduce, Paolo Pezzoli, and Fernando Barbosa. The track and field teams, led by Coach Dan Veach, also won repeated championships in the 1980s and 1990s.

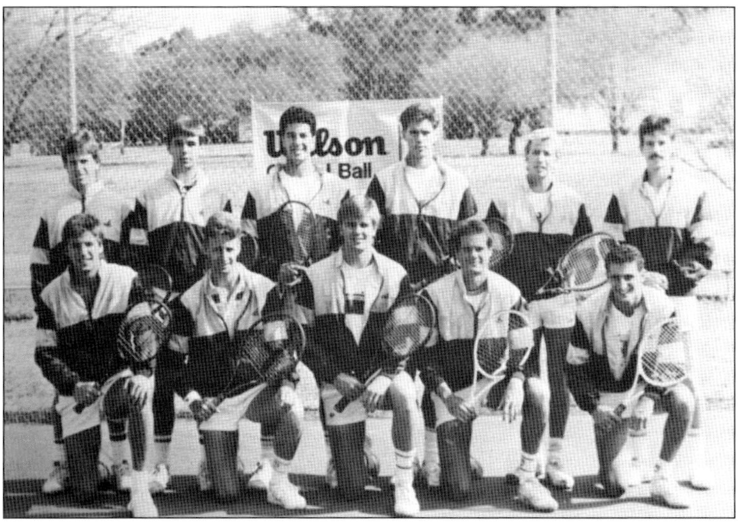

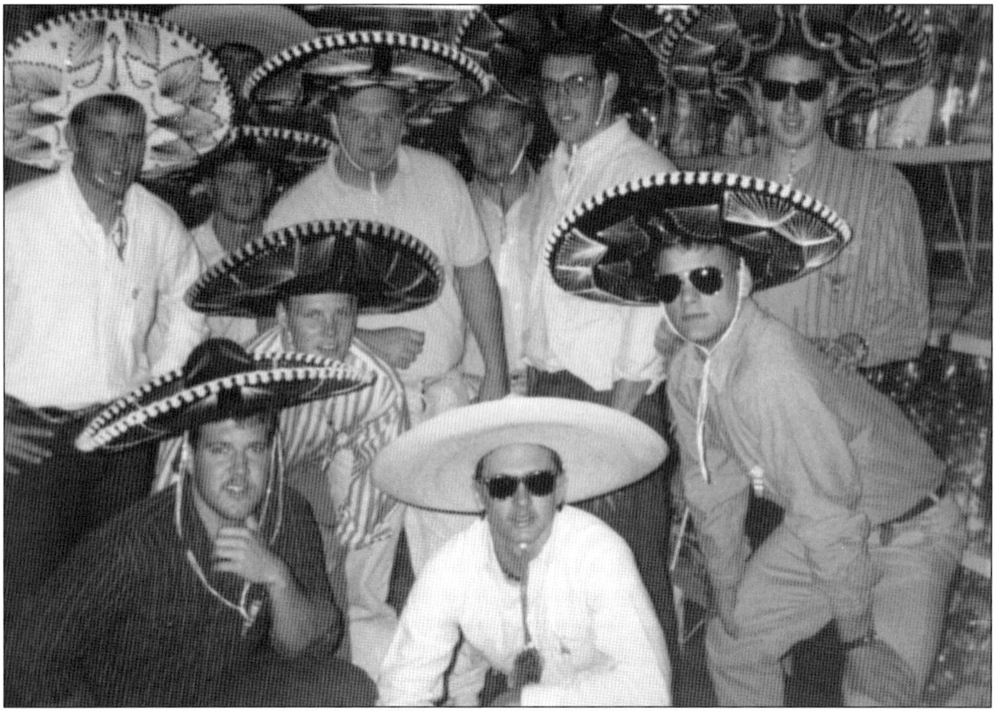

SAU football and baseball had notable achievements during the 1980s and 1990s. The Muleriders won eight games in 1990 and played in the Aztec Bowl in Mexico City, defeating that country's national all-star team while also touring the city and buying sombreros. Over the years, several SAU players went on to success in the National Football League, including Dennis Woodbury in the mid-1980s, and 15 years later, Jordan Babineaux. During 23 years, Coach Steve Goodheart's baseball teams compiled the winningest record in school history. Goodheart (second from left in the first row) and his 1987 team came in third in the College World Series. Goodheart had 764 wins, 416 losses, and 5 ties, for a percentage of .647, with 28 championship titles. Many of his players signed professional contracts.

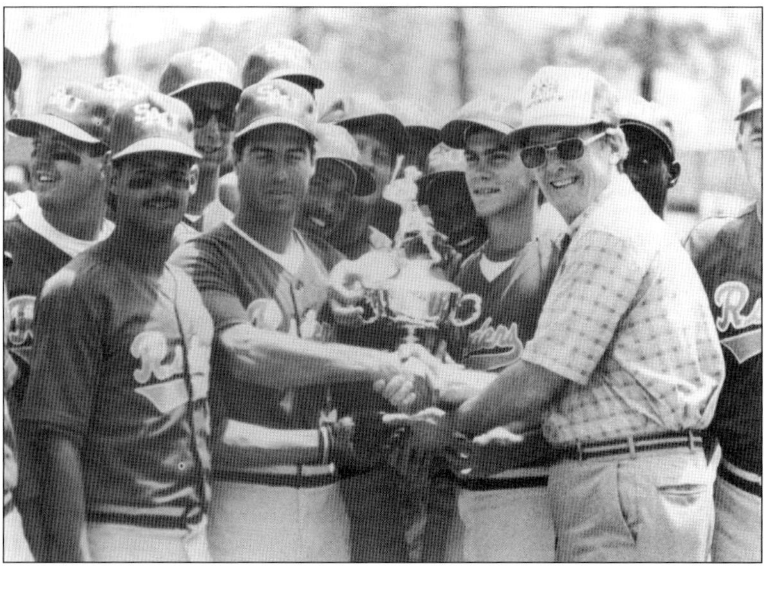

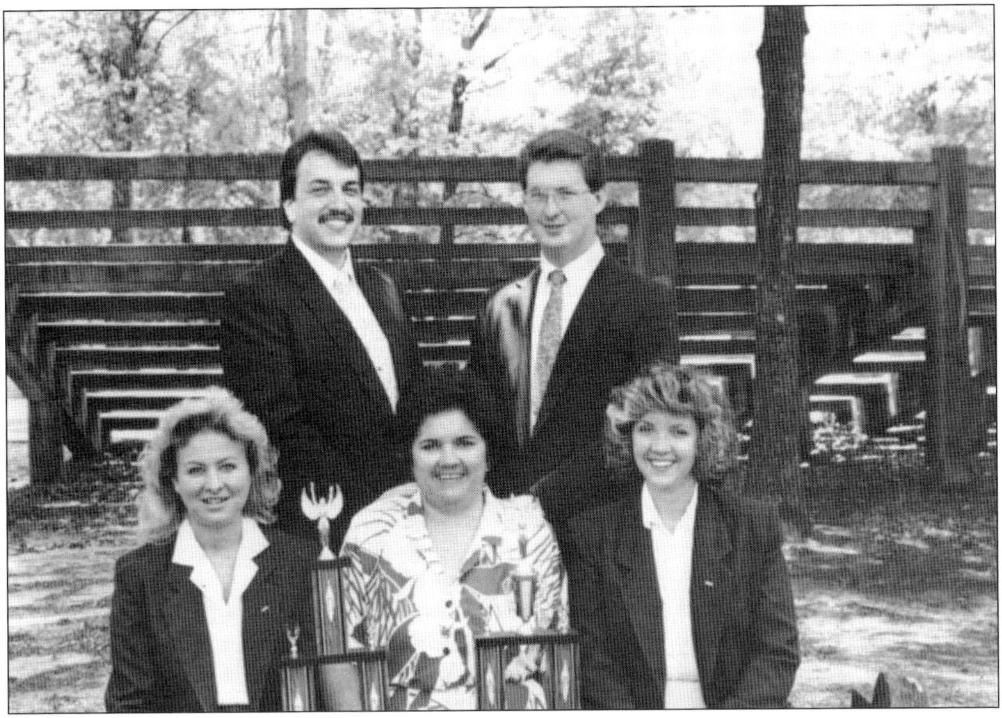

Among the most active student organizations were those in the School of Business. The Future Business Leaders of America–Phi Beta Lambda (FBLA-PBL) as well as Students in Free Enterprise, competed successfully in state and national contests. Wayne Floyd (above, second row, left) became FBLA-PBL's national president in 1988–1989; other students were, from left to right, (first row) Cari Vaughn, Kelly Williams, and Lisa Toms; (second row) Richard Collier. Long-time sponsor Dr. David F. Rankin (right, rear) was eager for students to meet the best economists in the country and helped persuade the Murphy Oil Company to sponsor an annual lecture, beginning in 1980, featuring such figures as Professor Ezra Solomon of Stanford University. Among notable student achievements was Michelle Belmont's winning economics essay, for which she received a $3,500 check from the famous economist and Nobel laureate Dr. Milton Friedman.

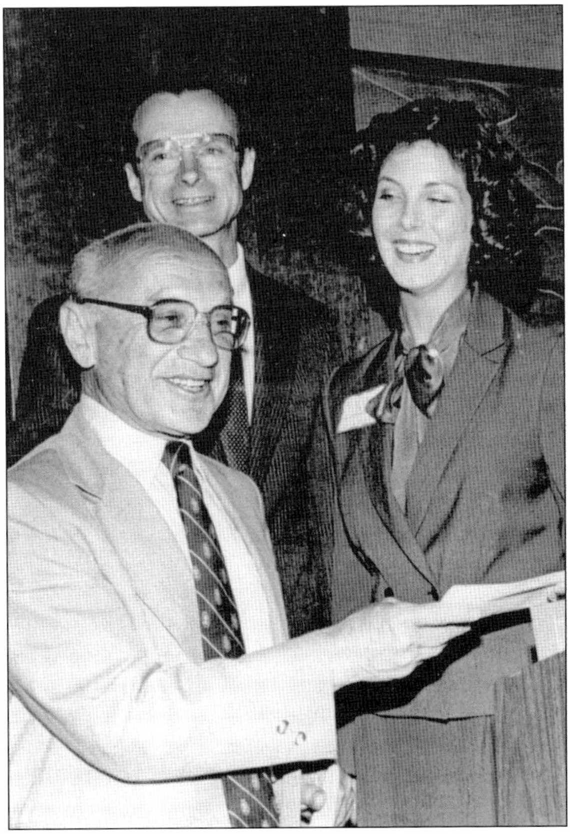

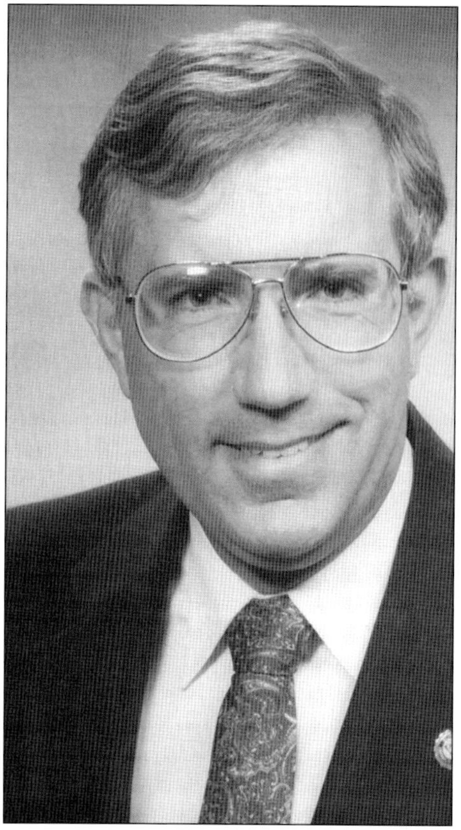

Dr. Steven G. Gamble became SAU's president in 1992. With a PhD in history from Texas Tech University, Gamble continued to teach one history class annually at SAU. He renovated numerous older buildings, gained approval for new master's degrees, laid the groundwork for new physical plant expansion, and increased enrollment. During the 1990s, international student enrollment grew to almost five percent of total enrollment. The largest number came from the South Asian nation of Nepal. The International Students Association produced a spring banquet each year with cuisine representative of the nationalities represented at SAU. Entertainments also featured music, dance, and songs from the students' cultures, such as a Nepalese dance.

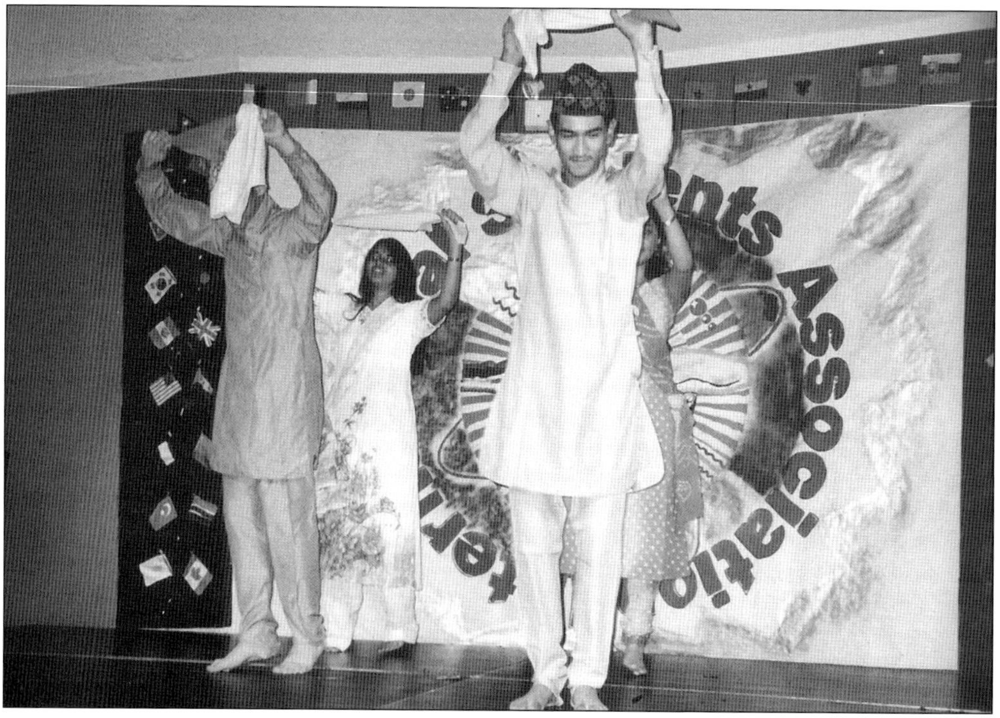

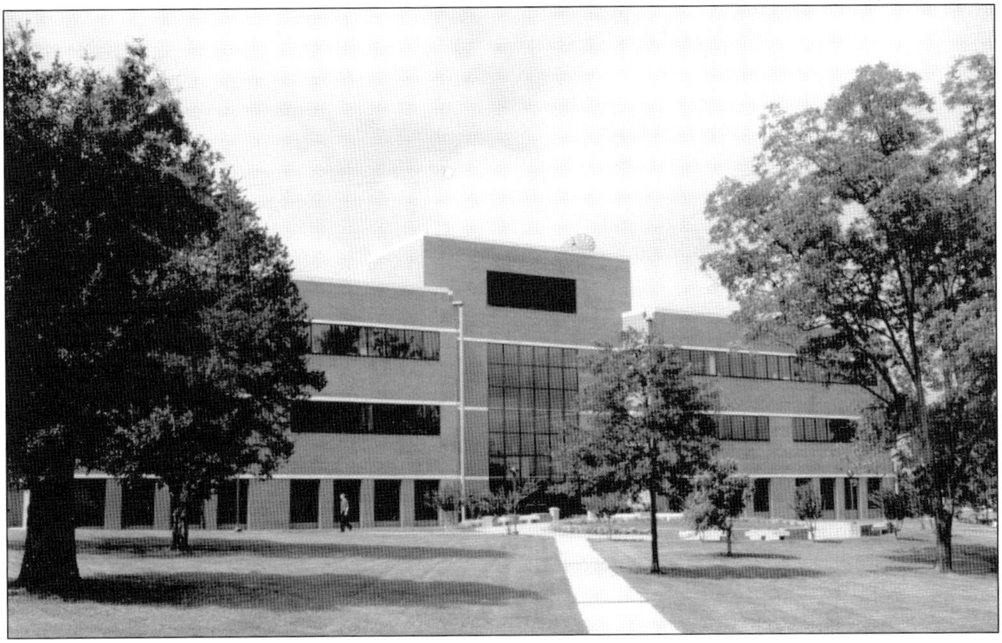

Just before Dr. Gamble became president, bond issues permitted SAU to fund two new buildings. The Business Building (above) was a three-story structure erected just north of the Wharton Nursing Building. The school was later renamed the Dr. David Rankin School of Business. Its lobby opened into a striking three-story atrium that led to offices, classrooms, seminar rooms, lecture halls, and computer labs. The new art building, named for Dr. Harold T. and Gene Lee Brinson (below), stood just north of Cross Hall and faced the mall between Magale Library and Harton Theater. Its exterior featured half columns built into the wall in a modest salute to the Georgian style that began with Overstreet Hall.

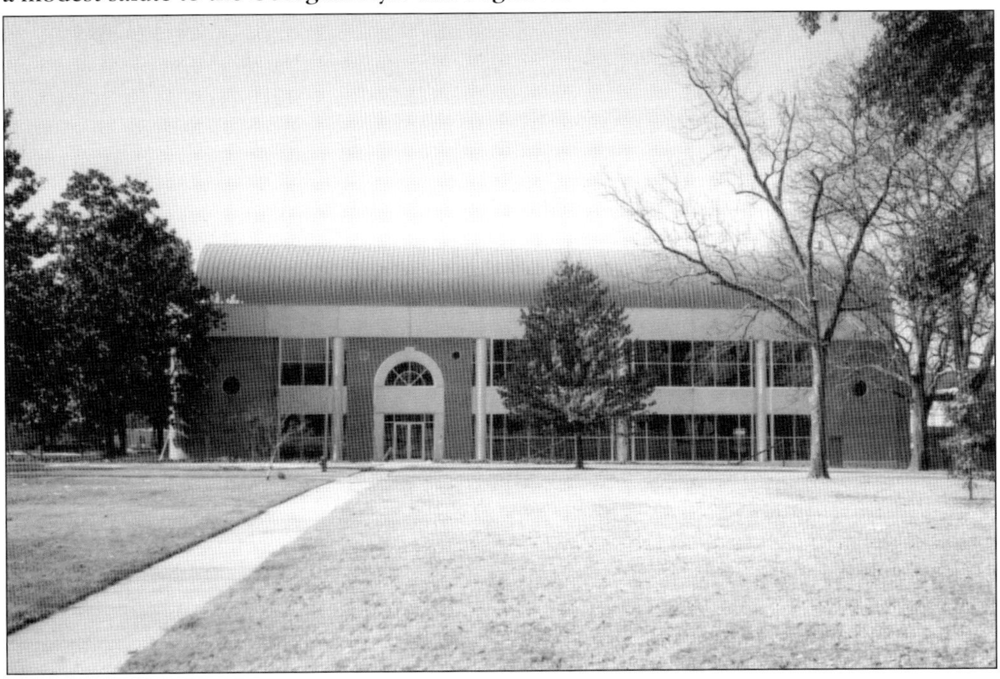

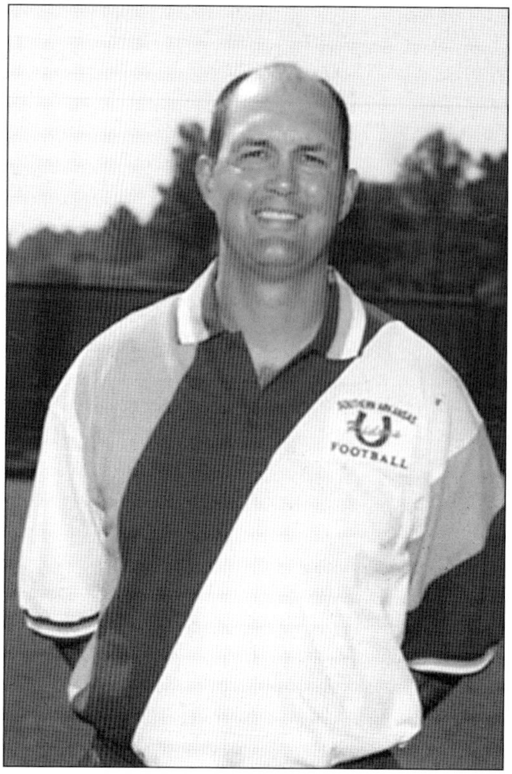

When the Arkansas Intercollegiate Conference dissolved in the mid-1990s, there was concern among Mulerider fans when SAU moved to the Gulf South Conference (GSC). Consisting of schools mostly larger than SAU, it was feared competition would overwhelm Mulerider teams. However, in 1997, during SAU's first year of eligibility, Coach Steve Roberts led the football team to a 9-2 season, a national ranking, and a GSC co-championship. Eventually, SAU athletics would become part of the new Great American Conference, consisting of small universities in Arkansas and Oklahoma. While Mulerider football moved in new directions, an old tradition was resurrected in 1993 when, for the first time in decades, fans saw a full-size mule at games. New agriculture department chair Dr. James Tollett, an SSC alumnus, gave Molly B to the school. A designated Mulerider brought the mascot to games. The first of a series of women Muleriders of Molly B was Kassie D. Ketcham.

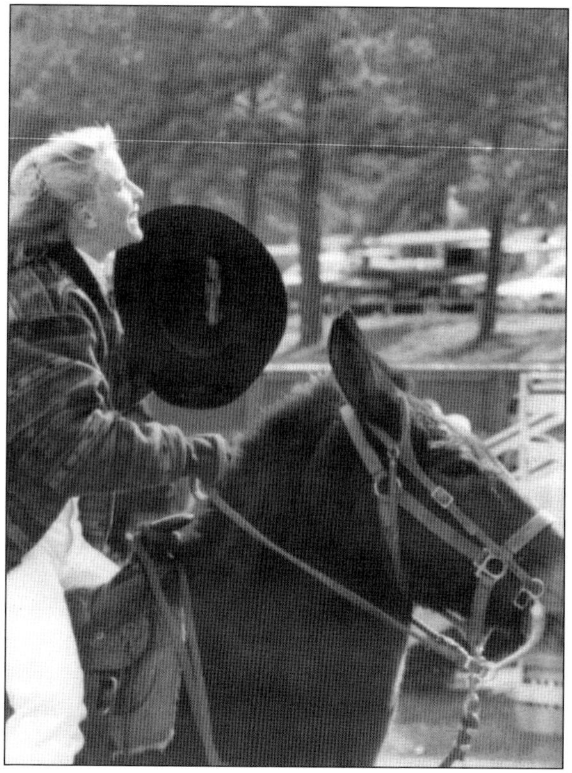

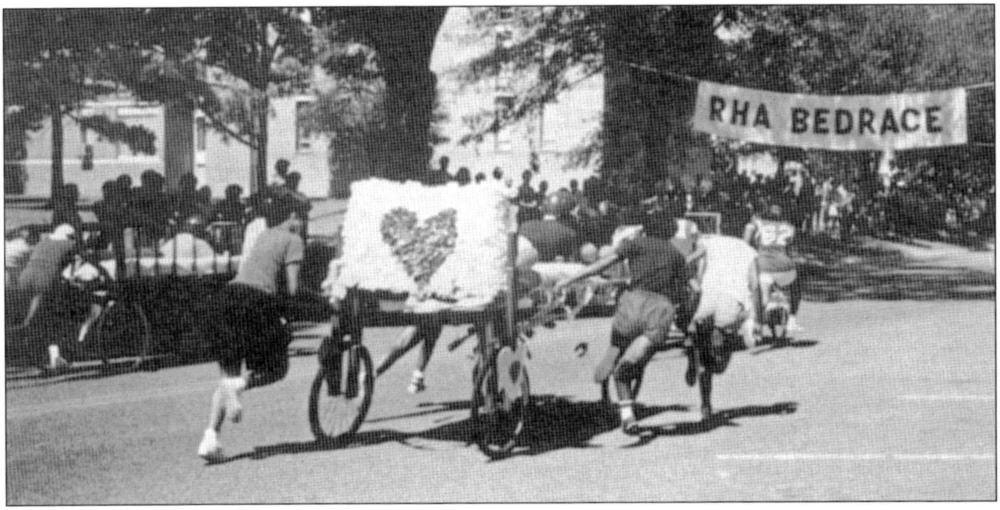

Assistant Dean J.B. Courson started an annual bed race in 1981, which became an instant tradition at SAU. The event grew ever larger as part of festivities during Parent's Day. Each residence hall entered the contest on East Lane Street with a "bed," a platform on top of bicycle tires ridden by a reclining student, as team members pushed the rickety structures at breakneck speed. Both exciting and hilarious to watch, the beds were as likely to careen off course as to cross the finish line. While this tradition continued unchanged, much began to change at SAU during the 1990s as the campus fully entered the age of the computer. Dr. Gamble turned Dolph Camp Hall into a technology center with a Computer Commons in an attempt to centralize access. But technological change was so rapid it could not be so easily contained.

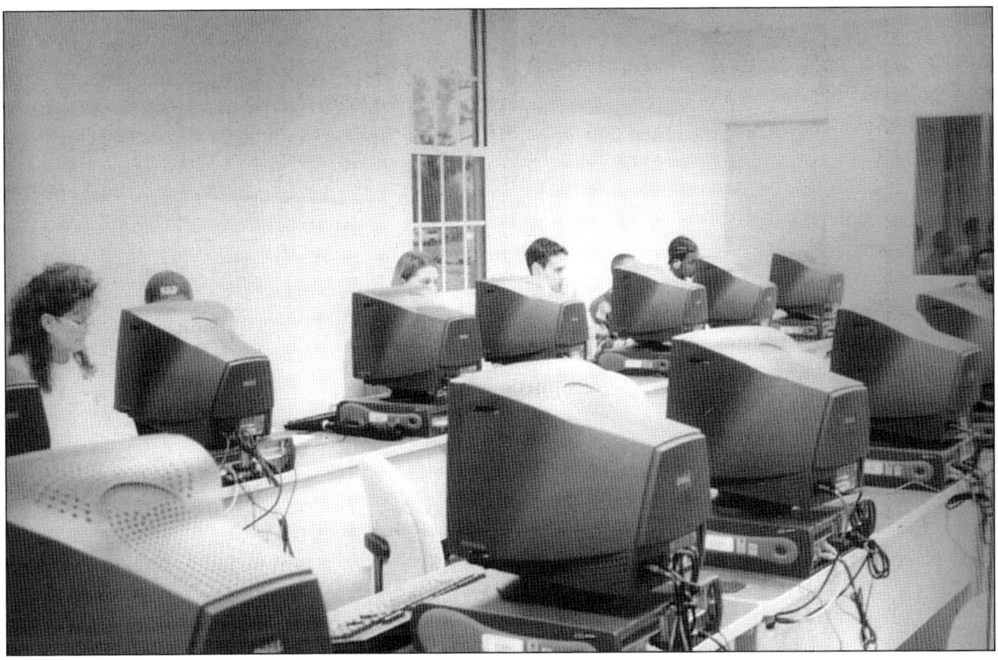

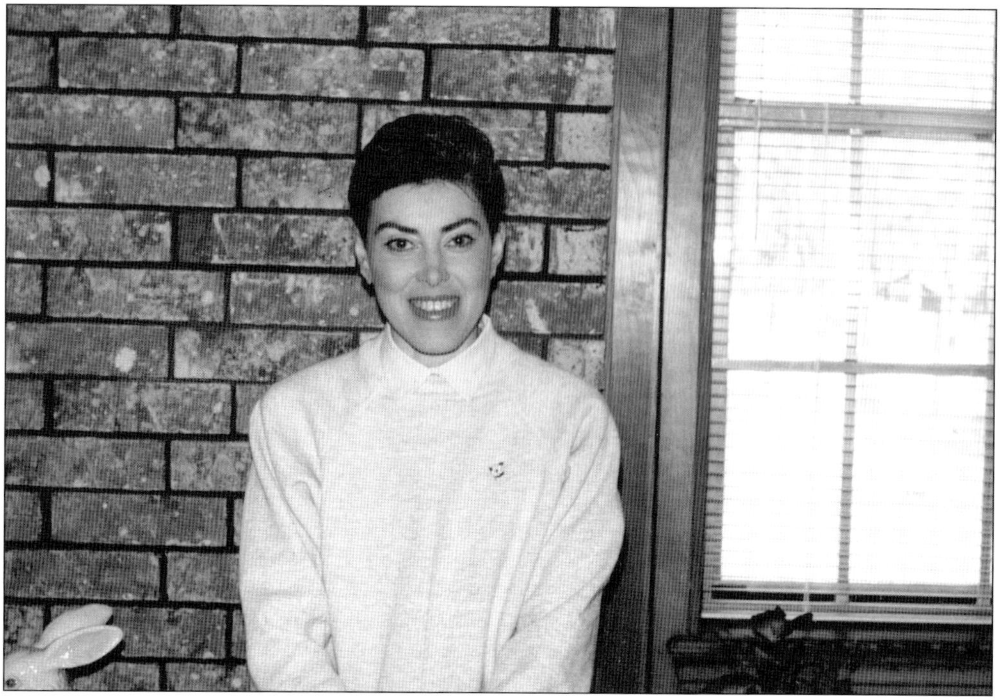

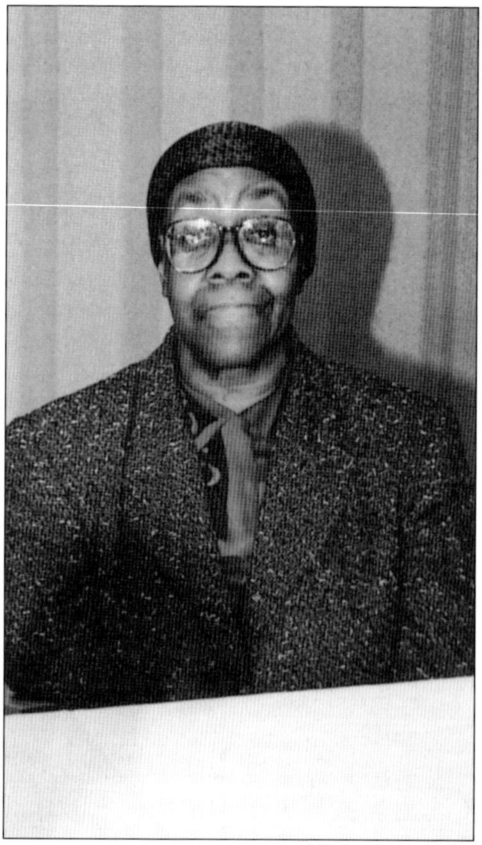

Dr. Elena Solovova from Moscow State Pedagogical University came to SAU in spring semester 1993 to begin the SAU Russian Exchange Program, the fruition of a long effort by Professor David Sixbey of the SAU history department. For more than 20 years afterwards, the agreement between the two universities brought scores of Russian professors and students to SAU.

In 1996, Gwendolyn Brooks, at age 79, delivered the Emerson-Crone Lecture. This annual lecture series began in 1993 with an address by famed historian Arthur Schlesinger Jr. Other famous scholars and humanists followed. Teacher and poet Gwendolyn Brooks received much acclaim for her poems over a long period. Awarded a Pulitzer Prize in 1950, she was named US Poet Laureate in 1985.

Dr. David F. Rankin became SAU president in 2002. He initiated an era of growth in facilities not seen since the 1960s and an expansion of university-owned land unequaled since 1910. He announced SAU's first capital campaign—the Blue and Gold Vision—that partially funded 25 projects, including 10 new buildings, at a cost of $130 million over his 13 years as president and essentially built a new campus. The first new building was the Don W. Reynolds Campus and Community Center. Built through a $12 million gift of the Reynolds Foundation and a $2 million match from friends of SAU, the structure opened in 2005 and quickly became the center of student activity with a cafeteria, post office, bookstore, and meeting rooms, including the Grand Hall for receptions and special dinners.

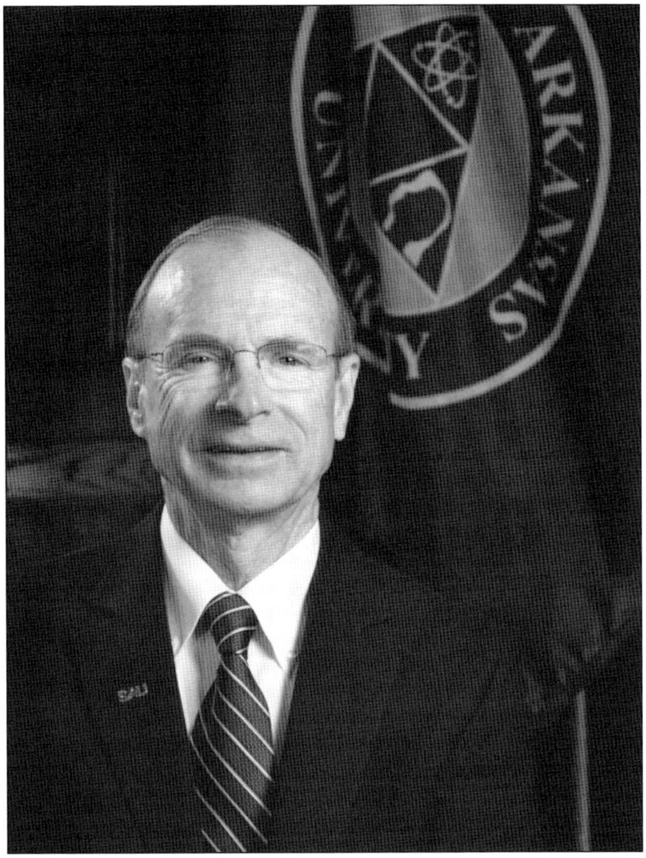

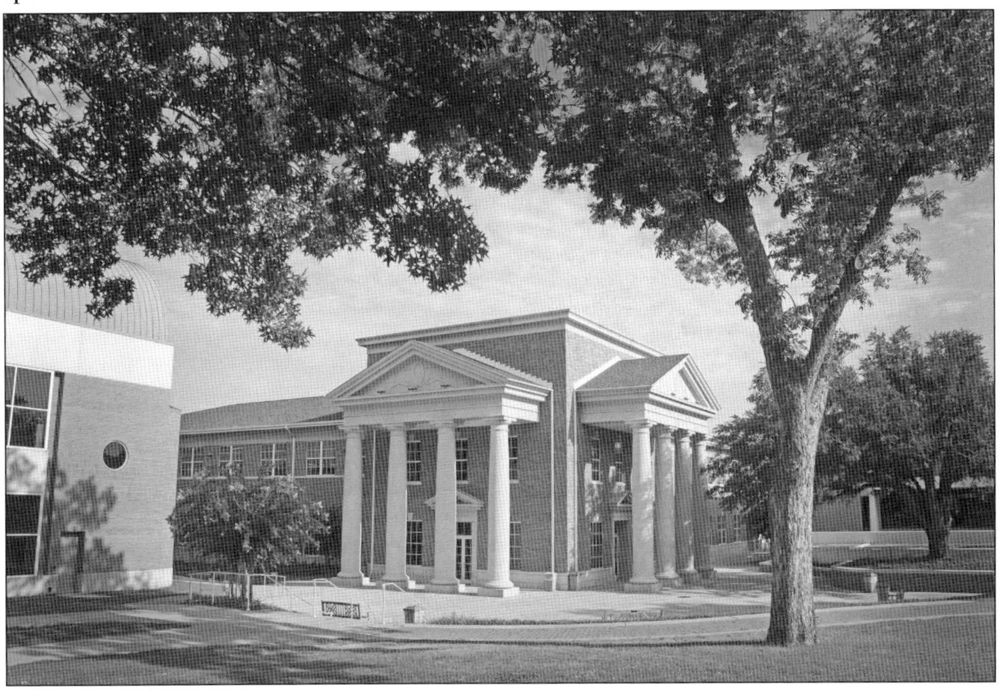

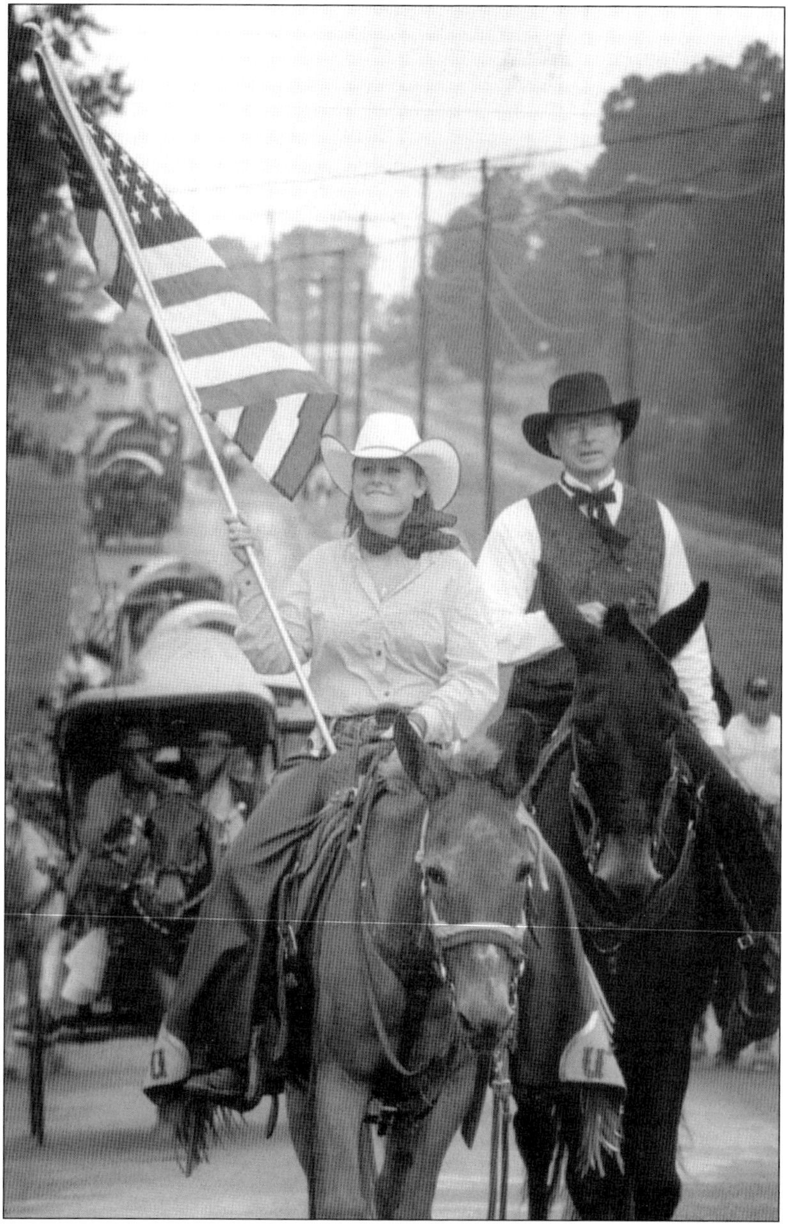

SAU's centennial year of 2009 was marked by various celebrations, including a free concert by country and western star Tracy Lawrence, a former SAU student, on April 1, 2009, exactly 100 years after Act 100 established SAU's ancestor, the Third District Agricultural School. However, no centennial event was more spectacular than the Great SAU Muleride to McNeil on September 19, 2009. Molly, the SAU mule mascot, ridden by Sunny Wilcox, the designated Mulerider, led the parade. Close behind was Dr. Rankin on another mule, followed by a procession of riders, buggies, and wagons that stretched for half a mile along the five-mile county road connecting Magnolia and McNeil. The event commemorated the legend that the TDAS football team selected their name, Mule Riders, in 1912 because they sometimes had to ride mules to McNeil's Cottonbelt Railroad Station where they boarded trains to travel to away games.

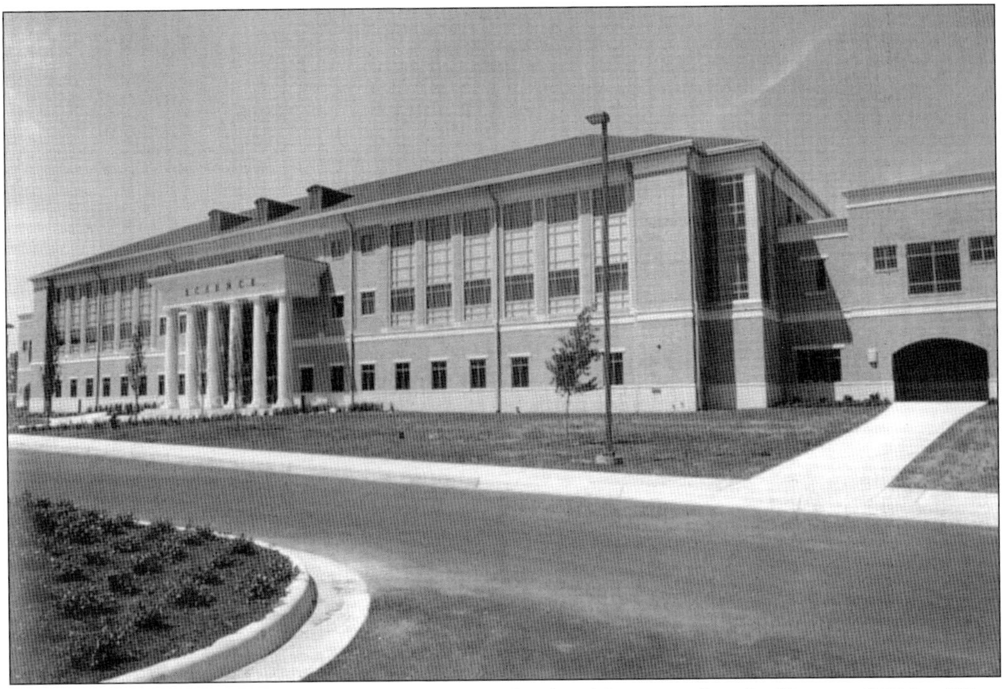

A new Science Center (above) opened in 2010. The 61,000-square-foot facility cost $17.2 million and took two years to construct. It provides classrooms, labs, and offices for the departments of biology and chemistry that moved from Overstreet Hall, as well as the physics department that moved from Wilson Hall. A separate facility immediately behind the Science Center was the National Resource Research Center. The 30,000-square-foot Agriculture Center (below) opened in 2013. It contains large lecture halls, classrooms, labs, and a special pavilion added to the rear of the building for the agriculture department, which moved from Childs Hall.

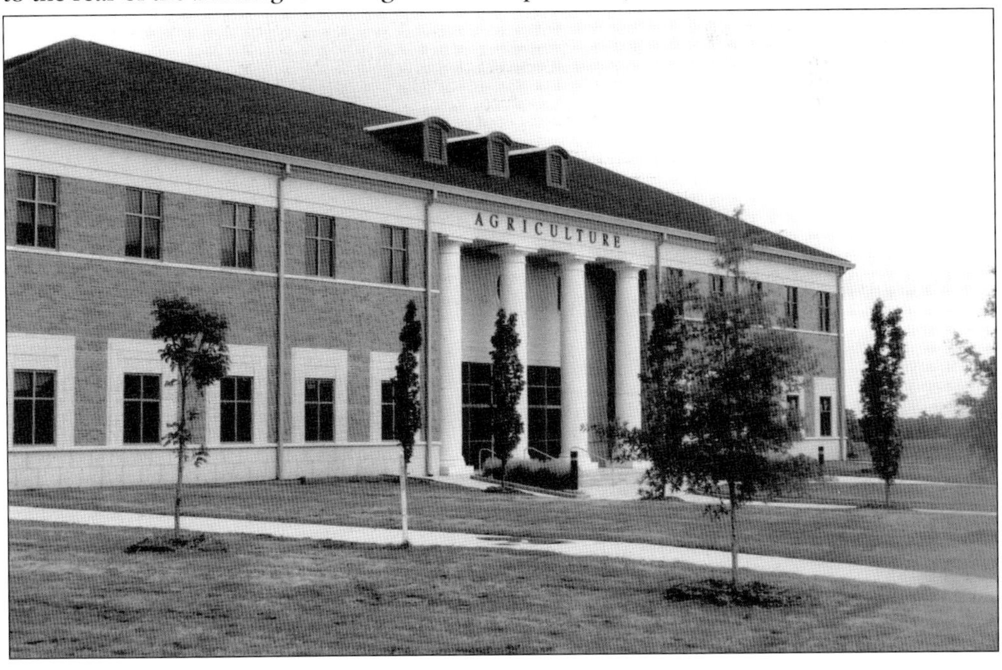

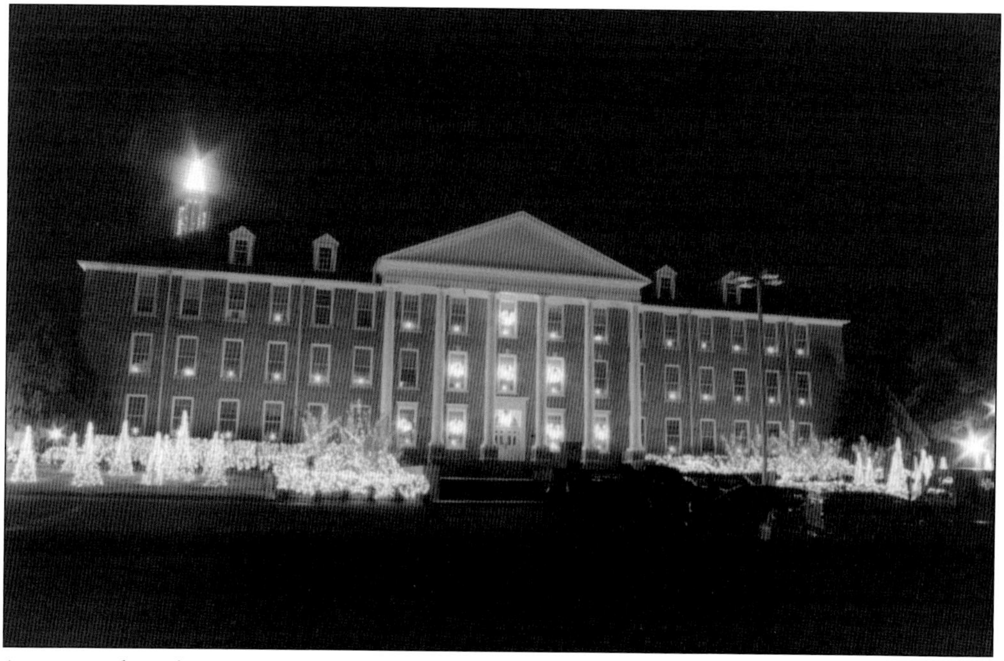

A spectacular Christmas decoration was added to campus in 1988 when the Bell Tower was lit with Christmas lights and made to look like a giant candle, seen here peeking over the roof of Overstreet Hall. The Christmas celebration grew larger each year as it received Magnolia's Christmas parade, which ended at the campus.

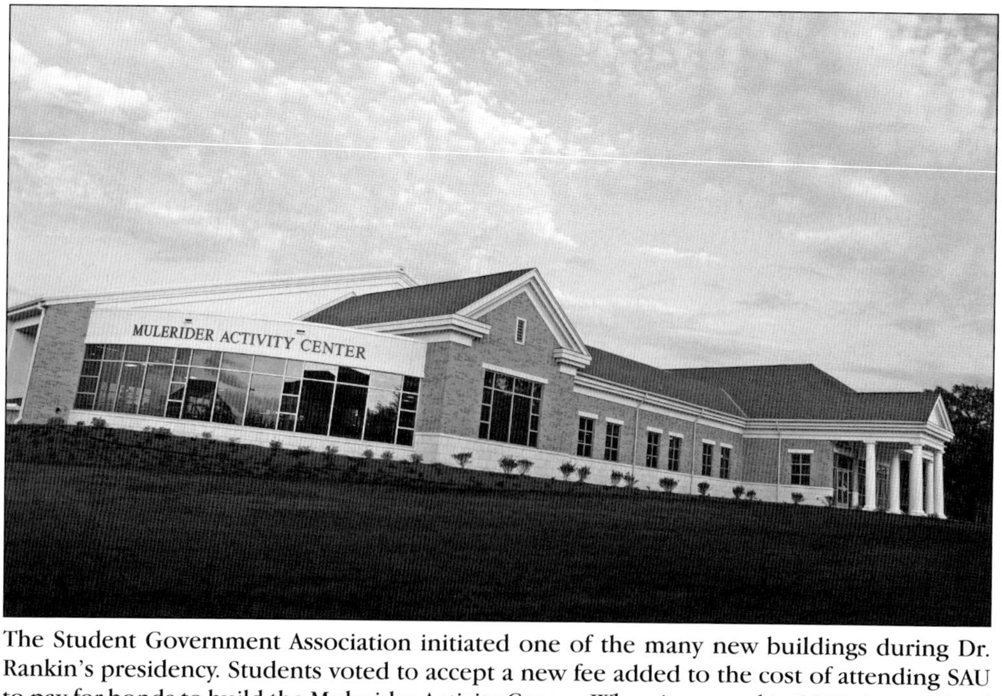

The Student Government Association initiated one of the many new buildings during Dr. Rankin's presidency. Students voted to accept a new fee added to the cost of attending SAU to pay for bonds to build the Mulerider Activity Center. When it opened in 2011, it contained almost every facility and all the equipment needed for physical fitness, including a full-size basketball court for intramural competition.

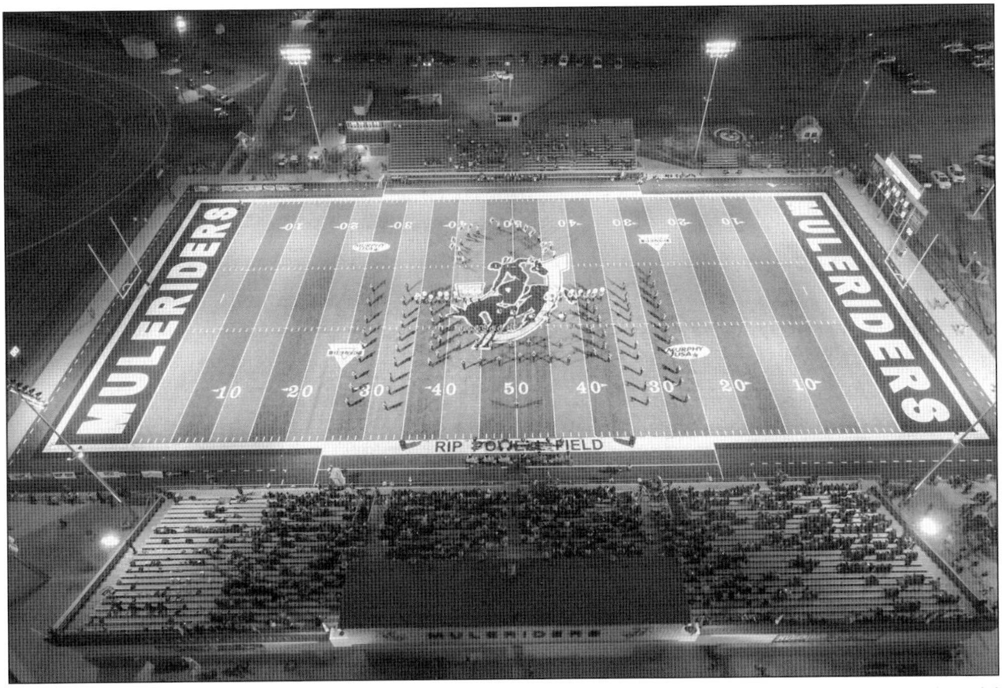

Improvements in athletic facilities were an important element of Dr. Rankin's Blue and Gold Vision. The football field at Wilkins Stadium, named for former college president Colonel Wilkins, had been used since 1949. The field was renamed for former coach Raymond "Rip" Powell and resurfaced with artificial turf and an arresting graphic at midfield of the school's long-used symbol, a rider in Western garb atop a wildly bucking mule. The baseball field had also been long used, but lacked suitable facilities. A grant from the Willard and Pat Walker Charitable Foundation helped add lights, seats, a press box, a concession stand, locker rooms, offices, dugouts, and public restrooms. Walker Baseball Stadium's field was renamed Goodheart Field for long-time coach Steven Goodheart.

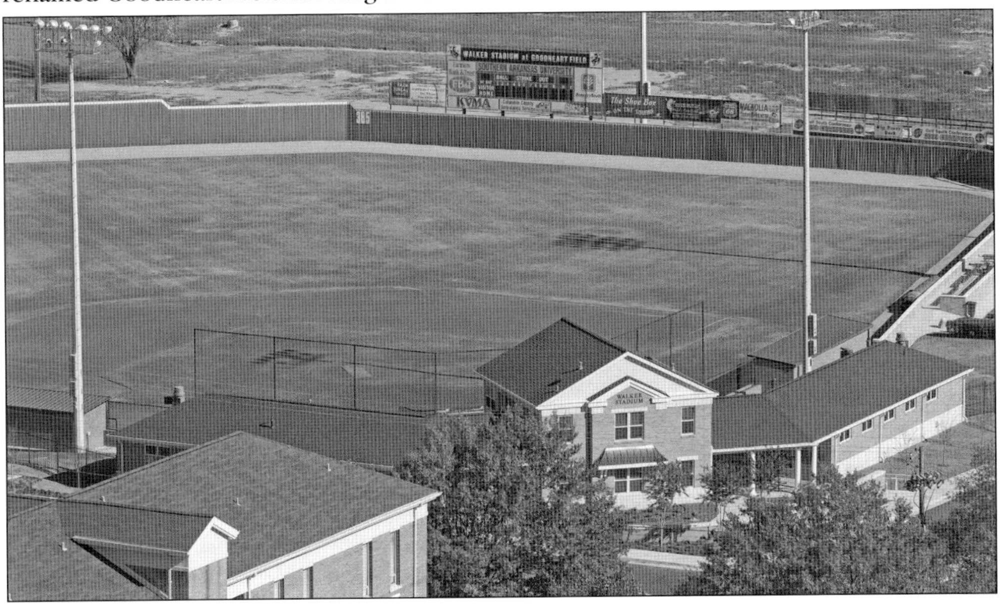

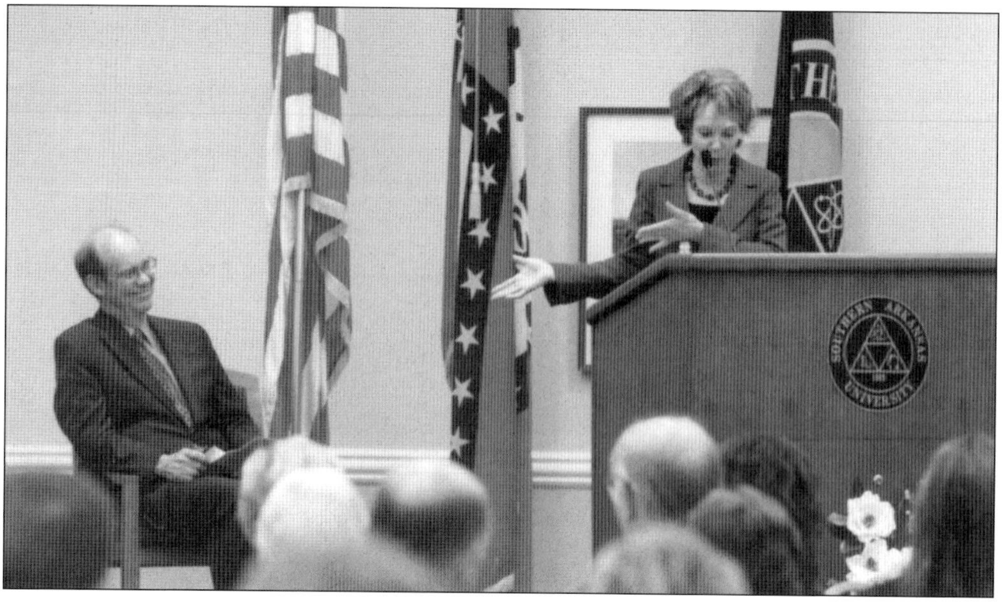

In 2005, Farmers Bank and Trust of Magnolia established a Distinguished Speaker Series to bring speakers of national and international prominence to the SAU campus and to support the SAU Foundation. Farmers Bank and Trust bore the expense of the speakers' fees, and the foundation received the proceeds of ticket sales, usually upwards of $30,000 each year. Among the many well-known speakers have been David and Julie Eisenhower (above) and James Carville (below). Other speakers have included the former prime minister of Israel Ehud Olmert, television host of *America's Most Wanted* John Walsh, retired US Army general Jack Keane, author James Bradley, and other well-known personalities.

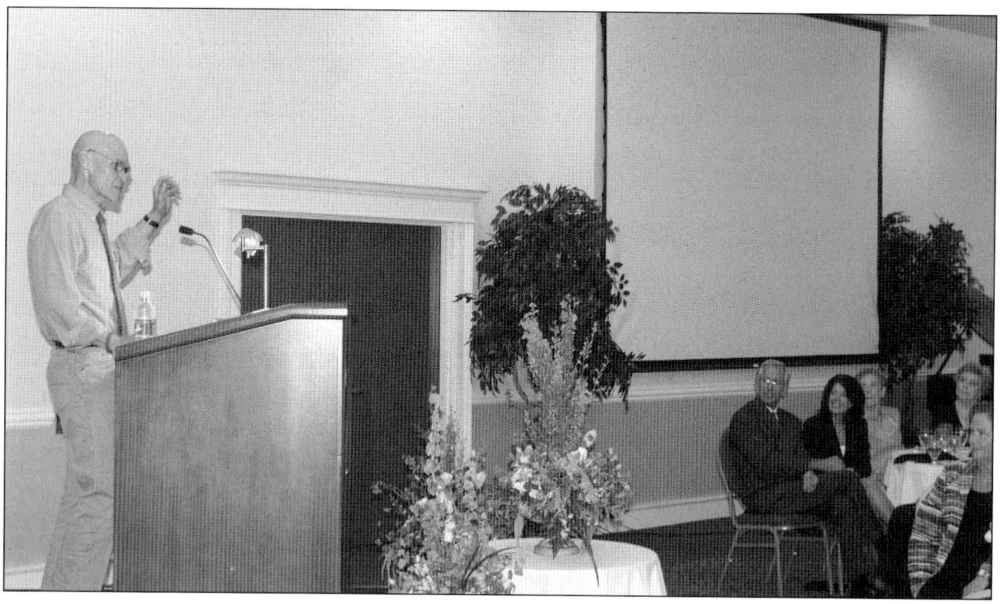

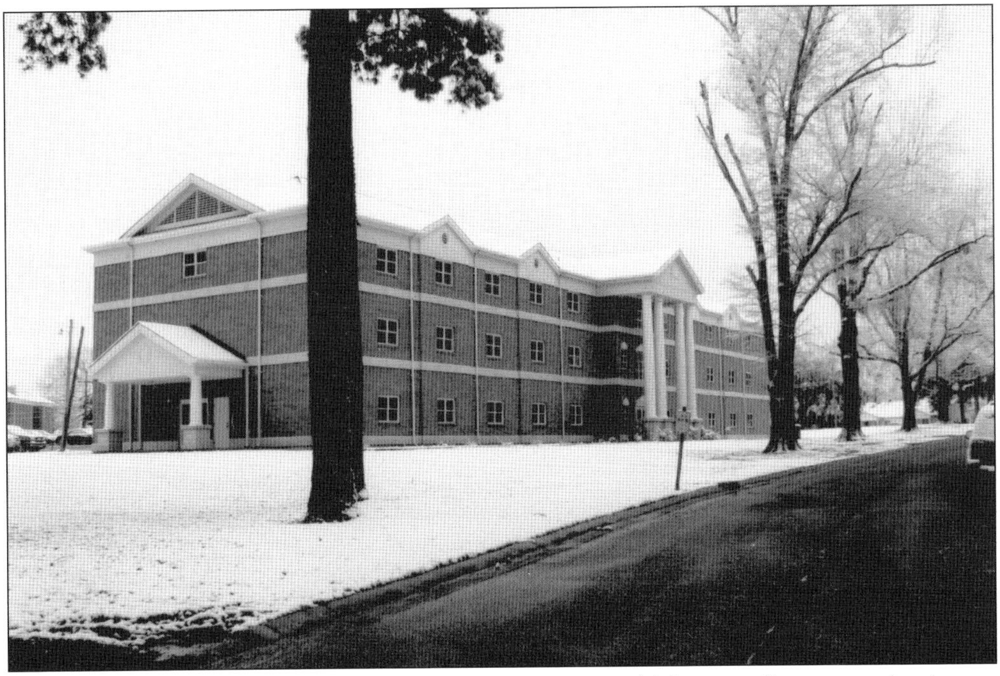

Dr. Rankin sought to assure that all new buildings would have pediments and columns at their entrances, consistent, as far as possible, with the Georgian architectural style first employed at Overstreet Hall. Fincher Hall, a residential hall for freshmen, continued that tradition and honored Harold and Dorothy Jeanne Fincher, among the most generous of all endowment donors for more than 25 years.

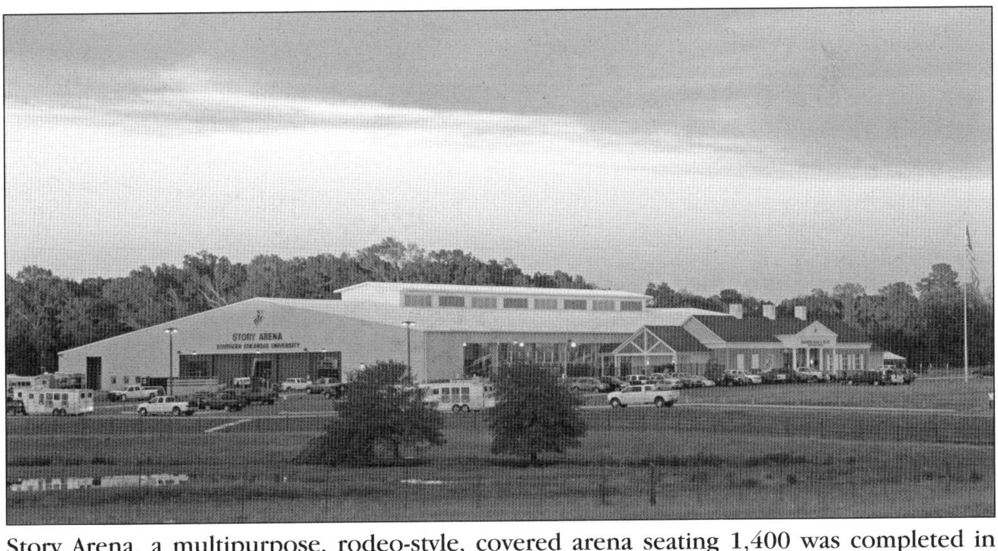

Story Arena, a multipurpose, rodeo-style, covered arena seating 1,400 was completed in 2014. It hosts SAU rodeo team competitions and other events. It was made possible by the generosity of Theral and Jan Story, whose $2 million gift was the largest individual gift in SAU history.

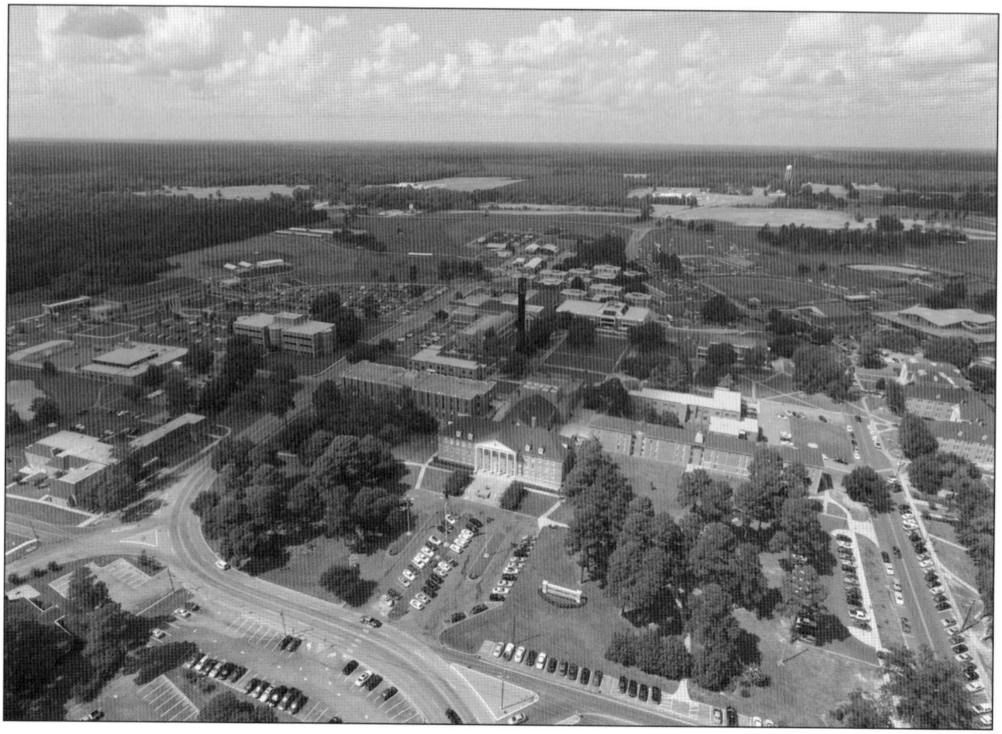

This 2014 aerial photograph of the SAU campus, centered on Overstreet Hall, shows some of the numerous buildings the campus had acquired since that main administrative building was completed in 1945. In 2016, the campus had 10 residential halls for students, and others under construction, in addition to apartments in University Village. It had 10 buildings dedicated to instruction, and four for recreation, as well as others for athletics.

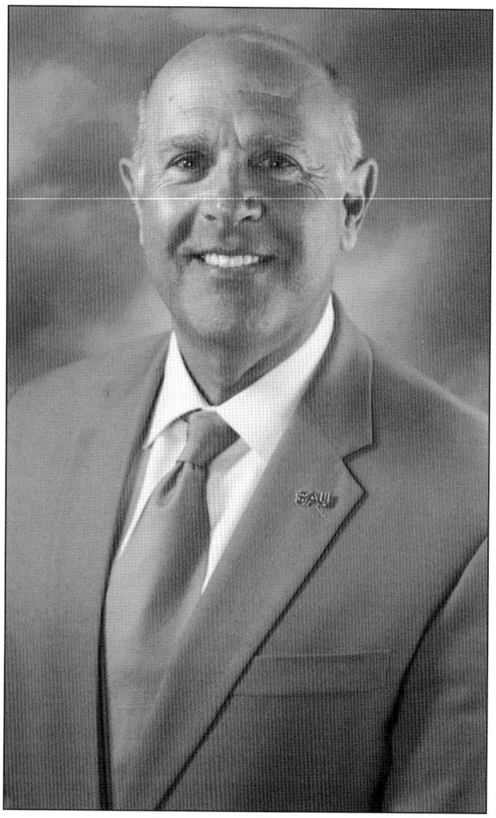

When Dr. Trey Berry became SAU's new president in 2015, the school was experiencing remarkable growth, both in programs and enrollment. Among the newest programs were game development and animation design, marine biology, cybersecurity, and engineering. Enrollment increases made SAU the fastest growing university in Arkansas. The total number of students attending SAU in 2016 was 4,771.

BIBLIOGRAPHY

Willis, James F. "The Farmers' Schools of 1909: The Origins of Arkansas's Four Regional Universities." *Arkansas Historical Quarterly* 65 (Autumn 2006): 224-49.

———. *Southern Arkansas University: The Mulerider School's Centennial History, 1909–2009*. Xlibris Corporation, 2009.